WHAT IS DEMOCRACY AND HOW DO WE STUDY IT?

WHAT IS DEMOCRACY

AND HOW DO WE STUDY IT?

EDITED BY
Cameron D. Anderson and
Laura B. Stephenson

UNIVERSITY OF TORONTO PRESS
Toronto Buffalo London

© University of Toronto Press 2021
Toronto Buffalo London
utorontopress.com
Printed in the U.S.A.

ISBN 978-1-4875-8858-8 (cloth)   ISBN 978-1-4875-8859-5 (EPUB)
ISBN 978-1-4875-8857-1 (paper)   ISBN 978-1-4875-8860-1 (PDF)

Library and Archives Canada Cataloguing in Publication
Title: What is democracy and how do we study it? / edited by Cameron D. Anderson and Laura B. Stephenson.
Names: Anderson, Cameron D. (Cameron David), 1973– editor. | Stephenson, Laura Beth, 1976– editor.
Description: Includes bibliographical references and index.
Identifiers: Canadiana (print) 20200341863 | Canadiana (ebook) 2020034188X | ISBN 9781487588571 (softcover) | ISBN 9781487588588 (hardcover) | ISBN 9781487588595 (EPUB) | ISBN 9781487588601 (PDF)
Subjects: LCSH: Democracy. | LCSH: Democracy – Study and teaching.
Classification: LCC JC423.W43 2021 | DDC 321.8–dc23

We welcome comments and suggestions regarding any aspect of our publications. Please feel free to contact us at news@utorontopress.com or visit us at utorontopress.com.

University of Toronto Press acknowledges the financial assistance to its publishing program of the Canada Council for the Arts and the Ontario Arts Council, an agency of the Government of Ontario.

 Canada Council **Conseil des Arts**
for the Arts **du Canada**

ONTARIO ARTS COUNCIL
CONSEIL DES ARTS DE L'ONTARIO
an Ontario government agency
un organisme du gouvernement de l'Ontario

Funded by the   Financé par le
Government   gouvernement    **Canadä**
of Canada   du Canada

Contents

CHAPTER ONE

Approaching the Study of Democracy

Cameron D. Anderson and Laura B. Stephenson

This book has its genesis in courses we offer to students at the University of Western Ontario. At both the undergraduate and graduate levels, we teach classes that are designed to expose students to the research process in the discipline of political science. Because the field is not homogenous with respect to the assumptions it makes when approaching a problem or the type of data that is used to evaluate a research question, the courses are naturally varied. Through experience, we found that the many differences in both approach and method can be difficult for students to perceive and understand. And, to be honest, why wouldn't they be? Political science includes a vast array of topics – covering everything from domestic institutions to theories of power to international trade agreements to war and conflict and voting behaviour, to name just a few. And within each of these literatures, commonly grouped into "international relations," "comparative politics," "Canadian politics," and "political theory," certain approaches and methods predominate. Our students, to the extent that they specialize, have very specific views of the discipline of political science. No wonder they're often overwhelmed when the full range of approaches is introduced!

Some of the confusion can be lessened by recognizing what actually distinguishes types of political science research. The first important distinction that needs to be understood involves the ends or goals of political scientists' work. In broad strokes, work in political science research aims to accomplish one of three things: *explanation, description,* or *prescription*. *Explanation* means seeking to provide an account of how and/or why something happened. *Description* typically focuses on outlining in great depth the features and elements of a particular concept or phenomenon. By contrast, *prescription* takes a position of emphasizing the normative dimensions of what should or ought to occur. Being aware of how researchers respond to the goals of political science research is central to thinking about how one might start to answer the central question that motivates this volume.

The end goals of research are related to how knowledge and learning are understood. Key terms relating to knowledge and learning in social sciences are ontology, epistemology, and methodology. While we don't wish to focus this chapter on a detailed discussion of these terms, we do think it is important to briefly review the central concepts and provide some insight into how social scientists go about developing positions on these terms.[1]

The concept of ontology concerns whether a social reality exists and whether this reality is knowable (della Porta and Keating 2008). Epistemology is a related concept that asks about the relationship between the researcher and the object of study. Another way to think of these concepts is that they are centrally related to many questions that underlie the research process. For example: What do social scientists know and how can we know it? What does it mean to know something? What can we know (objectively)? And, fundamentally, what is unknowable?

These are very abstract questions and concepts, so sketching out coherent responses to these questions is useful to provide clarity. Broadly speaking, there are two approaches to developing responses to these questions – positivism and interpretivism.[2] Researchers in the positivist tradition start with the ontological position or assumption that there is an independent social reality and that researchers can readily know, ask questions about, and study this social reality. Most research in the natural sciences follows this approach. By contrast, interpretivists respond to the ontological question by emphasizing the central importance of human subjectivity in perceiving and giving meaning to social reality. Put more bluntly, positivists' ontological position views social reality as an independent, objective, and knowable phenomenon while interpretivists conceive of social reality as intimately tied to the ideas, theories, and perspectives that the researcher brings with them.

Relatedly, these approaches answer questions of epistemology in a similar way. Positivists view the researcher as value-neutral and completely separate or independent from the social reality or phenomena being studied. By contrast, interpretivists understand the researcher as inherently bound by their own frames of reference, theories, and meaning, and they argue that these subjectivities preclude meaningful separation from the social reality being studied. In this sense, a researcher's own subjectivity is inherently linked to how and what they perceive about the social reality they are studying. Tying these camps back to the goals of social science research, we suggest that positivist-minded social science researchers strive for explanation and description in their work while interpretivists seek description and possibly prescription in their analyses.

We ought also to highlight the relationship between critical and interpretive approaches in political science research. We contend that critical approaches are broadly united in their identification of some (often unseen) social and/or economic force that generates and perpetuates inequality. Such forces can include gender, race and ethnicity, language, and/or religion. Critical approaches seek to highlight social and political inequality on the basis of these categories, often while seeking to propose amelioration of the underlying structure of inequality. Notably, we conceive of critical approaches as being methodologically diverse such that they may look to demonstrate social and economic inequalities empirically on the basis of these categories in a broadly positivist manner. Alternatively, critical approaches may seek to highlight the lived experiences, perspectives, and meanings of such inequality in a way that is consistent with the ontology and epistemology of interpretivism. In this sense, we conceive of critical theories as espousing a normative preoccupation and being analytically situated with either positivism or interpretivism.

In addition to distinguishing the end goals of research, we need to be aware of the methodological choices made by social science researchers. This helps us to properly understand the distinction between qualitative and quantitative methods in political science. For the most part, quantitative research follows a broadly positivist approach and seeks to "test," "prove," and "evaluate" using empirical data. In this way, it is often seen as more "scientific" and, indeed, quantitative research tends to use similar terms and language to the natural sciences. The quantitative approach emerges from the epistemological assumptions of positivists that social and political realities exist independently of the researcher and that testing or proving relationships between variables can be achieved. This type of research fits well with explanation, especially, and description, but it is less valuable for prescriptive or normative studies.

The other major methodological approach in political science is qualitative research.[3] Qualitative research is the predominant form of analysis for a wider variety of approaches and fields in political science, including explanation, description, and prescription. Some qualitative work aligns closely with the goals of positivist work and emphasizes explanation through testing or proving hypotheses. This kind of qualitative work clearly espouses a more positivist epistemological position regarding the independence of observation from the researcher. By contrast, other qualitative work leans much more on the interpretivist side of the epistemological fence. Such researchers assume that their subjectivity and perceptual limitations are very important because they shape how they perceive social reality. In these cases, the researcher is centrally involved in the collection and interpretation of data from the social world. The coincidence of research type, positivist or interpretivist, with methodological approach, quantitative or qualitative, has produced an interesting situation where some students come to believe that there are very distinct domains for methodological approaches.[4]

We staunchly disagree with this view of political science research. There are many different ways to approach research questions and many different types of analysis that can be conducted. There is no "right" way to answer any research question, because it depends upon the researcher's underlying assumptions about how knowledge can be gained. Further, some judgments about "good" and "bad" research come down to what scholars find compelling and convincing. Finally, research questions rarely have a single dimension. Insights provided by one approach can be fundamentally informative for another, even if they are very different.

What has always been important to us, and what spurred the development of this book, was the concern that students should know about and understand exactly the points we raise above. We think all students should be aware of the variety of ways in which political science research is conducted. Once we started to think about the best way to make that happen, we landed on the observation that while some research topics or questions are asked in all of the subfields of political science, each subfield may take a different approach to answering the question. We believe that all are of value for political science. We just needed to figure out a way to show students.

The problem, in our opinion, is that the approaches and methods that underlie research in political science are often implicit rather than explicit. Because of the tendency for researchers in a specific subfield to depend upon (or be drawn to?) a specific subset of approaches and methods, the deliberate process of making choices and decisions about those approaches and methods are often ignored or implicit. And yet those are fundamental to fully understanding the research! Further, as teachers, political scientists tend to focus on findings and conclusions rather than analysing the research process. We do not condemn political science professors for this. Indeed, this is a natural response when trying to cover the full breadth of a topic in a single semester (or even two). Some aspects of the research work covered in the course must be left out. But an unintentional effect of these pedagogical choices is that it may contribute to how undergraduate students learn about approaches and methods in the study of political science. A necessary remedy, we decided, was a set of studies that examined a single topic from a range of different approaches and methods, explicitly. We thought that this would show our students that what they were interested in could be studied in more ways, drawing on different approaches and methods, than they may have already encountered.

Our first step in making this happen was to gather our colleagues together to see if they agreed. Thankfully, they did! Even better, they were willing to work with us. We started with a co-taught undergraduate course that asked the same question each week and had answers provided by different faculty members using different approaches and methods. The enthusiasm for the course shown by both faculty and students convinced us that others might find the materials we used of value too, and so we undertook to develop those lectures into the chapters that make up this edited volume.

The research question we landed on has become the title of this book: What is democracy and how do we study it? Choosing to look at democracy simply made sense because it is a core, if contested, concept that spans the fields and eras of political science research. Political theory teaches us how the idea of democracy developed from the earliest philosophical writings, and considers questions about the fundamental principles underlying the concept. Domestic (Canadian) politics considers the workings of democracy in everyday life – how people choose leaders, what representatives do in office, how well the people are represented by their government, etc. Comparative politics pushes us to consider comparisons between different countries and aspects of government. How do we measure democracy and which countries are more democratic? Why does democracy fail in some countries and not others? How many ways can democracy be realized effectively? Finally, the international relations field studies interactions between states, including how democracy is promoted or spread and how democracy does or does not constrain states from certain behaviours.

This book is therefore designed to use a single research question to introduce students to different approaches to political science analysis. Instead of starting from a description of an approach or method, as many research methods texts usually do, the chapters each start with the same question (What is democracy and how do we study it?) and present research that addresses the question from a specific political science approach. Each chapter covers the same research design topics in order to make it easier for students to see where the approaches converge and diverge in their treatment of the question. The contributors span the fields of political science, and they generously agreed to let us "peek under the hood," as it were, to understand their approach to the question, how they conceptualized and operationalized the key ideas, and the method(s) they used in their analyses. As a result, each contributing chapter takes the reader through the research process of crafting a coherent answer to the volume's guiding question. A central benefit of reading the chapters in this book is that students will be able to gain an appreciation of the range of approaches to research in political science and be able to compare the conclusions more directly.[5]

We are particularly enthusiastic about the chapters in this volume because they incorporate approaches not always considered in research methods courses – those from the political theory field. Chapters 2 and 3 take a normative approach to discussing democracy. Charles Jones starts from basic principles and asks, "What is democracy?" He then considers classic arguments for and against. In contrast, Richard Vernon's chapter takes a different approach. He tackles the appropriateness of the connection between majority rule and democracy. It is often assumed that they go together – that majority rule is, in fact, democracy.

But is that the case? Vernon questions this assumption by systematically looking at alternative ways of deciding upon governments.

The second section of the book introduces positivist approaches to research. In chapter 4, Anderson and Stephenson explore official data on electoral turnout and public opinion data on participation to consider how important turnout is to assessing the democratic quality of a government. They take a multi-level approach, considering municipal, provincial, and federal elections. They also look at data from across Canada and find an interesting variation that they connect to inter-provincial differences. The next chapter, by Armstrong, deals directly with conceptualization and quantitative measurement. Here, the focus on conceptualization provides an interesting comparison to Vernon's chapter, and the discussion of analytic utility brings an added dimension to understanding research about democracy.

Still under the umbrella of positivist approaches to research, the next four chapters use various types of qualitative methods. Each author makes very conscious theoretical and methodological choices that alter the trajectories of how they develop their discussions. In chapter 6, Morrison takes a historical institutionalist approach to consider the longitudinal character of democratization, including sequencing, critical junctures, and incremental change. The next chapter, by Sancton and Alcantara, also takes an institutionalist approach but does so from a different angle. They challenge our ideas of what democracy is by looking at the development and impact of institutional rules determining membership in two non-traditional governance organizations. Leone and Morgan, both of whom have had experience in elected office, provide a very different take on democracy from a practitioner's point of view through a comparison of two cases in which the institutional design of political decision-making shaped the course of events. Their observations and experience bring to light aspects of democracy in practice that cannot be known without the type of data-gathering they were able to undertake.[6] Finally, Lyons's chapter asks whether democratic governments are thoroughly democratic by looking at the effects of changes in the institutional distribution of political responsibility among levels and bodies of government (or devolution) that are occurring in many jurisdictions and considering what that means for the quality of democracy.

Finally, we close the book by considering critical and postmodern versions of the interpretivist approach. The chapters by Bousfield and Biswas

Mellamphy challenge conventional ideas about democracy. Bousfield uses recent real-world events and the challenge of populism to question what democracy really means and why it is being threatened in many countries around the world. Biswas Mellamphy utilizes a critical contestation-oriented approach to explore democracy from a different perspective – one that focuses on the production, not elimination, of conflict.

HOW TO USE THIS BOOK

While we earlier outlined our intent and the approach we took in developing this book, here we would like to elaborate on how this volume can be used in political science classes. We offer two ideas in particular (but we would love to hear more!). The first is the way that we taught our own students at Western – as a course about democracy, a fundamental concept in political science. In this course model, each chapter provides material for one week of a one-semester course. Students read both the chapter and supplementary readings and discuss the material on its own, as well as in comparison to the materials from other weeks. We have gathered discussion questions and exercises (available at https://utorontopress .com/us/what-is-democracy-and-how-do-we-study-it-4) when we felt it would be useful for just this reason. Feedback from our students at Western indicated that this course was a great addition to their undergraduate curriculum and they were enthusiastic about us offering it again.

An alternative use for this book is as a companion to more traditional research design courses. For example, the topics typically covered in a research design course include understanding political science as a science, the importance of theory, distinguishing between quantitative and qualitative approaches, defining concepts, making measurement choices, choosing case studies and conducting comparative research, using surveys and official statistics, and conducting interviews and focus groups. Topics related to analysis specifically include what to do with qualitative data, how to understand univariate statistics, and inferential statistics. The chapters in this book would greatly complement student understanding in such a course by letting them see "research in action." For example, the Sancton and Alcantara chapter takes an explicitly institutionalist approach: they explain the theory that underlies institutions and how that approach structures their analysis. Another example is Vernon's chapter on majority rule. Conceptualization of ideas in research is a key first step to doing a good study, and his analysis of the place of majority rule in the concept of democracy is enlightening. Leone and Morgan's chapter highlights the value of comparative case studies by demonstrating how case studies can reveal details far different than what observations of institutions and rules may yield. One last example (each of the chapters has something unique to add to a discussion of methodology) is Biswas Mellamphy's chapter. Her explicitly critical approach challenges us to think about democracy in a new way, providing important insight into what can be gained from using different approaches to research. We think a traditional course on research methods would greatly benefit from the applied work that is presented in the chapters of this book.

NOTES

1 The interested reader might wish to reference Guba and Lincoln (2004) for a fuller treatment of these concepts.

2 While there are fine-grained differences between types of positivism and interpretivism, we will sketch the main parameters of each approach without delving into more nuance than is helpful.

3 Here we use the term "qualitative" to indicate research that does not make use of quantitative data (and therefore is non-quantitative).

4 We should note that positivist research traditions in the social sciences are often criticized as being inappropriate for the study of human social and political relations. The argument is generally made that we cannot hope to replicate in the social sciences the conceptual and causal precision that characterizes positivism in the natural sciences. Rather, the character of social relations, culture, and subjective understanding is simply too varied and conditional to allow for the strong application of positivist assumptions in the social sciences.

5 It should be noted that we consciously limit ourselves thematically in the chapters of this book. For instance, we do not address questions of what studying democracy looks like in the Global South, the influence of (de-)democratization in global powers on international relations, or the role of religion and democracy. These, of course, are highly relevant topics to the "What is democracy and how do we study it?" question, but appropriate answers to these lead us further afield from our central focus for this volume – variation within the field of political science to answer these questions.

6 The analytical approach employed in this chapter involves both explanation (positivism) of policy outcomes and the authors' own understanding

and interpretations of the events that they chronicle (interpretivism). As such, in a unique way this chapter reflects the coexistence of these otherwise divergent analytical frames.

REFERENCES

Della Porta, Donatella, and Michael Keating, eds. 2008. *Approaches and Methodologies in the Social Sciences: A Pluralist Perspective.* Cambridge: Cambridge University Press.

Guba, Egon G., and Yvonna S. Lincoln. 2004. "Competing Paradigms in Qualitative Research: Theories and Issues." In *Approaches to Qualitative Research: A Reader on Theory and Practice,* edited by Sharlene Nagy Hesse-Biber and Patricia Leavy, 17–38. Oxford: Oxford University Press.

PART ONE

Democracy in Theory: Normative Approaches

CHAPTER TWO

Democracy: What and Why?

Charles Jones

INTRODUCTION

This chapter investigates the meaning and value of democracy as a procedure of collective decision-making. We answer the question that guides this book – "What is democracy?" – by comparing the ancient Greek context with modern representative government. We then consider Plato's classic argument against democracy. This leads to a description of several important arguments in support of democracy. The aim is to give readers some sense of the way political theorists proceed when confronted with a fundamental and controversial value in the study of politics.

The discussion proceeds from the standpoint of analytical political theory. The political theorist's method consists in aiming for normatively significant conclusions about key political ideas by way of a specific range of methodological maxims, including careful conceptual analysis, sound argumentation, and clear writing. The case of democracy will serve to exemplify this method by describing the political theorist's demands for (1) analytical clarity about the concept of democracy and the various ways it can be interpreted, and (2) a careful outline and evaluation of arguments for and against democracy. The best way to reach a reliable assessment is to be open to the widest range of methods and approaches to the study of democracy, not only within political science but across related disciplines like history, philosophy, and the sciences of human nature, including psychology and biology.

Political scientists most often seek to describe and explain political activities (e.g., voting behaviour) and institutions (e.g., electoral systems). They want to know the way things are and why they are the way they are; they seek to describe the political world as it is and to explain how some political phenomena are related to others. But political science presupposes the conceptual and normative results of political theory. For example, political scientists might want to know whether democracy promotes economic growth or whether democratic countries are less likely than non-democracies to go to war with one another. Political theorists can clarify what should count as a democratic country or arena of decision-making in the first place. We need to know what characteristics make a country or a decision-making process democratic. How are decisions made? Who decides? How are opinions expressed in practice? Who puts those decisions into effect? We can know how democracies figure in the world only if we have a clear idea of what counts as democracy.

Political theorists consider arguments on all sides of key political ideas, values, and practices, from politics, power, authority, and democracy to justice, equality, welfare, and community. They pause to consider the complexities of the basic political concepts so that they can avoid confusion and bring into view a relatively clear idea for normative assessment. In the present chapter we first consider what democracy is before asking why it was widely thought to be undesirable and why it has become accepted by many as desirable. Even if there is a lot to be said for democracy, it is worth focusing as well on the puzzles involved in trying to set out a coherent conception of it.

DEMOCRACY: ANCIENT AND MODERN

What is democracy? A serviceable general answer is that democracy is a method of collective decision-making characterized by some kind of equality among the participants at a crucial stage of the decision-making process (Christiano 2006, 2). In modern democratic states, political equality is usually meant to characterize activities like choosing representatives, passing legislation, and implementing policies. If the question is "Who should rule?," the democrat's answer is "everyone": democracy is rule by the many. The belief that political power should be distributed equally leads to the demand that every citizen should have a right to an equal say in decisions to which they are subject.

Our word "politics" comes from the ancient Greek word "polis," meaning city-state; the word "democracy" is derived from the ancient Greek term for "rule by the people" (*kratos* by the *demos*). In fifth-century-BCE Athens, democracy was both an idea and a practice of political decision-making in which citizens regarded each other as political equals with the capacity to make binding collective decisions and thereby govern themselves (Dahl 1989, 1). If oligarchy was rule by the wealthy few, democracy was rule by the many; in practice, the many were the common people, the poor people.

Athenian democratic decisions were made by majority vote in an assembly of all citizens, each of whom was paid a day's wage to participate. There was significant emphasis on open discussion and debate aimed at promoting the public good. The Greeks called a public-spirited citizen a *polites* but reserved the term *idiotes* for someone concerned only with their own privately conceived self-interest. So our word "idiot" stems from the ancient Greek term for a private person who is not interested in politics. A line from a famous speech by the statesman Pericles (490–429 BCE) makes the point well: "We do not say that a man who shows no interest in politics is a man who minds his own business; we say that he has no business here at all" (Thucydides 1972, 147).

Consider some contrasts between ancient and modern democracies. Athenian democracy was direct, exclusionary, culturally homogeneous, and intolerant. Citizens in Athens participated directly in all major public policy decisions, but only about 10 per cent of the 300,000 people living and working there were entitled to citizenship. Women, slaves, and *metics* (non-citizen residents) did most of the productive work on which the community depended but played no role in political decision-making. Everyone shared Greek language and culture but unconventional beliefs and practices were not tolerated. By contrast, modern liberal democracies are indirect, inclusive, multicultural, and tolerant. With populations in the tens or hundreds of millions, we elect representatives to make decisions for us; all adults are included as equal citizens with the right to choose their representatives; our societies are multicultural and characterized by toleration for a wide range of religious and other "comprehensive" conceptions of the good life.

As a rough approximation we can say that a modern representative democracy aims to ensure the following: each citizen has an equal opportunity to participate in some way in the political decision-making process by making their views known; every citizen is entitled to seek election as a representative; representatives are chosen in free, frequent, and fair elections; citizens can learn about the options facing them by having access to independent media; citizens enjoy a basic right to freedom of speech, including the right to challenge political views in the public arena; and citizens can decide what items appear on the public agenda for debate (Dahl 2006, 4–18). Political practice does not always live up to these aims.

PLATO AGAINST DEMOCRACY

We have characterized democracy as an egalitarian decision-making procedure that, in both its ancient and modern forms, can be characterized as *rule by the many*. With the descriptive task accomplished, then, we can proceed to normative assessment. Our topic now is what can be said for and against democracy as a political decision-making procedure.

Let us begin with the critics of democracy. Robert Dahl helpfully describes three kinds of critic. The first, exemplified by Plato, sees democracy as possible but undesirable; the second, like Robert Michels, believes that democracy, whether desirable or not, is impossible; and the third type of critic sympathetically points to puzzles and problems that need to be addressed if democracy is to be a legitimate political ideal (Dahl 1989, 2). The sympathetic critic addresses such questions as, "What is the proper size of democratic decision-making communities?," or "If the people should rule, who should count as 'the people'?" Here, however, we focus on the most famous anti-democratic argument, put forward in the fourth century BCE by Plato in *Republic*, an argument that rejects democracy outright. The question of who is competent to rule generates Plato's famous argument against democracy: only a small minority is capable of ruling well, so we should reject an arrangement that distributes political power equally to everyone regardless of capability.

Plato's case is straightforward. He argues that ruling or governing is a skill possessed only by a small minority, so – given the overriding importance for everyone of having a well-governed state – the majority should be excluded from ruling. If we consider jobs like ship's captain or medical doctor that require knowledgeable, skilled practitioners, it seems obvious that we should seek their practical wisdom in the appropriate context. For example, if we want to travel safely by sea, we are much better off trusting our lives to the decision-making skills of a well-trained sailor rather than the mass of our fellow citizens who lack such skills. Likewise, in the medical case, when we seek a diagnosis and prescription for a health complaint, we are well-advised to seek the considered judgment of a doctor rather than poll the masses for their opinion. After all, the health of our bodies is at stake. But Plato's view is that, when it comes to governing, it is even more important to be guided by wise decision-makers – philosopher-kings and -queens who know the good for human beings – because their focus is the health of the body politic, a matter of greater consequence than the health of any individual citizen.

For Plato, navigation and medicine are like politics in that they can be done well only by those who possess teachable skills underwritten by a body of knowledge. Democrats are mistaken in their belief that there is no politically relevant ruling skill nor any knowledge underlying it (Plato 1992, Book 6, 488a–e). It is no wonder, he claims, that the democrat's equal distribution of ruling authority will give undue influence to ignorant people and that, consequently, democracies are prone to crashing onto the rocks. Applied to twenty-first-century representative democracies, the objection would be that political decisions are made by those who are good only at winning elections, when what we need is government by properly motivated people with advanced knowledge about public policies.

Underlying Plato's critique of democracy is a plausible set of criteria for political competence. Entitlement to rule should be given only to those who (1) know what ends the government should be pursuing, (2) are disposed to seek those ends, and (3) can figure out the best means to achieve them (Dahl 1989, 58). In other words, those who govern should possess knowledge of what is good for their society, they should be trustworthy, and they should have the technical skills necessary to achieve the public good.

This test of competence is reasonable, but Plato's objection is that democracy's assignment of equal decision-making power to each citizen is tantamount to falsely thinking that the moral and intellectual virtues of knowing the good and being able to bring it about are equally distributed throughout the population. On the contrary, says the objection, the average person is simply incapable of understanding what is in the public interest and, in any case, is motivated to promote their own individual good rather than the good of the community. In short, since democracy is rule by the ignorant, the unwise, the self-interested, it will fail to promote the good of the citizens.

Is there a coherent reply to Plato's critique of democracy? Insofar as the objection denies the political competence of ordinary people, any reply should present evidence that ordinary people are not as ignorant or selfish as the critique claims they are. At the very least it should support whatever is necessary for improved public understanding of complex issues – education, informed and respectful debate – along with elements of specialization and the use of expertise to provide sober advice (Dahl 1989, 77). And, as we will see below, it has been argued that political participation itself has educative and other improving effects on people; if so, elitist guardianship would prevent these positive features of democracy from being realized.

Can we identify a class of guardians who can both be trained to know the good for all and be trusted to implement it? On the question of knowledge, it is worth pointing out that there is no class of moral experts. In fact, in modern liberal democracies we are accustomed to what the political philosopher John Rawls calls "the fact of reasonable pluralism," the idea that reasonable people will continue to disagree about conceptions of the good or meaningful human life (Rawls 2005, 36). The most we can agree on, perhaps, is a conception of social or distributive justice, but even here we tend to believe that each person is perfectly capable of understanding and judging principles of justice: no one is properly denied access to participate in thinking about and deciding upon a view about the just society.

In any case we should ask how Plato's wise rulers are supposed to discover whether their decisions are protecting and promoting the interests of the ruled. As Aristotle, Plato's student, pointed out, the best judge of a house's quality is the user or tenant of the house, not the builder, "and it is the diner not the cook that pronounces upon the merits of the dinner" (Aristotle 1981, Book 3, Chapter 11, 1282a, 17–25). Likewise, each citizen is an appropriate judge of whether public policies help or harm them.

Technical expertise in public policy matters is highly controversial. It is now common to rely heavily on expert advice on monetary policy and some aspects of fiscal policy, but even here there is room for disagreement about the comparative value of goals like economic growth, employment, and the balance of trade. So technocrats should not be exempt from answering to the wider population on such normative questions. Even within experts' recognized realm of specialized competence, their opinions should often be treated with some scepticism. Consider acknowledged experts in social and political forecasting. While they are often confident in their predictions about what will result from an intervention, there is evidence to suggest that they are no better than non-experts in their forecasts (Tetlock 2005). The world is complicated in ways that make it difficult to assess risks. If we add to this the fact that every human being is susceptible to the same systematic biases in reasoning (Kahneman 2011), we are led both to scepticism about expert political judgment and to the need for constitutional protections from their likely mistakes.

Even if we bracket the issue of who is capable of knowing the public good, there would still be a problem of *trust*. Remember that rule by guardians would be rule by a governing elite who are not accountable to, or removable by, the ruling majority. So the question is why this elite should be trusted to look out for the good of all the others rather than looking out for their own good. The great nineteenth-century defender of representative government, John Stuart Mill, quite rightly emphasized that the only way for any person to ensure that their rights and interests are taken notice of is for each person to stand up for those rights and interests: we need to be both able and willing to protect ourselves. Mill encapsulates his view by asserting "that each is the only safe guardian of his [or her] rights and interests" (1861, 404). If this plausible claim is true, then Platonic guardianship is no way to protect the interests of the governed.

THE MARKET AND THE FORUM

Before outlining pro-democratic arguments, it is worth mentioning a helpful distinction between two conceptions of democracy: the market and the forum (Elster 1997). Democracy conceived as a *market* aggregates the brute preferences of individuals to reach a collective decision, thereby giving voters (i.e., political consumers) what they want. At election time, political parties offer options from which to choose and citizens vote for representatives who ultimately make the decisions. At its root, political equality means equal voting power for each citizen.

Democracy as a *forum*, on the other hand, encourages debate, deliberation, and discussion among citizens willing to listen to others and potentially change their preferences in response to reasons. On this view, political equality means each citizen having an equal opportunity to participate in democratic deliberation aimed at the common good (Swift 2014, 219). Defenders of the forum model would likely concede that the market model is relatively accurate as a description of representative democracy as we know it, but they would point out that two key features of that reality are impoverished debate and citizen incompetence. Moreover, private power exerts undue influence in the public sphere, threatening the equal-influence premise at the heart of democracy.

As we proceed, we should keep in mind that the soundness of arguments for and against democracy depend, to a significant extent, on whether democracy is conceived more as a market or as a forum.

ARGUING FOR DEMOCRACY: INTRINSIC REASONS

What can be said in a constructive way to support democracy as a political decision-making procedure? If we limit ourselves to actual political systems and states that exist or have existed, it could be argued that democracy "tends to produce the best feasible political system," all things considered (Dahl 1989, 83–4). In short, many would endorse former British prime minister Winston Churchill's point that democracy is the worst form of government except for all the other forms that have been tried.

But let us see whether there are stronger arguments available.

Here we should distinguish between intrinsic and instrumental reasons for democracy. An *intrinsic* reason says that democracy itself embodies a value, like freedom or equality, that we have good reason to accept, distinct from the results produced by democratic decisions. Democracy, according to this type of defence, is a form of freedom or equality, so if we value freedom or equality, we should be democrats. The decision-making procedure is justified quite apart from the consequences to which it might lead. An *instrumental* reason says that democracy is more likely than any other decision-making procedure to produce good or desirable consequences, such as greater overall happiness, better protection of citizens' core interests, or better-developed human beings. We will focus on two intrinsic arguments for democracy, appealing to freedom as autonomy and to equality; then we will address several instrumental arguments.

Freedom

Here we focus on freedom or liberty understood as individual *autonomy*. This is another word with ancient Greek roots: "auto" means "self," "nomos" means "law," "rule," or "convention." So autonomy means *self-rule*, literally "giving laws to oneself." It could be argued that democracy consists in individuals collectively ruling themselves, so it embodies a commitment to freedom as self-rule or self-government. The great eighteenth-century Swiss-French political theorist Jean-Jacques Rousseau defended such a view. He denied that freedom is simply the ability to do what you want: "the mere impulse of appetite is slavery, while obedience to a law which we prescribe to ourselves is liberty" (Rousseau 1993, *The Social Contract*, Book 1, Chapter 8, 196).

It is true that those in the minority – those on the losing side in a legislative vote – do not, strictly speaking, give laws to themselves and so seem not to be autonomous in the required sense. But the reply to this objection is that (1) no other decision procedure provides *more* autonomy to individuals than democracy, and (2) democracy gives every citizen the *opportunity* to participate in law-making on the same terms as every other citizen (Swift 2014, 214). If unanimity is an impossible requirement, then a commitment to autonomy seems to support democratic law-making as the best we can hope for in practice. No other decision-making procedure offers a greater opportunity for citizens to choose the laws under which they live.

Democracy is often thought to include both procedural and substantive requirements. Procedurally, it requires "one person, one vote" and majority rule; substantively, it secures basic liberties or rights such as freedom of expression and freedom of association (Simmons 2008, 105–6). Beyond "freedom as autonomy," therefore, we can identify a range of basic civil and political freedoms whose protection forms the core of liberal democratic theory and practice. The value of these basic rights and freedoms helps to explain why a defensible conception of democracy should not be equated with simple majority rule (see Richard Vernon's chapter in this volume). In modern constitutional democracies, decision-making by majority or plurality vote is often constrained by a constitutional document or framework, along with a recognized process of judicial review, with the aim of securing fundamental civil and political liberties. The idea, then, is that rights are constraints on majoritarian procedures with the aim of protecting individuals or minorities from majority imposition.

But it is arguable that this "rights as constraints" view misconceives their actual role in the self-conception and practice of democracy. As Elizabeth Anderson convincingly argues, such rights are best conceived not as constraints but as *constitutive* of democracy itself (Anderson 2009, 215–16). It is not as though individual rights serve to block democratic demands; on the contrary, democracy properly conceived *presupposes* those rights as a condition of its legitimacy. Consequently, it would be anti-democratic to deny any citizen such rights. Without freedoms of speech, association, and political participation, there would be no democracy at all.

Equality

A second intrinsic reason for democracy is that it embodies a commitment to treating each citizen as a moral equal. Insofar as democrats demand equal rights to participate in decision-making, they set out a conception of politics for a society of equals. The logic moves from the moral to the political spheres: we begin with a widespread moral commitment to equal consideration and derive from it the requirements of political equality such as "one person, one vote" and the right of everyone to run for office.

It bears repeating that the claim of equality is moral rather than purely descriptive. People are unequal in many respects, of course, including skills, talents, intelligence, appearance, and health. Moreover, they differ in terms of their personal, social, and cultural identities, which are grounded in features like race, ethnicity, gender, and sexual preference. But despite these many differences between us, we can assert that none of them justifies distributing political power unequally. Descriptive claims are not irrelevant, however, since democratic inclusion plausibly presupposes that all individuals possess the capacities to speak, to learn from others, and to develop reasoned opinions on matters of social concern.

Beyond equal consideration of interests, democrats assign primacy to each person's own perspective on those interests. Respect for persons demands that we recognize the capacity of individuals to make up their own minds about what makes for a worthwhile life (Waldron 2012, 193). To treat others as equals means not only counting them equally but asking them their opinion. Here we see the link between democratic legitimacy and the consent of the governed, a view memorably stated by Thomas Rainsborough in the 1647 Putney debates during the English Civil War: "the poorest he that is in England hath a life to live as the greatest he; and therefore truly sir, I think it's clear that every man that is to live under a government ought first by his own consent to put himself under that government" (quoted in Waldron 2012, 196). John Rawls extends this tradition of thinking by attributing to each person equally the capacity for a sense of justice that provides the starting point for reaching agreement on principles to underpin the main social, political, and economic institutions (Rawls 2005, 19).

Ronald Dworkin set out the following condition of government legitimacy: "No government is legitimate that does not show equal concern for the fate of all those citizens over whom it claims dominion and from whom it claims allegiance" (2000, 1). If equal concern for each citizen is necessary for a government to count as legitimate, what decision-making process is most likely to embody such concern? The answer is a process in which each citizen possesses the right to an equal say; in other words, a democratic process.

The close link between democracy and equality suggests that large-scale economic inequality can put democratic forms in danger. Political equality requires each citizen to have an equally effective say at some crucial stage of the decision-making process, but this is difficult to maintain in the face of large concentrations of individual and corporate wealth. Unequal wealth can translate into unequal political influence; if so, democracy can disappear in substance even if its formal mechanisms remain. The most obvious recent sign of this problem is the United States Supreme Court decisions in *Buckley v. Valeo* (1976) – in which money was judged a form of speech – and *Citizens United v. Federal Election Commission* (2010) – in which all limits were removed from the free speech rights (and therefore political campaign spending) of private corporations. A study of American billionaires argues that they exert a powerful yet unacknowledged – and therefore unaccountable – influence on the US political process, yet the policies they support tend not to be the policies favoured by the majority of their compatriots (Page, Seawright, and Lacombe 2018). In the present context, then, it is difficult to defend American representative democracy as expressing a strong commitment to equality.

Further evidence for this claim comes from the careful multivariate analysis of American political scientists Martin Gilens and Benjamin Page. They looked at 1,779 policy decisions and showed that, in general, policy has little to do with public opinion and a lot to do with corporate interests. They conclude that "economic elites and organized groups representing business interests have substantial independent impacts on US government policy, while average citizens and mass-based interest groups have little or no independent influence" (Gilens and Page 2014, 564). They argue that present-day America has only a weak claim to being called a democracy because, despite the presence of many democratic characteristics like regular elections and freedom of speech and association, "majorities of the American public actually have little influence over the policies [its] government adopts" (Gilens and Page 2014, 577). If their analysis is sound, the equality argument for democracy cannot get a foothold in the contemporary United States.

ARGUING FOR DEMOCRACY: INSTRUMENTAL REASONS

Does democracy produce better consequences than its alternatives? Let us consider several so-called instrumental reasons in support of democracy.

Good Decisions

Some argue that democracy produces good decisions. If democracy is political equality, it assigns – however imperfectly – some form of equal power to each citizen. The result is that representatives cannot simply ignore the interests of the governed (Mill 1861, Chapter 3). Amartya Sen (1999, 155–7) has argued, quite plausibly, that the fact there has been no famine in a democratic country with a free press is best explained by the further fact that, unlike autocrats, democratic leaders have strong incentives to listen and respond to information about the interests of citizens.

In other words, democracy has an "informational dimension": it sends messages about people's lives and condition to those in power (Waldron 2012, 193). But its accountability dimension ensures that rulers, who can be removed by the people, are motivated to process that information and act on it if they seek to retain power. So democracy improves the chances of decisions with desirable consequences. This can work in the other direction, however, when democratic majorities reject policies with significant long-term benefits because they judge the short-term costs are not worth bearing. The obvious example is popular resistance to climate-change policies that might preserve a habitable environment for our species in the future but require democratic publics to accept reduced living standards in the here and now (White 2007, 45; Barry 2005, 251–73).

Peace

Democratic countries tend not to go to war with one another. While it is not true that no two democracies ever fight, Steven Pinker, citing the multiple logistic regression studies by Russett and Oneal (2001), has argued that – especially since around 1900 – "pairs of countries that are more democratic are less likely to confront each other in militarized disputes" (Pinker 2018, 163). Protracted hostilities between democracies are rare. Perhaps internal appeal to consensus and the rule of law leads to external emphasis on these same norms. Or maybe democratically accountable leaders are more likely to think twice before starting wars that will cost both money and citizens' lives (Pinker 2011, 278). This would be consistent with the point made above about incentives, information, and accountability.

Of course, democracies are not necessarily good examples of civilized international conduct. The United States, for instance, has invaded, infiltrated, and attacked other countries, including the overthrow of democratically elected governments in Iran (1953), Guatemala (1954), and Chile (1973); and it initiated, carried out, or supported the killing of millions in places such as Korea, Vietnam, Cambodia, Laos, Indonesia, Guatemala, El Salvador, Nicaragua, Afghanistan, and Iraq (White 2012, 465–75, 514–16). Nonetheless, other things being equal, democracies are less war-prone than non-democracies.

Active Human Beings

Consider the supposed effects of democracy on the character of individuals (Mill 1861, Chapter 3). John Stuart Mill argues that participating in law-making produces in people more public spirit and an active character better able to think creatively about social problems and their potential solutions and more willing to take responsibility for decisions that affect them. Political participation, especially as understood on the forum model as government by discussion and compromise, seems likely to expose citizens to conflicting opinions and new information. The likely result will be better-educated individuals than would be produced by non-democratic systems.

CONCLUSION

We have seen how the tools of political theory – conceptual analysis, historical awareness, and argument evaluation – can shed light on a core idea of political science like democracy. Political theorists emphasize the normative dimension of politics. Beyond the essential descriptive and explanatory tasks of political science, theorists focus on evaluative questions: "Is democracy valuable and, if so, why?" and "How do different conceptions of democracy, such as market or forum, affect our views about its desirability?"

This chapter has only scratched the surface. Many questions remain to be considered. For example, if democracy is rule by the people, one obvious question is immediately suggested – namely, "Who are the people?" This question becomes especially important when we consider that, in multinational states like Canada, people disagree about who counts as the relevant decision-making population. Some argue that shared nationality is a necessary condition for a well-functioning democracy, but who decides which nation should have final authority when more than one nation exists within a given state boundary? Or consider the idea and practice of global democracy. If we accept democratic procedures within nation-states, shouldn't they be applied beyond state borders, perhaps even to the population of the entire globe? After all, decisions made by sovereign states affect many people beyond their borders who lack a say in those decisions. If democracy is political equality, why should outsiders be denied the equal respect we give to insiders? Democracy as a decision-making procedure does not settle the question of who should count as participants in the making of decisions.

REFERENCES

Anderson, Elizabeth. 2009. "Democracy: Instrumental vs. Non-instrumental Value." In *Contemporary Debates in Political Philosophy*, edited by Thomas Christiano and John Christman, 213–27. Malden, MA: Wiley-Blackwell.

Aristotle. 1981. *Politics*. Translated by T.A. Sinclair and Trevor J. Saunders. London: Penguin. (Originally composed ca. 330 BCE.)

Barry, Brian. 2005. *Why Social Justice Matters*. Cambridge: Polity Press.

Christiano, Tom. 2006. "Democracy." *Stanford Encyclopedia of Philosophy*. https://plato.stanford.edu/entries/democracy/

Dahl, Robert. 1989. *Democracy and Its Critics*. New Haven, CT: Yale University Press.

– 1998. *On Democracy*. New Haven, CT: Yale University Press.

– 2006. *On Political Equality*. New Haven, CT: Yale University Press.

Dworkin, Ronald. 2000. *Sovereign Virtue: The Theory and Practice of Equality*. Cambridge, MA: Harvard University Press.

Elster, Jon. 1997. "The Market and the Forum: Three Varieties of Political Theory." In *Deliberative Democracy: Essays on Reason and Politics*, edited by James Bohman and William Rehg, 3–34. Cambridge, MA: MIT Press.

Gilens, Martin, and Benjamin I. Page. 2014. "Testing Theories of American Politics: Elites, Interest Groups, and Average Citizens." *Perspectives on Politics* 12, no. 3: 564–81. https://doi.org/10.1017/s1537592714001595

Kahneman, Daniel. 2011. *Thinking Fast and Slow*. Toronto: Doubleday Canada.

Mill, John Stuart. 1977. "Considerations on Representative Government." In *Essays on Politics and Society*, edited by John M. Robson. Volume XIX, *Collected Works of John Stuart Mill*. New York: Routledge. (Originally composed 1861.)

Page, Benjamin I., Jason Seawright, and Matthew J. Lacombe. 2018. *Billionaires and Stealth Politics*. Chicago: University of Chicago Press.

Pinker, Steven. 2011. *The Better Angels of Our Nature: Why Violence Has Declined*. New York: Viking.

– 2018. *Enlightenment Now*. New York: Viking.

Plato. 1992. *Republic*. Translated by G.M.A. Grube and C.D.C. Reeve. Indianapolis: Hackett. (Originally composed ca. 380 BCE.)

Rawls, John. 2005. *Political Liberalism*. New York: Columbia University Press.

Rousseau, Jean-Jacques. 1993. *The Social Contract and Discourses*. Translated by G.D.H. Cole. London: Dent. (Originally published in 1762.)

Russett, Bruce, and John Oneal. 2001. *Triangulating Peace*. New York: Norton.

Sen, Amartya. 1999. *Development as Freedom*. New York: Anchor.

Simmons, A. John. 2008. *Political Philosophy*. Oxford: Oxford University Press.

Swift, Adam. 2014. *Political Philosophy*, 3rd ed. Cambridge: Polity Press.

Tetlock, Philip E. 2005. *Expert Political Judgment*. Princeton, NJ: Princeton University Press.

Thucydides. 1972. *The Peloponnesian War*. London: Penguin. (Originally composed ca. 410 BCE.)

Waldron, Jeremy. 2012. "Democracy." In *The Oxford Handbook of Political Philosophy*, edited by David Estlund, 187–203. Oxford: Oxford University Press.

White, Matthew. 2012. *Atrocities*. New York: Norton.

White, Stuart. 2007. *Equality*. Cambridge: Polity Press.

CHAPTER THREE

Is Majority Rule Democratic?

Richard Vernon

In the United Kingdom ironically inclined political theorists can buy T-shirts on which the following words are printed: "I'm a political theorist, I solve problems you didn't know you had, in ways that you can't understand." The last part seems rather harsh: political theorists, in general, are no more obscure than other social scientists, in general. But the first part is right on the mark: political theorists do raise "problems you didn't know you had," or, more formally put, they seek to problematize what is familiar. Political discourse is packed with highly significant words such as freedom, equality, rights, justice, democracy. Often it is assumed that the meaning of these words is obvious. Equally often, political actors seek to persuade their audience that one or an other meaning is obviously the right one. But the discipline of political theory, which is critical through and through, rests on the premise that what appears to be obvious is not. In the discourse that surrounds us, words that are freighted with meaning pass without reflective attention; and political actors seek to monopolize words with multiple possible meanings as though only one possible meaning was worth our attention. In both regards, political theorists would claim that their essentially critical stance is valuable: in the case of taken-for-granted meanings, it is important to unsettle conventional understandings so that our sense of what is important is enlarged; and in the case of discursive monopoly, as we may term it, it is important to open up discourse to alternative meanings. Behind all this is a deep assumption that what we can do is governed and constrained by what we can think, and that what we can think is governed and constrained by what we can say. Because of this, political theorists attach the most fundamental (moral and political) importance to their role as, above all else, critical interpreters of political terms.

The critical method generally employed by political theorists is really not all that different from a common-sense approach to problem-solving. Faced with a problem, our natural first move is to identify a range of possible solutions and then to compare the merits, and respective likelihood of success, of the alternatives. One thing that may make political theory look different from ordinary problem-solving is that in canvassing the range of possible meanings for a term political theorists often look beyond the context at hand – for example, to the history of political thought. This does not mean that they are historians. There are also historians of political thought, whose aim is to recover the specific context of problems to which classical texts responded; for political theorists, what *we* are trying to do is exactly the same as what Hobbes or Locke or Rousseau was trying to do – that is, to make sense of the conceptual controversies of the day; and if those famous antecedents can help us it is not because they enjoy authority but because they can contribute valuably to the range of alternatives that critique must take seriously. Another thing that may make political theory look unusual is the recourse to thought experiments, artificial examples designed to test how readers will respond. Political theorists use these devices, however, not because of any love for the abstract, but exactly because they recognize that reality is a complex of many variables, so that we have to resort to artifice if we're to figure out what any one variable is doing. In order to evaluate the appropriateness of an argument, it is sometimes necessary to test with counterfactuals or hypothetical cases how that argument might withstand the specifics of a different context. Thought experiments may also be a tool of social and political critique. The social contract tradition is the most familiar example – theorists such as Locke and Rawls evaluate institutions by asking if they are the kind that we would choose if we were in a position to do so.

All of that is intended as an introduction to the topic of this chapter: the principle of majority rule. Its place in the idea of democracy is among the things that seem unassailably secure. There is a widespread, taken-for-granted assumption that taking a vote, and assigning a win to the alternative with the largest number of votes, is, simply, what democracy is about. But while that assumption is widespread, critical evaluation of it is quite rare. If majority rule is democratic, why is it? Moreover, while majority rule seems to have a secure place in the idea of democracy, it can't be said to be equivalent to it, because other normative variables such as equality and fairness are also held to be essential to it. So what follows below is a process of questioning. Is majority rule essential to what democracy is, and if so how does it relate to other things deemed essential to it? The account is sceptical of several of the claims made for the majority principle. Eventually, though, it gives a qualified endorsement to one view of its importance.

First, though, let me set aside two matters that are important but not central to this inquiry. One is a distinction between the majority principle in the strict sense and a looser use of it that is common. In the strict sense a person or a party or a position enjoys a majority by virtue of having received more votes than all the other alternatives voted on. In a less strict sense, the person or party or position may have received more votes than any other single contender: this is often (and more properly) called enjoying a "plurality." The second is that what counts as a majority (in either of those two senses) is often going to depend on the system of voting that is employed (Black 1958). On this there is a fascinating literature stemming from the French scientist Condorcet and the English mathematician Dodgson (better known as Lewis Carroll, author of the *Alice* books). These issues are not discussed here, not at all because they are unimportant, but because they concern ways of counting numbers, whereas the question addressed here is more basic still: Why do numbers count at all? Or, put differently: Why is more better than less?

Although, as noted above, the connection of democracy with the majority principle now seems natural, even a brief look at history shows us that once, and for a long time, it was very far from natural-seeming, and in fact needed quite strenuous special justifications (Heinberg 1932). The original decision-making ideal, in various contexts and traditions, seems to have been unanimity. To say that a group approves of something, according to the original (and still understandable) belief, can only be to say that all members of the group approve. Otherwise, are we not in effect saying that dissenters don't really count as members of the group? But, unanimity being very rare, the need and the desire to make collective decisions, rather than doing nothing at all, led to the adoption of majoritarian substitutes. So, sometimes, after a vote, dissenting minorities were asked to confirm their acceptance of the majority view, in order to confer on it the legitimacy that it would otherwise lack. Alternatively, the majority was deemed to be not only the larger but also the saner or wiser part of the electorate, so that – anticipating later ideas of hypothetical consent – the majority could be held to give voice to what dissenters would have agreed to had they been saner or wiser. What we need to note here is that neither of these expedients amounts to a justification of majority rule itself. They endorse a unanimity principle, and grudgingly accept (very!) rough approximations to it.

In looking for a starting point for this enquiry, often one encounters something like the remark, attributed to Winston Churchill, that democracy is the worst system apart from all the others. Similarly, majority rule is sometimes defended by way of comparison with clearly unsatisfactory contenders. What are those alternative contenders? One is the unanimity principle, from which, we have just seen, the majority principle is (historically) descended. Now, we do still look for unanimity in certain contexts, typically ones involving small numbers of people who need to get along together, so that it's overridingly important to make everyone happy. A group of friends deciding where to go for dinner would be deeply reluctant to pick a place that anyone in the group hated. But as groups become larger and decisions more consequential, a unanimity rule would become objectionable because, in effectively giving veto power to minorities opposed to proposed changes, it would become an instrument for preserving the status quo. That would please conservatives, of course, but also strengthen the hand of radicals who, hoping to provoke revolution, preferred the status quo to moderate reform. The same goes, though obviously to a lesser extent, to the requirement for "supermajorities" – that is, for majorities greater than 50 per cent plus one of the votes cast; there is a case to be made for supermajorities in special contexts in which some degree of status-quo bias is reasonable – for example, in constitutional matters, in which much of the point of constitutions would be lost if change were to become too easy. Constitutions don't mean anything if they're no different from ordinary laws. Supermajorities are often required for the approval of electoral reform too, on the grounds that stability in voting systems is desirable: in the 2009 British Columbia referendum, for example, the proposed reform failed because the rules required 60 per cent approval in at least 60 per cent of the province's electoral districts.

The second not-too-hard-to-dismiss alternative is rule by the wise, or "epistocracy" as it is sometimes called (Estlund 1997). Now the first objection to this would likely be based on the moral value of equality, to which we turn next. But before we get to objections of a moral kind, there is a logical problem or paradox. How do we know who the wise people are? We can't tell if they're wise unless we can evaluate their views, or decide who among us is wise enough to do so. But if we can evaluate their views, or decide who among us is in a position to do so, then surely we must be wise enough to rule ourselves? It is true that in certain contexts we place our trust in professional qualifications, so that most of us trust (for example) duly accredited climate scientists without being personally able to evaluate their evidence. But there are no duly accredited authorities on politics, and the idea that there could be begs all the questions about politics, which is itself a process of deciding who has authority to do what, in a context of disagreement about what it would be right to do.

What about the positive case for majority rule, though? As noted above, it must surely have to rest on the value of equality. If we take a vote, each person having one vote, then the outcome reflects equal power. Compare it with a situation in which only some people could vote, or in which some people had more than one vote. We would regard such situations as being hopelessly biased, and as inconsistent with a general value, equality, that (in some form or other) almost everyone, these days at least, would endorse. So do we have our answer? Not quite, for there are other ways of giving expression to the value of equality, in some respects, perhaps, more fully.

One of these is the practice of compromise (May 2005). This is a topic that was once oddly neglected by political theorists, but which has recently been interestingly explored. There are various kinds of compromise. Suppose I want a, b, and c, and you want b, c, and d: we can settle on what we both want – that is, b and c, giving up a and d. Or suppose I want a and b, while you want c and d: we can each give something up while accepting something from the other, settling on b and c. Or suppose neither of us can accept anything in the other's list, but we both think e is better than anything on the other's list, and so we settle on that instead. What these have in common is that in each case both parties' views get to be reflected in the final decision. Now in what sense is that less respectful of equality than a majority vote? At the time of writing, the

United Kingdom is in the process of coming to terms with a referendum in which a 52 per cent majority voted to leave the European Union, 48 per cent voting to remain. Without wanting to take sides here, we might say that a compromise theorist would recommend a "soft Brexit" – that is, a renegotiated relationship with the EU that would preserve some of the benefits that the 48 per cent evidently valued. Would that be less egalitarian than simply giving the majority what they want, or, arguably, more respectful of the equal value of those in the minority? It must be noted, though, that although a compromise or mid-point outcome might be defended in this way, there is no guarantee that a majority would endorse it if it were presented for a vote.[1]

The second possible alternative, as a way of institutionalizing equality, may be more surprising: lotteries. Strange as it may seem now to use lotteries as a decision-making tool, they were widely used in the past. Aristotle approved of their use in adding a democratic element to constitutions – a random distribution of offices would give extra weight to the demographically more numerous (hence poorer) class of citizens. A particularly elaborate lottery system was used by the city-state of Venice for many centuries, as a way of defeating electoral corruption – voters can be bought, the Venetian political class recognized, but chance can't (Manin 1997, 63–7). In the US constitutional debates of the late eighteenth century, it was proposed that the Electoral College, which was charged with the task of picking presidents, should be filled by random selection from the electoral roll (80). Even today, "sortition" theorists (as they are called) continue to press for a more extensive use of lottery-like devices to fill public positions (Goodwin 2005) – precisely because it would enhance equality, on the grounds that it would generally equalize chances to exercise influence, as well as on Aristotle's demographic grounds.

The point of the above two paragraphs was not to recommend alternatives to majority rule. The point was to show that we need more than a bare appeal to the value of equality if we are to justify it. We need to show that majority rule satisfies equality in a way that other possible expressions of equality do not. That brings us to the heart of this topic. In democratic theory there are two proposals that offer to satisfy this condition. I shall term them "utilitarian" and "deliberative," and discuss them below.

The "Utilitarians" were a group of philosophers and social reformers in (mainly) nineteenth-century Britain who came to advocate (among other things) political democracy. Actually their reasons rather resembled the "saner part" view from the distant past, for they believed that majorities would have the good sense to resist the special (or "sinister") interests that in their view corrupted politics (James 1981). But in later political theory, the "utilitarian" label has come to be attached to an idea of democracy that reflects the Utilitarians' basic principle, "the greatest happiness of the greatest number." We want political decisions to maximize happiness, and minimize unhappiness, on the largest practicable scale. And we can easily see how this connection might be thought to work. If twenty people disagree about something, and take a vote to settle it, then if thirteen vote pro and seven vote con then as an outcome there are thirteen happy people and only seven unhappy ones. So that looks good. And here's another utilitarian-good thing: remember that even if you have lost in *that* vote, in a stream of decisions over time, majorities are (obviously) larger than minorities, so your statistical odds overall of being in a majority are long-term positive.

That view faces two severe objections. Taking the second claim first, if there were an even chance of any given person being in a minority or in a majority over time, then yes, your odds would be good. But majorities and minorities do not form in infinitely fluid ways. There are consistent voting affiliations, based on such things as class and region and traditional partisanship, that last for generations, and the claim that (say) a left-inclined voter in Texas has better-than-even-odds at seeing their policy preferences winning over time is plainly false. But it is the first claim that is fatal to the "utilitarian" view as it is taken to be here. That view would work if (in addition to having equal chances of winning or losing over time) everyone stood to gain or lose to an equal extent from the outcome of the vote. But that, too, is obviously false. Women have more to gain or lose from a vote on abortion than men do. Indigenous people who rely on fishing for subsistence have more to gain or lose from conservation decisions than others do. Parents with young children have more of a stake in school-board decisions than childless people or empty-nesters do. Now, if we had a way of measuring how much "more" one group would be affected than another would be, then we could solve this problem – we could not only count up the numbers on one side and the other but also factor in their respective levels of happiness and pain. But we can't do that, because we don't have a metre for happiness or pain.

The problem here is sometimes termed the "intensities problem": while we can give each person one vote, we have no way of knowing (or measuring) the degree of intensity with which any given voter will respond, positively or negatively, to any given issue. Is there a solution? One, of a very pragmatic kind, is to rely on voter turnout. We can assume, perhaps, that those who feel intensely will turn out to vote, while the relatively indifferent will stay home. (If that is a good response, it's also a good reason, by the way, not to adopt compulsory voting, which would remove intensity of interest as a factor.) That seems a bit precarious as a solution, however, given that the propensity to vote may be affected by factors other than the intensity of interest. It may be affected, for example, by the sense of personal efficacy, which is in turn correlated with social and economic variables, which we might not want to play a part in affecting democratic outcomes. (For another look at turnout and democracy, see chapter 4 by Anderson and Stephenson in this volume.)

Another response is that we should try to anticipate issues regarding which particularly intense interests are likely to come into play (Brighouse and Fleurbaey 2010). Some degree of local self-government, for example, might be an implication, if we assume that people living and working on the main street have a stronger interest in the speed limit there than truck drivers passing through have. Another important implication leads us to the idea of personal rights. There may be things that you have a stronger interest in than anyone else could legitimately have: who you associate with, for example. If so, we may want to give some classes of decision the form of constitutional control that is embedded in the idea of rights. This is a significant provisional result: quite often, rights are thought of as things that constrain the operation of democracy, because they take issues off the table and prevent majorities from settling them. The defence of rights often falls to courts, which in many countries take decisions that strike down decisions made by democratically elected legislatures. But if we are justifying majority decisions on "utilitarian" principles as defined above, then we should also believe in rights, and endorse ways of protecting them, given that people predictably have such uneven stakes in the outcomes of many decisions.

The main rival of the utilitarian view is what is generally called deliberative democracy (Gutmann and Thompson 1996). The main difference between the two approaches is that deliberative democrats don't regard voters as coming to the election with a set of given interests or desires, hoping to get them satisfied. Rather, they come to the process with proposals to offer, and they are open in principle to changing their minds if their proposals meet with effective criticism or they hear of better ones. So the process is not meant to register everyone's list of demands, but to register "the force of the better reasons." So when a vote is taken at the end it is one that reflects a wider range of reasons or views or information than any one voter enjoyed at the beginning. Something like this view was held by Aristotle, who relied on it in advocating a democratic element in constitutions: "When they [the people] meet together," he wrote, "their perceptions are quite good enough" (Aristotle 1941, 1191). The condition that he states is important: the voters must "meet together," for there is held to be something about their interaction that improves their eventual decision.

It is fascinating to speculate about the kinds of things that might take place when decision-makers interact (Waldron 1995). But our focus here is on the majority principle, and so we need to ask how it is that this process changes our view of the eventual vote. It is tempting to say that the vote is the outcome of the discussion, but that simply isn't true. The vote only expresses the majority's view of the outcome of the discussion – that is, what the discussion led to. Suppose we say, what I think *is* true, that interaction brings more information to the table: the vote still only reflects what the majority makes of this richer information base. The minority evidently doesn't share the majority's interpretation of what to make of it. And we can't put their dissent down to self-interest or stupidity, because obviously we might discount the majority's view in exactly the same fashion.

Now is there any reason to think that the majority judges the reasons and the evidence better? Here some theorists turn to the famous "Condorcet Jury theorem," an argument developed in the eighteenth century by the Marquis de Condorcet, who reasoned that if each voter has a better-than-even chance of being right about something, then the majority of a group has a still better chance of being right about it (Dahl 1989, 135–52). Jeremy Waldron (2012) uses the simple analogy of black and white balls in a jar. Suppose 70 per cent of them are black and 30 per cent are white: the more you take out the more likely it is that the composition of the sample will represent the composition of the whole. So the more people we ask, assuming each one is likelier to be right than wrong, the sounder our decision will be. One evident downside is that if we assume that each has a less-than-even chance of being right, then the logic works the other way – the majority vote is still more likely to be wrong than any individual voter, picked at random, is likely to be. But an even more generally decisive problem is that the Condorcet model is basically unsuitable to a deliberative situation in which voters "meet together." It only works if each voter votes independently. Suppose, to simplify, there were two very persuasive speakers in our group of fifty voters, and we all followed one of them or the other: then the vote would reflect two opinions, not fifty, and so the accumulative logic wouldn't apply.

There is a less ambitious version of the deliberative argument that does not depend on finding reasons to think that majorities are more likely than minorities to get it right. It is simply an argument about incentives (Vernon 2001). Suppose that, in order to win, you only had to persuade an all-powerful king. All you would have to do is figure out what kinds of reasons are likely to appeal to him. But suppose instead that, in order to win, you had to find reasons that would appeal to several million people: then you would have an incentive to find reasons that would appeal broadly and from many different points of view. You would be maximally incentivized to be persuasive. Now of course, your opponent would be similarly incentivized, and there is no way of knowing which of you is going to be more successful. But whether you or your opponent wins, whatever the winning position turns out to be, it will (if you've both done your work, as you've been incentivized to do) have been given the best possible justification. That means, not that the better set of reasons will have won, but that the majority will have been voting for good reasons, and that the minority will have been given reasons for their defeat. That is desirable, not because it requires us to think that the better view is going to win, but because it expresses a sort of civic respect. There are going to be winners and losers, but winners owe losers a reason, and majority rule may be a better way to secure this than any other way of doing things.

But although that proposal is less ambitious than the full deliberative case, it may still be way too ambitious. It is applicable when there is a political culture that permits and encourages a spirit of mutual persuasion. It doesn't rule out a political culture in which there is partisanship; it is quite consistent with the ineliminable political fact that we want our side to win. But it does depend on desiring to win for the right reasons. Soccer teams want to win, and while they are happy to accept quite a bit of luck they would prefer not to win just because, although they were playing badly, the goalie on the other side was struck by lightning at a crucial moment. Analogously, political partisanship is admirable to the extent that it cultivates persuasive skill, and ceases to be admirable when it loses any interest in reaching out beyond its already-committed base. No theory of majority rule applies when political contestation reaches that level. From a deliberative point of view, especially, the outcome of such contestation isn't superior in any way to a lottery outcome.

Is there a still less ambitious position to fall back on? One is suggested by a provocative paper by Adam Przeworski (1988), a Polish political scientist who wrote about democratic transitions in former Soviet Bloc countries. He wondered at one point: How do we know when the transition to democracy has actually happened? And it occurred to him that the answer was very simple: it's when we don't know who's going to win this time. Before, whatever paraphernalia of decision-making was paraded, we knew who was going to win. And then a point came when the outcome was in doubt. That, in Przeworski's view, is the democratic moment, the moment when the outcome of public decision-making becomes "contingent" or unpredictable. So how does this relate to majority rule? It relates to it very closely, in that controlling majorities, which are large and heterogeneous, is very hard to do. Domination depends on the use or threatened use of reliable instruments. You can dominate me if you can reliably propose to deploy against me something that I fear. But, except perhaps in exceptional circumstances, you can't deploy the threat of majority disapproval against me, or at least not without the threat of counter-mobilization by me and my friends. So domination becomes very uncertain, and, when achieved, insecure, because holding on to majority support is just as hard as gaining it in the first place.

That is of course a very minimal or negative sort of defence, and it seems to take us back to "the worst system but for all the others" (i.e., other systems in which domination is easier to achieve). In fact, if preventing domination is the *only* value in play, majority rule is no better – and arguably less effective – than the lottery system operated by Renaissance Venice, mentioned above. But the defence doesn't actually rule out some of the more attractive views that we have discussed. The *practice* of engaging in political competition for majority support may itself be an educative one, even if we cannot say that there is a strong case for the rightness of any *particular* majority decision. The practice of majority rule may contribute over time to a political culture of civic respect in which we come to recognize the need for persuasion. That idea, it must finally be mentioned, gives no weight to a majority decision as such, but it approves of the use of majority rule as a way of fostering political relations, within an ongoing democratic polity, of a uniquely valuable kind. So there is no inconsistency in holding a minimalist and somewhat sceptical view of majority rule while also hoping that the practice of majoritarian decision-making might modify political culture in desirable ways. In political as in personal cases, it is a good thing that people should learn to give reasons for what they want from others, and there is no institution better than majority rule that can promote (without guaranteeing) that learning process.

NOTE

1 At the time of writing, opinion polling suggests that an overall majority would disapprove of the compromise on the table: for analysis, see Bellamy (2019).

REFERENCES

Aristotle. 1941. *The Basic Works of Aristotle.* Edited by Richard McKeon. New York: Random House.

Bellamy, Richard. 2019. "Was the Brexit Referendum Legitimate, and Would a Second One Be So?" *European Political Science* 18, no. 1: 126–33. https://doi.org/10.1057/s41304-018-0155-x

Black, Duncan. 1958. *The Theory of Committees and Elections.* Cambridge: Cambridge University Press.

Brighouse, Harry, and Marc Fleurbaey. 2010. "Democracy and Proportionality." *Journal of Political Philosophy* 18, no. 2: 137–55. https://doi.org/10.1111/j.1467-9760.2008.00316.x

Dahl, Robert. 1989. *Democracy and Its Critics.* New Haven, CT: Yale University Press.

Estlund, David. 1997. "Beyond Fairness and Deliberation: The Epistemic Dimension of Democratic Authority." In *Deliberative Democracy: Essays on Reason and Politics*, edited by James Bohman and William Rehg, 173–203. Cambridge, MA: MIT Press.

Goodwin, Barbara. 2005. *Justice by Lottery.* Exeter, UK: Academic Imprint.

Gutmann, Amy, and Dennis Thompson. 1996. *Democracy and Disagreement.* Cambridge, MA: Harvard University Press.

Heinberg, John Gilbert. 1932. "Theories of Majority Rule." *American Political Science Review* 26, no. 3: 452–69. https://doi.org/10.2307/1946465

James, Michael. 1981. "Public Interest and Majority Rule in Bentham's Democratic Theory." *Political Theory* 9, no. 1: 49–62. https://doi.org/10.1177/009059178100900103

Manin, Bernard. 1997. *The Principles of Representative Government.* Cambridge: Cambridge University Press.

May, Simon Cabulea. 2005. "Principled Compromise and the Abortion Controversy." *Philosophy and Public Affairs* 33, no. 4: 317–48. https://doi.org/10.1111/j.1088-4963.2005.00035.x

Przeworski, Adam. 1988. "Democracy as a Contingent Outcome of Conflicts." In *Constitutionalism and Democracy,* edited by Jon Elster and Rune Slagstad, 59–80. Cambridge: Cambridge University Press.

Vernon, Richard. 2001. *Political Morality: A Theory of Liberal Democracy.* London: Continuum.

Waldron, Jeremy. 1995. "The Wisdom of the Multitude." *Political Theory* 23, no. 4: 563–84. https://doi.org/10.1177/0090591795023004001

– 2012. "Democracy." In *The Oxford Handbook of Political Philosophy,* edited by David Estlund, 187–203. Oxford: Oxford University Press.

PART TWO

Analysing Democracy: Positivist Approaches

CHAPTER FOUR

Evaluating a Democracy: Are Citizens Engaged?

Cameron D. Anderson and Laura B. Stephenson

INTRODUCTION

Democracy is commonly thought to mean "rule by the people." Indeed, one of the defining features of a functioning democracy is the collective exercise of choosing the government through free and fair elections. Also known as turnout, voting in elections is central to legitimizing the selection of democratic governments and to fulfilling the notion of democracy as rule by the people. Whether in long-established democracies like Canada or fledgling democracies such as Ukraine, Indonesia, or Bolivia, voting in elections to select one's government is a substantial if not symbolic indicator of democracy in practice. Indeed, elections feature prominently in definitions of democracy. For example, Freedom House, an international organization known for scoring the "democratic-ness" of countries, focuses on political rights and civil liberties. It judges the quality of a democracy, in part, by the extent to which elections of government officials are free and fair; essentially, whether its citizens are able to participate in legitimate and meaningful elections (Freedom House 2018).

Some would argue that a defining element of democracy is public participation in the selection of government or government representatives (Dahl 1989; Lijphart 1997). From this, it follows that the extent to which citizens choose to be involved in the selection of their government may be an important indicator of the health of a representative democracy. Fewer people involved in choosing a government means fewer voices are shaping government decision-making and this has the potential to affect representativeness (Lutz and Marsh 2007). If declining turnout means fewer citizens are choosing to engage in democracy, then the quality of democracy, as rule by the people, could be viewed as weakened.

But is this a valid assumption? Does lower turnout necessarily mean less support for democracy? Perhaps lower turnout does not reflect badly on democratic quality because it is not related to whether citizens support democracy. What we really need to understand are citizens' attitudes toward democracy and the extent to which citizens' support the principles and performance of democratically elected governments.

In this chapter, we evaluate whether judging democracy on the basis of turnout levels is justifiable. To do so, we not only examine turnout rates and democratic support at the national level in Canada but we also consider democratic elections at subnational levels of government – provincial and municipal. We believe that exploring engagement at more than one level aids in elucidating the complexity and nuance of the democratic experience in a multi-level country such as Canada. We also take a behaviouralist approach, consider the existing research on the subject of turnout at different levels of government, and use two types of data to investigate the issue. In the pages that follow we elaborate on the assumptions and process of our research approach, outline what we know about the decision to turn out from other researchers, analyse data to understand more about attitudes toward democracy at different levels of government, and compare these attitudes to what we know about turnout. Finally, we reach some conclusions about the suitability of using turnout as a measure of democratic health.

OUR APPROACH

The behaviouralist approach to answering a research question in political science can also be described as positivist, post-positivist, or scientific.[1] Simply put, such an approach looks to explain phenomena by following agreed-upon procedures of scientific inquiry. The behavioural approach began in the first half of the twentieth century. Commonly referred to as the "Behavioural Revolution," political scientists (and social scientists more generally) began to study questions in political science with an eye to increasing the rigour imposed by adopting standards commonly associated with the hard sciences (Dahl 1961). Writing in 1961, Robert Dahl noted that the behavioural research approach in American political science had become so successful and popular that it was joining the ranks of the political science establishment.

Two important assumptions underlie this approach to political science, and they are rooted in our responses to the questions of ontology and epistemology. The first is a belief that political phenomena can be observed. That is, we can identify particular events (e.g., the development of protests over approval of the Trans Mountain Pipeline) and make the empirical observation that these events did in fact occur and can be analysed. For example, regardless of our perspective on whether or not the Trans Mountain Pipeline is a good public policy choice, we can and indeed ought to treat these events as something that can be explained. In this sense, then, we treat political phenomena as occurring independently from the political science researcher and our perceptions of these phenomena. Social and political phenomena are objectively real and knowable.

The second assumption is that there can be a separation between political science researchers and the political or social phenomena that they study. For example, we can and should study pipeline protests without having to participate in or take a position on either the pipeline or the protests – objective observation is possible. Essentially, we conceive of our role as researchers as independent from the events that we study and this independence allows for a degree of objectivity in thinking about and understanding political phenomena.

In addition to these assumptions, there are two key features of the behavioural approach. The first is that it draws upon *empirical theory*, which can be defined as "a set of interconnected abstract statements, consisting of assumptions, definitions and empirically testable hypotheses, which purports to describe and explain the occurrence of a given phenomenon or set of phenomena" (Sanders 2010, 25). The theory developed about social or political phenomena must include abstract statements that posit how a phenomenon proceeds as well as scope conditions or parameters delineating the extent to which the theoretical statements pertain to other domains. For example, a theoretical statement about the causes of pipeline protests in Canada will likely only relate to that phenomena and have little or no relevance for legislation regulating health care or banking.

The second key feature of behavioural work is that it seeks to provide an *explanation* for social or political phenomena. As Sanders (2010, 25) outlines, "an explanation is a causal account of the occurrence of some phenomenon or set of phenomena." The goal in explanations of social or political phenomena is to posit logical arguments that account for why something happened. In this sense, the goal is not simply to describe the features of social or political phenomena but to go further and account for the conditions required for their occurrence.

Agreement on these two features of behavioural analysis has resulted in the widespread adoption of the scientific method in social science. Far more detailed introductions of the scientific method and related research design topics are available elsewhere (for example, see King, Keohane, and Verba 1994; Frankfort-Nachmias and Nachmias 2010). It is sufficient to say here that the following steps apply:

1. Draw on theory to generate specific hypotheses or predictions about political phenomena.
2. Prepare to investigate or test the hypotheses empirically by:
   – defining key terms and concepts, and
   – developing valid measures and means of operationalizing these concepts.
3. Collect data for the investigation that reflect the theory and hypotheses being assessed, being careful to document the procedures followed.
4. Evaluate the data in light of the hypotheses. Are the expectations from the hypotheses borne out in relationships observed in the collected data? The goal at this stage of the research process is to establish empirically verified statements about political phenomena and assert levels of uncertainty about those statements.
5. Drawing upon the evaluation of the hypotheses, clarify the implications of the empirical findings for broader theories about political phenomena.

It is important to note that the data used for such an analysis could take many forms, and the process of collection could involve running individual-level surveys, conducting experiments (in which respondents are randomly assigned to treatment and control conditions), or simply gathering aggregate statistics (such as census data, government statistics, or other population-level data). Behaviouralists often draw upon quantitative and statistical methods to test their theories and hypotheses about political phenomena, but it is also possible for researchers to use qualitative data. Indeed, this is part of the central argument put forth by King, Keohane, and Verba (1994) and others (e.g., Brady and Collier 2010). The key to the behavioural approach is not the type of data used but the fact that the appropriate data needed to evaluate the hypotheses are gathered in a transparent, generalizable, replicable, and rigorous fashion. Behaviouralists seek to generate empirical theory that can explain political phenomena. The approach dictates adherence to a codified process of inquiry broadly understood as the application of the scientific method to the study of social and political phenomena.

WHAT MOTIVATES TURNOUT

The central research question we want to investigate is what turnout levels might indicate about the quality of a democracy and citizens' satisfaction with democracy. As noted in the introduction to this chapter, voting is a key activity in representative democracies; the degree to which people choose to abstain from voting can therefore signal their (dis)-engagement with democracy. Following this logic, less citizen engagement in democracy should also mean that citizens are less supportive of democracy, less satisfied with their democracy, and less interested in government. This perspective does not reflect the majority of research into the causes and correlates of turnout. Therefore, before we assess the relationship between turnout and democratic satisfaction and consider what this indicates about democracy more generally, we first explore some of the scholarly work on turnout and develop some background for assessing electoral turnout in Canada.

Why is it that people turn out to vote? Rational choice theory (RCT) provides one answer, based on the assumption that individuals are utility maximizers. Utility maximization means that individuals behave and make choices in ways that will result in the greatest benefit to themselves. For RCT, participating in an election is the result of a calculation based on a relatively straightforward set of factors summarized in the following equation:

$$\text{Decision to turn out} = p(B) - C$$

Here, the decision to turn out is positive if the equation is greater than zero and negative otherwise. In this equation, B is the benefit from having a favoured candidate win the election, and p is the probability of casting the winning ballot to elect a preferred candidate. Because the terms are multiplied by each other, the benefit of a candidate winning is discounted by the probability of casting the winning ballot (which, in most elections, is extremely small). Think, for example, of the most recent federal election in Canada. The winning margin for most candidates simply made any single person's decision to vote or not irrelevant.[2] The C term in the equation references any and all costs associated with turning out to vote, such as the time it takes to go to the poll, the effort involved in gathering information about where and how to vote, and the time spent following the campaign to become informed about the different candidates. Given these three elements, RCT would suggest that voting is an irrational act – the probability of casting the decisive winning vote is so low that the benefits accrued from turning out are always exceeded by the costs of voting.

However, despite the power of the cost-benefit analysis, we know that people do vote. Acknowledging this fact, researchers have struggled to understand why. The most common explanation is that voters get another benefit, separate from which candidate is successful, from the act of voting. Downs (1957) proposed that there is a long-run participation value that individuals derive from living in a democracy that can outweigh the costs. More formally, Riker and Ordeshook (1968) proposed the addition of a D term to the calculus of voting to incorporate the benefits accrued from voting, regardless of the outcome (and therefore not subject to the p term). They listed a number of possible definitions of the term, such as "satisfaction from affirming allegiance to the political system" and "satisfaction of affirming one's efficacy in the political system" (28). Essentially, D represents any non-rational benefit that accrues from the act of voting itself. A sense of duty to vote implies that in the individual voter's mind their participation is important and that they have a responsibility to participate in democracy. Adding the D term to the original turnout equation produces this new variation:

$$\text{Decision to turn out} = p(B) - C + D$$

A decline in turnout around the world has been documented by many, including the World Bank in a World Development Report (2017, 228). This decline has challenged researchers to rethink turnout in terms of what has changed, since the RCT approach would predict consistency. Importantly, researchers have shown that the voting rates of young people are responsible for much of the change (Blais and Rubenson 2013). So what accounts for this change in behaviour? Before we can evaluate the meaning of abstention in terms of democracy, we need to consider what research has shown about the causes of the decline in turnout.

Three theories have been prominent. The first is that there is a life cycle effect (Blais and Rubenson 2013). Citizens who are young (under thirty) tend to turn out at lower rates than citizens in their forties, fifties, and sixties, after which turnout rates tend to decline (perhaps for reasons of health or mobility). From this view, young voters may be less likely to turn out because the issues that are often central in elections (e.g., taxes, health care, transportation) are less relevant to younger voters, and therefore their potential benefit from choosing between candidates is less.

The second explanation focuses on the nature of the elections. Franklin (2004) and Johnston, Matthews, and Bittner (2007) are proponents of this view, which holds that if elections are exciting and competitive then people are motivated to turn out. Furthermore, people can develop specific attitudes toward elections that can carry throughout their lifetime, meaning that experiences when first voting can shape later turnout behaviour. This is known as a period effect.

Blais and Rubenson (2013), however, have a different take on the issue. Their research supports the third argument, that the decline in turnout among young people represents a generational change. The generational effect emphasizes that the political culture of one's youth affects their attitudes toward voting, and that those cultures may vary over time. According to this line of argumentation, a central reason differentiating turnout rates among young and older generations is feelings of duty to vote – older generations developed a stronger sense of responsibility to turn out in democratic elections and younger generations simply have less of this internal sense of duty (Blais and Rubenson 2013); these generational differences will carry over to decrease the voting behaviour of older people over time. Blais et al. (2004) also demonstrate that attention paid to politics is similarly less among young people, which is another component of their generation's orientation toward the democratic system.

This last explanation comes closest to suggesting that lower turnout can be a symptom of weaker democracy, as it suggests that the bond between citizens and the democratic process may have eroded such that citizens no longer feel that their involvement is important or necessary in electoral democracy. Given that representative democracies tend to require elections, this kind of trend is troublesome and points in favour of using turnout as a measure of democratic quality.

However, is this argument universally true? Considering elections at different levels of government calls this conclusion into question. It is well-known that supra- and subnational elections typically have lower turnout. Confronting this trend with respect to European Union elections, Reif and Schmitt (1980) developed the idea of "second-order" elections, ones that are simply less interesting and important for voters because the jurisdictions are or can be perceived to be less important. In this view, turnout is lower simply because people are less motivated to take part. This would be consistent with the idea of weaker democracy, but the appropriateness of the "second order" label for all non-national elections has been seriously questioned at the subnational level (Cutler 2008). With respect to local elections, Rallings and Thrasher (2007) found that differences in turnout between elections at the national and local level in England were eliminated when mail ballots were allowed, suggesting that reducing the costs of voting with mail-in ballots can overcome the challenge of lower-salience elections. This finding supports the rational choice model of costs and benefits and suggests little in terms of the quality of democracy. Henderson and McEwan (2015) argue that understanding subnational turnout requires understanding region-specific variables, such as regional attachment and regional autonomy, in order to understand the variation in turnout across subnational elections. The extant research, then, accounts for the (usually lower) levels of turnout at non-national elections without sounding the alarm about the quality of democracy.

Which view is correct? If low turnout is in fact an indicator of a weaker democratic environment, then we should see differences in attitudes toward the levels of government that are consistent with turnout rates. In other words, if we see that Canadians express the same interest and engagement with their government at different levels but participate to varying degrees, or vice versa, then there is no cause for concern. If, however, we see that attitudes do vary in sync with turnout, then the reverse seems more likely.

DATA AND METHODS

When studying turnout, there are two main sources of data: aggregate statistics and individual-level survey data. Aggregate turnout statistics are typically collected and available in a democracy like Canada from public agencies tasked with administering elections (such as Elections Canada at the federal level or the comparable bodies that exist in each province). These agencies are responsible for ensuring that the list of electors is up-to-date, that campaigning for elected office is done fairly and legally, and that the ballots in each constituency are counted accurately and efficiently. At the conclusion of each federal and provincial election, these public agencies produce detailed and exhaustive reports of public participation in the election and it is from these publicly available documents that aggregate turnout rates can be gathered for individual constituencies and for the electorate as a whole.

Individual-level survey data largely come from public opinion surveys designed to gather information about the political attitudes, identities, and behaviours of respondents. The same kind of public opinion polls commonly discussed in the media (conducted by Forum, Pollara, or Ipsos, for example) are valuable sources of data for studying turnout. In fact, the development of public opinion survey techniques has been a big part of the development of the behavioural approach discussed above. Individual-level surveys enable researchers to make inferences, or empirically based statements, about a population from a much smaller sample of the population. To be of use in scholarly research, individual-level surveys need to be evaluated in terms of a number of important characteristics, including random selection and representativeness. The principle of random selection means that everyone in a target population (all Canadians, for instance) has an equal probability of being contacted, which reduces or eliminates bias in the composition of the sample. Closely related is the goal of representativeness, which means that those who complete the survey mirror the target population (usually evaluated along certain predetermined indicators, such as age, gender, education, and possibly income). Following these two principles ensures that a survey sample reflects as closely as possible the population it is meant to allow inferences about.

Of course, the match between sample and population is rarely perfect. An important consideration is survey mode – the method used to contact potential participants to complete a survey. Individual-level surveys can be conducted in person, over the phone (either landline or cell phone) with a human interviewer, over the phone (either landline or cell phone) with an automated questioner (interactive voice response), online through a web browser, or with paper mail-in forms. There are two important considerations related to mode. The first is *sampling error,* which is closely related to representativeness – depending on the survey method used, not everyone in a population may have an equal chance of being selected into the sample. Online survey samples, for example, could be biased because of differential access to computers (perhaps under-representing lower income or older segments of the population). Similarly, conducting a telephone survey without including cell phone numbers can lead to bias by ignoring segments of the population who only have cell phones. The other issue is *non-response error,* which is bias introduced because of systematic differences in who agrees to complete a survey. Again, this error can be a function of different modes of surveying respondents.

Mindful of these considerations, researchers must also be aware that survey research presents a unique challenge for studying turnout in that it relies on self-reporting.[3] There is always the possibility that respondents are not truthful, and this is especially relevant for turnout, as individuals might think that they should vote or that there is a social expectation of voting and want to avoid being judged negatively. Survey researchers interested in turnout are aware of these dynamics and some have designed question wordings to lessen the effects of social desirability by introducing a preamble and new response categories. A preamble, which is a statement posed before the survey question, can reduce the presumed negativity associated with not turning out. For instance, the

Canadian Municipal Election Study includes the following preamble before its turnout question: "In each election we find that a lot of people were not able to vote because they were not registered, they were sick or they did not have time. Others do not want to vote." This wording tells respondents that it is understandable if they did not vote and flags some possible reasons.

The second technique follows up on the preamble by allowing respondents to provide reasons for not voting. The Making Electoral Democracy Work (MEDW) project (Blais 2010) included a survey experiment to test whether having the traditional yes/no turnout question response options yielded different answers than options that allowed expanded responses, such as "I thought about voting this time but didn't" and "I usually vote but didn't this time." These options indicate that the respondent considered voting or had voted in the past and that they gave some degree of consideration to the act of voting this time around. Morin-Chassé et al. (2017) found that, on average, reported turnout was more than seven percentage points lower when the additional options were allowed. Including these kinds of measures in the construction of survey questions on turnout may help to lessen the incidence of social desirability biases among respondents. While there are no perfect means of lessening social desirability biases on survey questions about turnout, the awareness of these tendencies is important for understanding turnout rates in surveys.[4]

DOES ABSTENTION MEAN WEAKER DEMOCRACY?

To address our research question – whether turnout should be considered as a measure of democratic health – we proceed in two parts. First, we provide some basic aggregate data about turnout rates at different levels of government in Canada. Then, we look at survey data to understand whether attitudes toward democracy correspond and differ accordingly.

Figure 1 plots turnout in Canadian federal and provincial elections in Quebec, Ontario, and British Columbia since 1984.[5] The general decline mentioned above is evident in the figure. It is also notable that the highest and lowest lines are both provincial elections. There does not appear to be systematically lower turnout in provincial elections.

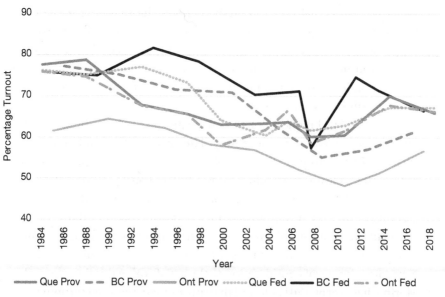

Figure 1. Federal and provincial turnout (British Columbia, Quebec, and Ontario)

This is in contrast to the second-order election theory and more in line with the findings of Cutler (2008). However, and somewhat ironically, the one province that does have lower provincial turnout than federal turnout is Ontario, which informed Cutler's empirical work.

Given these trends, it makes sense to look closer at Ontario for our analysis. Adding the municipal level, figure 2 plots turnout in federal, provincial, and municipal elections among Ontario voters since 1981. Again, we see the general decline in turnout, as well as a clear difference in the level of turnout across the three levels of government – turnout in federal elections is highest while turnout in municipal elections is lower than in either of the other levels.

If turnout is a measure of democratic health, then surveys of Ontarians should reveal different attitudes toward democracy at each level that correspond to the observed aggregate turnout trends. It is important to acknowledge that the data we are using for our analysis are not perfect. In an ideal world, we would be able to look at people's attitudes toward democracy and know (truthfully) whether they voted in elections at each level of government, but such measures are not available – neither validated voting nor perfect questions about the quality of democracy. As is common for behavioural researchers, we look for reasonable indicators of the phenomenon we are trying to

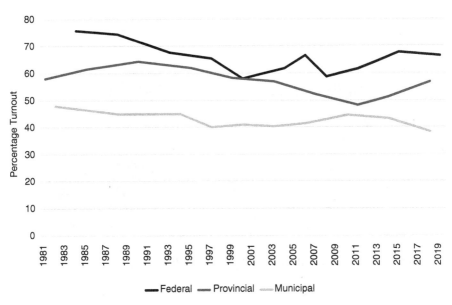

Figure 2. Turnout in Ontario

examine. In this case, we look at satisfaction with democracy, the perceived importance of elections, interest in politics, and feelings of duty to vote across different levels. We do not, unfortunately, have reliable measures of turnout that correspond to more than a single election. This is because recalled vote responses from elections that happened months or years ago are likely faulty (Weir 1975). Therefore, we investigate Ontarians' attitudes about the three levels of government and look to see whether they correspond to the patterns observed in the aggregate turnout data.

We can use MEDW data to look at satisfaction with democracy at different levels of government. This data is particularly appropriate because respondents were asked about more than one level of government in the survey. Figure 3 shows reported satisfaction with federal and provincial democracy among Ontarians gathered at the time of the 2015 federal election and the 2011 provincial election.[6] What is very interesting is that during the provincial election, the reported levels of satisfaction with each government were very close, but during the time of the federal election, satisfaction with Ontario's democracy was significantly lower. While it is possible that the time difference between the surveys could account for this disparity, it is also possible that the salience of the election at hand inflates reported satisfaction, in one of two ways – either provincial satisfaction at the time of the Ontario election or federal satisfaction

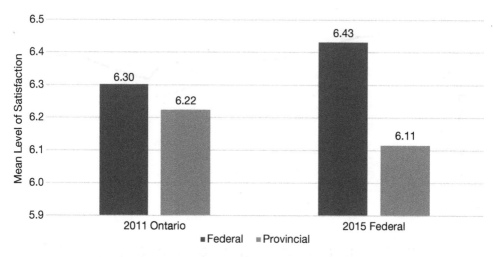

Figure 3. Satisfaction with democracy (MEDW data)

at the time of the Canadian election. Nevertheless, on the basis of this measure, there is no evidence that turnout indicates a weak democracy, at least in the eyes of the people it is meant to serve.

We can turn to other measures to investigate this finding further and incorporate the municipal level. First, we are able to use data from the Toronto Election Study (TES) (McGregor, Moore, and Stephenson 2014) to look at interest in politics at the different levels of government.[7] It is helpful that we have measures of interest in all three levels of government in the same survey, answered by the same people, as otherwise we could not be sure whether other factors might be shaping attitudes. It would not be useful to look at interest in the federal level asked one year, interest in the provincial level asked another year, and interest in the municipal level asked in yet another year, as the responses could be drawn from completely different samples of people[8] and there may be unique events that affected views at each time.[9]

The TES survey asked individuals about their level of interest in federal, provincial, and municipal politics on a scale from 0 (not at all interested) to 10 (very interested). We find that overall levels of interest are moderate and comparable (the mean or average reported value is 6.1 for municipal, 6.2 for provincial, and 6.4 for federal). While the

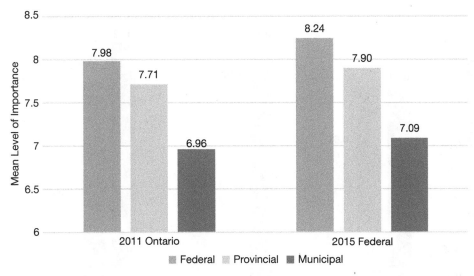

Figure 4. Importance of election (MEDW data)

small variation that exists is significant – interest in politics goes up with the level of government, similar to turnout – the overall low levels are not encouraging.[10]

Next, we can look at the perceived importance of the election. Figure 4 shows the mean (or average) scores for the importance of each election from the MEDW data, again from the Ontario and Canadian elections (measured on a 0–10 scale). The pattern fits our expectations exactly, and corresponds to the turnout levels – the municipal election is seen as the least important and the federal election as the most.[11] Again, we see some evidence that turnout levels reflect attitudes toward politics at each level.

Finally, figure 5 displays the frequency of expressions of duty to vote in elections at different levels of government in three different elections (drawn from the TES and the MEDW projects). The surveys asked respondents, "Is voting first and foremost a duty or a choice" at different levels of government? What the data show is the proportion of the sample that answered "duty." Without exception, the results displayed in figure 5 suggest that the lowest level of duty to vote is found at the municipal level.[12] That said, a majority of respondents in all surveys indicate that voting in municipal elections is a duty. Again,

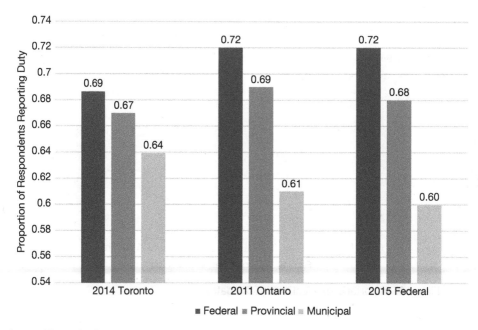

Figure 5. Comparing attitudes across levels: Duty (vs. choice) to vote (TES and MEDW data)

these data do not contradict the idea that citizens are less engaged with elections at lower levels of government.

We focus on Ontario data because turnout in that province differed between levels of government, and we want to see whether attitudes correspond. The flip side, of course, is that the weaker differences in turnout in other provinces should also correspond to weaker attitudinal differentiation by levels. To check this, we can again use MEDW data from Quebec and British Columbia to consider responses during the 2015 federal election. From figure 1, we see that turnout in the federal election in BC was 70 per cent while in Quebec it was 67.3 per cent; provincial turnout around that time in BC was 57.1 per cent (2013) and 61.2 per cent (2017) and in Quebec it was 71.4 per cent (2014). Although the trends in these provinces are not as clear over time as in Ontario, we can consider whether attitudes toward politics at each level correspond to the observed behaviour (greater importance of the federal level in BC and the provincial level in Quebec). First, satisfaction with democracy is significantly different at the provincial and federal levels in both provinces (p<0.05), but opposite to what observed turnout would predict (5.7 [federal] vs. 5.6 [provincial] in Quebec; 6.0 vs. 6.1 in BC; compare with figure 3 for Ontario). The perceived importance of the elections is also statistically different in both provinces, and the provincial level is more important in Quebec (7.5 vs. 7.6) while the national level is more important in BC (8.2 vs. 7.8; compare with figure 4 for Ontario). This corresponds to what we observe from turnout. Finally, while there is essentially no difference in perceived duty in Quebec, there is in BC (69 per cent of the sample reported duty at the federal level vs. 66 per cent at the provincial level; compare with figure 5 for Ontario). These additional data show that, once again, satisfaction does not appear to track with turnout levels, and that there is inconsistency between what we observe regarding actual turnout levels and duty. Only the importance of elections tracks with expectations.

EVALUATING THE DATA

We began this chapter with a clear research question and, on the basis of existing research, we developed expectations for what we would find in opinion surveys if election turnout levels are appropriate measures of citizen engagement and, in turn, democratic health. The data we have analysed show that, first, a turnout difference between levels of government does not exist everywhere. Only Ontario shows the expected pattern consistently over time. Second, our analysis of citizen attitudes in Ontario shows that for several measures (interest in politics, importance of elections, and feeling a duty to vote) the pattern corresponds to different levels of turnout for elections at the federal, provincial, and municipal levels. However, when we look at a measure of satisfaction with democracy, we find inconsistent results. Finally, when we look at data from BC and Quebec to see if attitudes correspond to the trends in turnout in those provinces, we also find a mix of results.

How can we answer our research question in light of these findings? Most basically, we can urge caution in using turnout as a measure of democratic quality. It seems true, as the second-order election theory proposes, that people are often less engaged in democracy at lower levels. However, less engagement is not necessarily the same as dissatisfaction. Indeed, it is possible that people are not as involved in democracy at certain levels of government but still retain a comfortable measure of satisfaction with the functioning of democracy at that level. In the classic definition of democracy, this would suggest less representation of the people. But if people are not perturbed by this trend, then perhaps our understanding of democratic quality is insufficient.

CONCLUSION

We have outlined a number of aspects of behavioural research in this chapter. From its perspective on what can be known, to how we can gather information about social and political phenomena, behaviouralism is a multi-faceted research approach that can be found in almost all subfields of political science. Yet there are limits. As we note above, there are many potential problems with survey data and the use of survey data in behavioural work is best done with an eye to minimizing these concerns. As behavioural researchers, we find this approach, grounded in empirical theory and evidence, to be most satisfying for the study of social and political phenomena.

NOTES

1 The term "post-positivist" is used by some in the positivist camp who soften some of their ontological, epistemological, and methodological assumptions about studying social phenomena. Specifically, post-positivists often adhere to the broad goals of explanation and causation but acknowledge a greater role for subjectivity in the study of social phenomena and a more probabilistic understanding of causation.

2 This is not to say that voting is unimportant. If many people chose to coordinate their behaviour and either vote or not, the outcome might change. The point to be made is that the decision of a single individual has a very small probability of actually changing the outcome of the election.

3 In some countries, such as the United States, researchers are able to validate the voting records of survey respondents, such that the researcher can find out who actually did vote rather than just who reported voting. This is not possible in Canada at this time.

4 All public opinion analyses in this chapter use data that are weighted for demographics and vote intent.

5 These data come from publicly available election records from the election management bodies for Canada, British Columbia, Ontario, and Quebec.

6 These data come from surveys conducted as part of the MEDW project (Stephenson, Blais, and Kostelka 2017). Satisfaction with democracy is

measured on a scale ranging from 0 to 10. Data are available online at https://dataverse.harvard.edu/dataverse.xhtml?alias=MEDW.

7   Data from the TES are available online at http://www.torontoelectionstudy .com/data.

8   While the principle of random sample selection should mean that average attitudes recorded across different samples of the same population should be the same, having the same people answer questions at the same time is the best way to guard against various sources of bias.

9   Ideally we would have a panel study that surveyed the same people at different times but those are relatively rare and unavailable in this case.

10 The differences between provincial and federal interest and municipal and federal interest are significant at p<0.01. The mention of "significance" here references how confident we can be that average levels of interest are actually different from one another. A significance level of 0.01 would suggest that 99 times out of 100 a similar difference between these levels of interest would occur if we replicated the survey with a new sample.

11 The differences between reported importance at each level of government are significant from each other for each election (p<0.01).

12 It is interesting that, somewhat contrary to our findings, Galais and Blais (2016) find that feelings of duty do not often vary between levels of government, and that when they do the difference is driven by identity more than rational considerations. However, their finding does fit with those of Henderson and McEwan (2015).

REFERENCES

Blais, A., E. Gidengil, and N. Nevitte. 2004. "Where Does Turnout Decline Come From?" *European Journal of Political Research* 43, no. 2: 221–36. https://doi.org/10.1111/j.1475-6765.2004.00152.x

Blais, A., and D. Rubenson. 2013. "The Source of Turnout Decline: New Values or New Contexts?" *Comparative Political Studies* 46, no. 1: 95–117. https://doi .org/10.1177/0010414012453032

Brady, H.E., and D. Collier, eds. 2010. *Rethinking Social Inquiry: Diverse Tools, Shared Standards*, 2nd ed. Lanham, MD: Rowman & Littlefield.

Cutler, F. 2008. "One Voter, Two First-Order Elections?" *Electoral Studies* 27, no. 3: 492–504. https://doi.org/10.1016/j.electstud.2008.01.002

Dahl, R.A. 1961. "The Behavioral Approach in Political Science: Epitaph for a Monument to a Successful Protest." *American Political Science Review* 55, no. 4: 763–72. https://doi.org/10.1017/s0003055400125924

– 1989. *Democracy and Its Critics.* New Haven, CT: Yale University Press.

Downs, A. 1957. *An Economic Theory of Democracy.* New York: Harper and Row.

Frankfort-Nachmias, C., and F. Nachmias. 2010. *Research Methods in the Social Sciences*, 6th ed. New York: Worth Publishers.

Franklin, M.N. 2004. *Voter Turnout and the Dynamics of Electoral Competition in Established Democracies since 1945*. Cambridge: Cambridge University Press.

Freedom House. 2018. "Freedom in the World 2018." Accessed 25 July 2018. https://freedomhouse.org/sites/default/files/FH_FITW_Report_2018 _Final_SinglePage.pdf.

Galais, C., and A. Blais. 2016. "Do People Feel More of a Duty to Vote in Some Elections?" *West European Politics* 39, no. 4: 755–77. https://doi.org/10.1080 /01402382.2015.1104994

Gray, M., and M. Caul. 2000. "Declining Voter Turnout in Advanced Industrial Democracies, 1950–1997: The Effects of Declining Group Mobilization." *Comparative Political Studies* 33: 1091–120. https://doi.org/10.1177 /0010414000033009001

Henderson, A., and N. McEwen. 2015. "Regions as Primary Political Communities: A Multi-Level Comparative Analysis of Turnout in Regional Elections." *Publius: The Journal of Federalism* 45, no. 2: 189–215. https://doi .org/10.1093/publius/pju040

Johnston, R., J.S. Matthews, and A. Bittner. 2007. "Turnout and the Party System in Canada, 1988–2004." *Electoral Studies* 26, no. 4: 735–45. https:// doi.org/10.1016/j.electstud.2007.08.002

King, G., R.O. Keohane, and S. Verba. 1994. *Designing Social Inquiry: Scientific Inference in Qualitative Research*. Princeton, NJ: Princeton University Press.

Lijphart, A. 1997. "Unequal Participation: Democracy's Unresolved Dilemma." *American Political Science Review* 91, no. 1: 1–14. https://doi.org /10.2307/2952255

Lutz, G., and M. Marsh. 2007. "Introduction: Consequences of Low Turnout." *Electoral Studies* 26, no. 3: 539–47. https://doi.org/10.1016/j.electstud .2006.10.001

McGregor, R.M., A.A. Moore, and L.B. Stephenson. 2014. The Toronto Election Study [dataset].

Morin-Chassé, A., D. Bol, L.B. Stephenson, and S.L. St-Vincent. 2017. "How to Survey about Electoral Turnout? The Efficacy of the Face-Saving Response Items in 19 Different Contexts." *Political Science Research and Methods* 5, no. 3: 575–84. https://doi.org/10.1017/psrm.2016.31

Rallings, C., and M. Thrasher. 2005. "Not All 'Second-Order' Contests Are the Same: Turnout and Party Choice at the Concurrent 2004 Local and European Parliament Elections in England." *British Journal of Politics and International Relations* 7, no. 4: 584–97. https://doi.org/10.1111/j.1467 -856x.2005.00207.x

Reif, K., and H. Schmitt. 1980. "Nine Second-Order National Elections – A Conceptual Framework for the Analysis of European Election Results." *European Journal of Political Research* 8, no. 1: 3–44. https://doi.org/10.1111 /j.1475-6765.1980.tb00737.x

Riker, W.H., and P.C. Ordeshook. 1968. "A Theory of the Calculus of Voting." *American Political Science Review* 62, no. 1: 25–42. https://doi.org/10.1017 /s000305540011562x

Sanders, D. 2010. "Behavioural Analysis." In *Theory and Methods in Political Science*, 3rd ed., edited by D. Marsh and G. Stoker, 23–41. Basingstoke, UK: Palgrave Macmillan.

Stephenson, L., A. Blais, D. Bol, and F. Kostelka. 2017. "Making Electoral Democracy Work" [dataset]. https://doi.org/10.7910/DVN/RR0NNQ, Harvard Dataverse, V2, UNF:6:aOzmLmOonAKPSFq1guPLkg==

Weir, B.T. 1975. "The Distortion of Voter Recall." *American Journal of Political Science* 19, no. 1: 53–62. https://doi.org/110.2307/2110693

World Bank. 2017. *World Development Report 2017: Governance and the Law.* Washington, DC: World Bank. https://doi.org/110.1596/978-1-4648-0950-7

CHAPTER FIVE

Conceptualizing and Measuring Democracy

David A. Armstrong II

INTRODUCTION

Throughout this volume, all of the authors provide a conceptual under-standing and definition of democracy. Here, I take a step back to think about what it means to conceptualize the idea of democracy – what the major features and dimensions of the idea are and what pitfalls should be avoided. For me, the question "What is democracy?" is not about pro-viding the definition of democracy. Rather, it is about considering how institutions and behaviours that relate to democratic governance can help us understand when other political phenomena (like development, war, or repression) happen. To that end, I will not offer a single conceptual definition of democracy; instead, I will focus on the kinds of different conceptual definitions that have been used to separate democratic from autocratic regimes in quantitative political science studies. One of the main themes of the discussion that follows is the attempt to understand the analytical utility of these different ways of conceptualizing democracy. That is, how useful are the various ways of thinking about democracy when what we want to do is either (a) explain democracy using other variables (e.g., development) or (b) use democracy to predict other things (e.g., conflict)?

The discussion that follows depends heavily on the comparative evaluation of data by Munck and Verkuilen (2002) and the advice about conceptualizing and measuring democracy put forth by Bollen (1990).

Looking through this lens, I discuss the history of measuring democracy, pointing out both the more and less rigorous projects that have come to prominence over the years. Finally, I walk through some of my own work that implements the advice offered by Bollen with the aim of predicting and understanding the use of state repression.

APPROACH

I would argue that there are two main ways of producing a measure of democracy (or regime type). These would fall under the headings of user-developed typologies or scales, on the one hand, and more systematic data-driven exercises, on the other. My own work focuses heavily on the latter approach, but I discuss both below.

Since antiquity, scholars have considered the similarities and differences in how people are ruled. Among the most famous of these is Aristotle's typology of rule based on the "correctness" of the constitution and the number of people ruling (Lord 2013). Aristotle looked around the world as systematically as he could and devised a typology that captured what he saw as the main features of different kinds of rulers. More recently, a similar exercise was undertaken by Raymond Gastil in creating Freedom House's *Freedom in the World* report (Gastil 1979). Gastil, mostly through his own personal knowledge, placed countries on a seven-point scale measuring both political rights and civil liberties. While Gastil had a whole constellation of activities, events, and behaviours in mind when considering a country's position on the scale, the aggregation of those factors was the result of Gastil's own thinking rather than any objective measurement of each component piece. In both of these cases, the researcher brought a great deal of knowledge, but also personal preferences and biases, into the process of conceptualization and measurement.

One benefit of an approach like this is that it can be relatively easy. There are no herculean efforts required to collect data on every aspect of the process. As a researcher, you bring the sum total of your knowledge and whatever other research you see fit to the categorization effort. But one of the problems with this approach is that the measurements often reflect our own biases and subjective understandings of the world as well as our own preferences about the nature of rule.

The alternative method for measurement uses quantitative analyses. This means using tools developed by mathematicians and statisticians to understand how different measures of democracy relate to each other and to other socio-political phenomena. Further, these tools can be used to develop summary measures of democracy that allow us to evaluate and investigate the evolution of democracy over time and space. This work is also generally committed to a positivist world view. This means that understanding is generated, and "truth" revealed, through the analysis of empirical evidence. I will talk more about how these tools are used below. One benefit of using these tools is that they tend to mitigate the subjectivity and biases that can creep into less formal and systematic typologies. However, there is no guarantee that this will be the case. Lipset (1959) famously produced a quantitative measure of democracy that, through its conceptualization, had a clear anti-communist bent. Another benefit of quantitative measurement is that there are means for gauging how well the data fit our conceptual understanding. I find these compelling reasons for making the choice to use quantitative measurement tools to capture the "democraticness" of different countries.

Before jumping into my discussion, allow me to lay out the parameters of this investigation in the broadest terms. The measurement of any concept, democracy or otherwise, will rarely exist in a vacuum. Estimating the relative "democraticness" of countries provides interesting insights into how different states can manage and adapt to the changing preferences of their citizens. That said, the end goal is often something larger in scope, where we take the measures we derive and use them either to predict other measured phenomena (e.g., we might use democracy to predict respect for human rights like Davenport [2007]) or as an outcome to be predicted by other measured phenomena (e.g., using natural resource rents to predict democracy like Ramsay [2011]). If our goal is to use our measure of democracy in future quantitative investigations, we have to be cognizant of the "analytical utility" of our particular conceptualization of democracy.

For a concept to be analytically useful, it must be the case that it is sufficiently broad to capture important variations across space and time. On the other hand, the concept must be narrow enough that it is not related to the other variables in our investigation by definition. This latter point is fundamentally important for quantitative studies. If we defined democracy in such a way that the definition included people being free from torture (a not entirely unreasonable proposition), there would exist a built-in relationship between democracy and torture. If we were trying to predict the use of torture, we could no longer use our conceptualization of democracy to do so. Quantitative analysis requires that the outcome and explanations not be related by definition. For example, if we defined political participation to include voting, among other things, and then tried to predict whether or not a person voted by their level of political participation, there would be a built-in relationship between those two variables. Finding such a relationship is not particularly interesting. On the other hand, imagine we found that more media consumption leads to a higher likelihood of voting. This is more interesting because there is no necessary relationship between media consumption and voting (people can consume media and vote or not). In the discussion that follows, we will pay considerable attention to the analytical utility of the different ways of conceptualizing and measuring democracy.

CONCEPTUALIZING DEMOCRACY

There are many different ways to conceptualize democracy. These range from the classical Athenian variety to more modern ideas, like deliberative and competitive authoritarian regimes (see Held [2006] for a good overview).

Perhaps the most rigorous general advice about conceptualizing democracy comes from Bollen (1990). His first piece of advice to us is to provide a theoretical definition of democracy. For Bollen, the definition is "the extent to which the political power of the elites is minimized and that of the non-elites is maximized" (Bollen 1990, 9). Note that this definition itself is reasonably abstract. It does not mention indicators or other aspects that will be required for more concrete operationalization. What it does do, however, is define the relative balance of power for citizens and governments.

Other scholars have provided quite different theoretical definitions of democracy, though they contain overlapping pieces. For example, Schumpeter (2003, 250) argues that "the democratic method is that institutional arrangement for arriving at political decisions in which individuals acquire the power to decide by means of a competitive struggle for the people's vote." Weber (1978) suggested that democracy was, in essence, an elected dictatorship. The requirements are similar to those of Schumpeter – elites vie for votes in periodic, competitive elections. Weber saw the right of citizens to dismiss ineffective leaders as the only real right of citizens and as the only piece of political power worth surrendering to them. Lipset (1959) defined democracy, quite simply, as free, fair, and competitive elections carried out on a periodic basis. The closest that Cutright got to a theoretical definition was to say that "a politically developed nation has more complex and specialized national political institutions than a less politically developed nation" (1963, 255). Most modern conceptions of democracy take Dahl's definition and subsequent operationalization as their points of departure: "a key characteristic of a democracy is the continuing responsiveness of the government to the preferences of its citizens considered as political equals" (1971, 1). More recently, Przeworski et al. (1996, 39) defined as democracies "all regimes that hold elections in which the opposition has some chance of winning and taking office." Polity IV (Marshall, Gurr, and Jaggers 2017) is one of the most widely used operationalizations of democracy. Rather than define democracy, the authors are trying to define and measure what they call "authority patterns" – that is, "a set of asymmetric relations among hierarchically ordered members of a social unit that involves the direction of the unit. The direction of a social unit involves the definition of its goals, the regulation of conduct of its members, and the allocation and coordination of roles within it" (Eckstein and Gurr 1975, 22).

Bollen's second piece of advice is to identify the important dimensions of the theoretical definition. That is, we should be as precise as possible when trying to identify the pieces of the democratic puzzle. Dahl states that a necessary condition for continued responsiveness is that citizens be able to formulate preferences, make them known to others, and have them considered by the government equally relative to all others. There are eight "guarantees" that are needed to ensure citizens can meaningfully engage their governments:

1. Freedom to form and join organizations.
2. Freedom of expression.
3. Right to vote.
4. Eligibility to hold elected office.
5. Right of political leaders to compete for support/votes.

6. Alternative sources of information are available.
7. Free and fair elections.
8. Institutions for making government policies depend on votes and other expressions of preferences (Dahl 1971, 3)

These eight guarantees and the extent to which they are protected constitute the first dimension of democracy (or what Dahl calls "polyarchy") – contestation. Further, he states that this dimension is not sufficient on its own. For it to be indicative of democracy, these guarantees must be extended to and taken advantage of by the citizenry, which comprises the bulk of the adult population. Bollen adopts the same eight guarantees as fundamentally important to understanding and measuring democracy, but splits those guarantees into two underlying dimensions – political rights and political liberties. He writes,

> Political rights exist to the extent that the national government is accountable to the general population and each individual is entitled to participate in the government directly or through representatives. Political liberties exist to the extent that the people of a country have the freedom to express any political opinions in any media and the freedom to form or to participate in any political group. (Bollen 1986, 586)

In a similar vein, Lipset suggests certain conditions that must be met for a country to be a democracy: "(a) a 'political formula,' a system of beliefs, legitimizing the democratic system and specifying the institutions – parties, a free press, and so forth – which are legitimized, i.e., accepted as proper by all; (b) one set of political leaders in office; and (c) one or more sets of leaders, out of office, who act as a legitimate opposition attempting to gain office" (Lipset 1959, 72). In this case, democracy requires those in power to consider and respect the rights of those out of power. The relevant dimensions for Polity's democracy variable are "the presence of institutions and procedures through which citizens can express effective preferences about alternatives and leaders ..., the existence of institutionalized constraints on the exercise of power by the executive [and] the guarantee of civil liberties to all citizens in their daily lives and acts of political participation" (Marshall, Gurr, and Jaggers 2017, 14). Przeworski et al. (1996, 5) also use the two dimensions of participation and contestation, though they argue that "contestation, in turn, entails three features: 1) ex ante uncertainty, 2) ex post irreversibility and 3) repeatability."

Bollen, then, instructs us to use multiple indicators to measure the important dimensions and explain how they were created. He uses three indicators (variables) to operationalize each dimension. For political liberties, the three indicators are "subjective ratings of press freedom, the freedom that political parties have to organize and oppose the government and the extent of government sanctions imposed on individuals or groups" (Bollen 1990, 14). For political rights, they are "fairness of elections, whether the chief executive came to office via an election, and the effectiveness and elective/non-elective nature of the national legislative body" (14). Lipset (1959) proposed two criteria to measure democracy (though he conflates democracy with stability). In Europe, democracies are those states that have (1) been democracies since the First World War and have not had any moves toward totalitarian government over the past twenty-five years (meaning no fascist or communist party got more than 20 per cent of the vote). In Latin America, the criteria were relaxed slightly to include as democracies those countries with generally free elections for much of the time since the First World War. The problem here is that there is no clear definition of what makes a democracy to begin with. In fact, Lipset just groups together more and less democratic countries by fiat.

Cutright (1963) uses aspects of both legislatures and chief executives as his main indicators where multi-party legislatures with sizable minorities garner the most points on the former dimension and elected executives score highest on the latter. Similarly, Przeworski et al. (1996) also focus on legislatures and chief executives using four indicators – elected legislatures, elected chief executives, multiple parties in the system, and observed alternation of power. This last criterion is an addition to Cutright's in an effort to not identify as democracies countries with single-party control since independence. The Polity project uses several of the same indicators as well, though the criteria they use are a bit more comprehensive, including constraints on unilateral action by the chief executive and the competitiveness of political participation (Marshall, Gurr, and Jaggers 2017).

Bollen also encourages us to specify the relationships between each dimension and the indicators and to report estimates of reliability and validity.[1] Oftentimes, scholars do not necessarily identify which indicators correspond with which dimensions. In fact, several of these conflate the two dimensions (e.g., Polity).

Many of the projects discussed thus far do little to identify the reliability of the indicators employed. In fact, among the projects discussed above, this is true of all but Bollen (1990). One project that is especially good on this dimension is the Varieties of Democracy project (Coppedge et al. 2017). I have not discussed this project before now because it does not have a single abiding definition of democracy; instead, the project attempts to measure several different types of democracy identified by other authors (including Dahl's polyarchy). This project, however, does use a rigorous measurement model to identify the reliability of all indicators for each different type of democracy. Others have also tried to identify the reliability of indicators for the Polity project (Treier and Jackman 2008) and for Freedom House (Armstrong 2011). The general result is that the indicators used by these projects demonstrate high degrees of reliability.

Validity is also an important concern that relates mostly to the extent to which the new measure works in the way we might imagine it should. We would expect the new measure of democracy to have face validity – the measurements should correspond with what we know about the world from previous research. It should also have convergent validity – it explains things we know democracy should explain – and divergent validity – it should not be related to things with which we know democracy is unrelated. In essence, all of the studies make some attempt to evaluate convergent validity as they use democracy as either a dependent or independent variable in models with other variables. Further, most also make some attempt at evaluating face validity. That said, there are other impediments to validity. One of the most important is conflation of democracy with other ideas (e.g., multi-partyism, economic development, health, or stability). Cutright (1963) and Lipset (1959) both suffer from this problem by conflating stability and democracy. The Freedom House Freedom in the World project (Freedom House 2017) also suffers from conflating democracy with other normatively positive outcomes, though in its defence, its goal is not to produce a minimalist measure of democracy either.

Subjective measures can also have reduced validity. Both Lipset (1959) and the Freedom House project under the management of Gastil (1979) had a notably anti-communist bent in terms of how they assigned scores to different countries. Other studies, like the current incarnation of Freedom House's Freedom in the World project and Varieties of Democracy, use expert evaluations to score the components of their measures. The latter of these projects pays considerable attention to inter-coder reliability and uses expert aggregates, which should minimize the effect of bias in any one expert.

In sum, there is wide variation in the extent to which measurement exercises use the most rigorous practices available to ensure the quality of their measurements. By and large, this has not had noticeably negative effects on the discipline. As scholars move back and forth between different measures of democracy, there seems to be reasonable convergent validity across measures. This is likely due to the near total reliance on Dahl's conceptualization of polyarchy and its attending two-dimensional structure. After a brief technical discussion, I will walk through some of my own research on the topic and how it fits with Bollen's advice.

PUTTING THE PIECES TOGETHER

I want to provide the very basic foundation of how measures of democracy are constructed. I will try to keep the technical details to a bare minimum. Many of the earlier attempts at measurement (pretty much up through Przeworski et al. [1996], though excluding Bollen's work) used a variant of the summated rating model (SRM) to generate measurements.

Whether you know it or not, you've been subjected to this kind of measurement exercise countless times already in your life. Everyone who has taken a test has been an observation in a summated rating scale. The argument is that we have several indicators of an underlying latent trait. In the test example (let's say you are taking a math test) the idea is that each question helps assess one aspect of your mathematical knowledge. Using just one question would not work because there are lots of idiosyncratic reasons that someone might answer a single question incorrectly. Instead, we use lots of questions that tap different aspects of the knowledge we are trying to assess and we do so with questions of varying difficulty. The grade you get on the test is simply the sum of all the points you got on the individual questions. We assume that this overall score tells us more about your knowledge than any single question could (i.e., it reduces measurement error) and provides a value that allows us to better compare the level of knowledge you have relative to your peers.

With democracy, we do the same thing. Each democracy indicator (variable) is like an answer to one question on a test. It may tell us something, but it is an error-laden measurement. That is, the score that we observe has something to do with the underlying trait of democracy, but there are other non-democracy factors contributing to the values on that variable too. These non-democracy factors we call "measurement error." By taking the sum (or equivalently, the average) of the variables for each country (or country-year), we can reduce the measurement error relative to any one of the variables individually. More formally, we could write:

$$\text{Indicator}_j = \text{True Score} + \text{Measurement Error}_j$$

That is to say, the indicator we observe is a function of the true value of what we're trying to measure (e.g., democracy) and some idiosyncratic measurement error. If we have enough indicators, the measurement errors will cancel each other out, leaving the true score (or something close to it) behind.

The statistical details get a bit more complicated for some of the more recent work. Researchers are using tools like factor analysis and item response theory, which are more complicated and sophisticated implementations of the basic idea presented in the equation above. This is not the place to mount a full introduction to those tools, but if you see scholars talking about them, the basic idea behind their use is the same.

RESULTS

To demonstrate how this works in "real life," I want to walk you through some of my own research that attempts to measure democracy and understand its relationship to other political phenomena (Armstrong 2009). Above, I mentioned that my answer to the question "What is democracy?" relies on understanding how the behavioural and institutional aspects of government, particularly as they relate to democratic practices, help us understand other phenomena. So, to study democracy is to study the way that democracy helps us understand the other actions and attributes of states. To that end, I want to describe my work as it relates to the study of democracy and state repression. Specifically, I will describe how I think the "democraticness" of governments can help understand why they might or might not use repressive tactics against their citizens.

The dependent variable, the phenomenon I'm trying to explain, is state repression. State repression is defined quite narrowly here as the state violating its citizens' rights to be free from torture, political imprisonment, forced disappearance, and extra-judicial killing (Cingranelli and Richards 1999). I propose that one of the main explanations for why states choose to repress or not has to do with the nature of the regime (i.e., democracy). There is a rich quantitative literature regarding the link between democracy and repression (Stohl and Lopez 1984; Poe and Tate 1994; Davenport 2007; Hill Jr. and Jones 2014).

First, following Bollen's (1990) advice, I can define democracy. I define democracies as regimes having a rich set of constraints on unilateral decision-making on the part of the chief executive. Democracies are thought to be relatively peaceful places with low levels of repression, at least relative to more autocratic regimes. In autocratic regimes, when leaders feel threatened, either from within or without, they can easily increase repression because they are solely in control of the security forces who carry out such orders. In democratic regimes, leaders do not have the same unilateral control over the state's repressive agents.[2] They would often need explicit support from the courts or legislature or at least implicit support from the electorate for those changes to be successful.[3]

As Bollen suggests, I can identify the important underlying dimensions of my definition. There are two main dimensions on which I focus. Both of these capture constraints on tenure-maximizing leaders. I call the first "veto," following Davenport (2007). This dimension captures the institutional constraints on unilateral decision-making by the chief executive. If the chief executive needs the assent of a legislature (particularly one controlled by an opposition party), an independent judiciary, or sub-federal units, changes in policy will happen more slowly or not at all. The other dimension I call "voice." A leader wants herself or her party to retain power. Transgressing the rights of the citizenry is often a quick way to lose support and votes. As such, the more competitive elections are and the more people vote, the more democratic a place is considered to be.

I follow Bollen's advice and measure each dimension with several indicators. I use five indicators to operationalize voice. The Polity IV project (Marshall, Gurr, and Jaggers 2017) supplies the first two indicators – competitiveness of executive recruitment[4] and the competitiveness of political participation.[5] Competitiveness of executive recruitment is measured on a three-point ordinal scale ranging from hereditary selection or similar (1) to election (3). Competitiveness of political participation is measured on a five-point scale, which ranges from repressed competition (1) to competitive (5). I also use the democracy measure offered by Alvarez et al. (1996), wherein a country is considered a democracy if legislative and executive offices are filled through elections, more than one party exists, and power has alternated from one party to another in the past. Bernhard et al.'s (2001) dichotomous measure of democracy is also included. This involved an original coding effort to operationalize the definition of polyarchy set out by Dahl (1971). Finally, I use the data produced by Vanhanen (2000) and modified by Gates et al. (2006). Here, competition (the percentage of legislative seats held by all but the largest party) is multiplied by participation (the percentage of adults who voted). However, countries with competition scores less than thirty necessarily score zero on the new indicator. See Armstrong (2009, 405n3) for a discussion of the transformation done to the Vanhanen measure.

For veto, I also use five indicators. The first indicator is the checks measure from Keefer (2002). This measures the number of institutional checks on the executive as well as the nature of those checks (e.g., cohesiveness of governing coalitions and ideological distance between the government and opposition parties). Keefer and Stasavage (2003) suggest that this is a reliable measure of the number of checks on the chief executive. The executive constraints variable[6] (Marshall, Gurr, and Jaggers 2017) is a seven-point scale ranging from unconstrained executive (1) to executive parity with or subordination to the legislature (7). In addition to the two mentioned above, I use the political constraints measure developed by Henisz (2002).[7] This measures the "feasibility of policy change" by looking at the position of the legislative house(s) and the executive. This quantitative variable has a 0–1 range. I also use the sub-federal veto identified in this same dataset. Though it is perhaps slightly less relevant here, the variable still captures the extent to which the executive can be stymied by other institutional actors. The final variable I use is the law and order variable from the PRS Group (2009). Law and order captures the effectiveness and institutionalization of the legal system – an important check on the chief executive.

Note that for each indicator, I give a sense of how it is "coded" – meaning how the numbers are applied to different aspects of the polity. Further, as Bollen suggests in his fourth piece of advice, I give a citation for each indicator used. This would often lead to the raw data, but in other cases, it would certainly lead to a more fulsome explanation of how the variable was initially created. While Bollen does not talk about this explicitly, it is good practice to also release the data used in the investigation so others can verify your results without going through the trouble of gathering and combining all of the original data. Further, it is clear from the discussion how each indicator relates to each dimension. One thing that I have not yet discussed is how these two dimensions might be related. There is not necessarily any relationship between the voice and veto measures, though it is very likely that, empirically, the two tend to correlate quite highly. The model I use to generate the measurements allows for a possible relationship between both dimensions of democracy.

Next, I have to attend to the reliability and validity of the indicators.[8] First, the indicators do seem to capture the sorts of things they need to for each of the relevant dimensions. The veto indicators largely cover constraints on the chief executive and the voice indicators cover broadly the ease and regularity with which citizens can use the vote to censure leaders. The method I use to generate measurements operates on essentially the same idea discussed above. Specifically, though the details are well beyond the scope of this discussion, it is a Bayesian mixed-data factor analysis (Quinn 2004). For more information about the method and how the analysis was conducted, see Armstrong (2009).

Table 1 gives estimates of the reliability. These give us a sense of how much better our understanding is of the indicator when we use the latent variable to predict it. The numbers are bounded between zero and one with one meaning the variable is perfectly reliable and zero meaning the variable is perfectly unreliable. What we find is that the Alvarez et al. measure along with Polity IV's competitiveness of participation and competitiveness of executive recruitment are the most reliable indicators. Presumably, this has something to do with the alternation-of-power aspect of the Alvarez et al. measure. The alternation of power is an indicator of the willingness of citizens to replace one set of governing elites with another through elections. The more likely this is to happen, the more that leaders should fear the wrath of their constituents. For veto, Polity IV's executive constraints measure is clearly the most reliable, with both

Table 1. Reliability estimates for indicator variables

(a) Voice		(b) Veto	
Variable	Reliability	Variable	Reliability
Log (Gates)	0.90	Log (Checks)	0.65
Alvarez et al.	0.88	Political Constraints	0.69
Bernhard et al.	0.42	Exec. Constraints	0.98
Competitiveness of Exec. Recruitment	0.81	Law and Order	0.13
Competitiveness of Participation	0.82	Sub-federal Veto	0.00

the log of checks and balances and political constraints demonstrating reasonably high reliability as well. This, again, makes sense because it captures the extent to which the chief executive faces real constraints against unilateral action. Law and order and the sub-federal veto are both potentially useful variables, but they are not actually reliable indicators of the same construct underlying checks and constraints.

Next, I probe the validity of the indicators. Our first check is face validity. By that, I mean to assess whether it tends to agree with what we already know (or at least think we know) about the world. The ten countries with the lowest scores on average voice are Cuba, Libya, Rwanda, Somalia, Afghanistan, Brunei, Saudi Arabia, North Korea, Bahrain, and Qatar (in that order, starting with the lowest). On the other side, the ten best countries with respect to voice are Belgium, Italy, Denmark, the Netherlands, Finland, Norway, Iceland, the Czech Republic, Sweden, and Austria. I would argue that this squares relatively well with our impressions of the world. All of the high-voice countries are consolidated democracies and all of the low-voice countries are authoritarian regimes. I also undertake a similar exercise with regard to veto. The lowest ten countries on the veto measure are the Democratic Republic of the Congo, Somalia, Iraq, Uzbekistan, Libya, North Korea, Syria, Swaziland (now Eswatini), Qatar, and Saudi Arabia (starting with the worst). The ten best countries on veto are Iceland, Luxembourg, Slovakia, Belgium, Australia, Denmark, Canada, the United States, Finland, and the Netherlands. Again, this list is not surprising.

Checking convergent validity can be accomplished by looking at the effect of democracy (voice and veto) on repression. There is a considerable strand of research in comparative politics that finds a positive relationship between democracy and state repression. Replicating Davenport and Armstrong (2004), I find that the relationship between repression and democracy is non-linear in roughly the same way as the original study. That is, when both dimensions of democracy are at their highest values, predicted repression is at its lowest values. Since the Polity variable conflates both ideas, this finding confirms the theoretical ideas set forth in Davenport and Armstrong (2004). Voice and veto are both correlated at around 0.9.[9] If we treat them as a single variable combining the two dimensions together and use this new combined variable to replicate the Davenport and Armstrong study, the model with the new measurement outperforms existing models in both substantive and statistical ways. First, these variables provide a more nuanced story about the relationship between democracy and repression. The two dimensions of democracy used provide a clearer operationalization of the underlying causal mechanisms. Second, the new measures outperform previous measures as they provide a stronger prediction of the dependent variable than other alternatives. That said, this new model confirms the original substantive finding – that democracy only reduces repression when it gets to its highest values.

CONCLUSION

As this volume shows, there are many ways to study democracy. The quantitative study of democracy has a rich history in the political science discipline and it is particularly useful if the reason for measuring democracy is to include it as a variable in an empirical model. Bollen (1990) provides lots of advice for people who are trying to measure democracy in a quantitative way.

The alternative to the rigorous quantitative measurement of democracy has not proved especially successful. The alternative would be subjective measurement, perhaps like the typologies produced by Aristotle (which are categorical in nature) or the early Freedom House ratings conducted by Gastil (1979), who tried to provide a bit more numerical precision. These sorts of subjective measurements can be used in empirical studies, but there is little opportunity to evaluate the reliability of these measures. Further, they can often suffer from subjective biases, as we see, for example, in Lipset's (1959) work, which had a clear anti-communist orientation. The Varieties of Democracy group uses expert surveys but mitigates the bias by collecting expert data on several indicators (Coppedge et al. 2017). The expert responses are aggregated at the indicator level and then the reliability of those indicators is evaluated. The benefit of using experts or other subjective evaluations is that it is often cheaper and, in principle, permits retrospective evaluations. This method of using multiple experts evaluating multiple indicators seems like a good compromise.

The quantitative study of democracy stands in more or less stark contrast to other ways of studying democracy. Using quantitative measures often requires the ability to measure indicators that are at a sufficient level of abstraction to capture meaningful variation across a wide range of countries and over a long period of time.[10] The major disadvantage of this kind of quantitative study is that it cannot attend to the nuanced but sometimes important differences between specific regimes. In these sorts of cases, qualitative work would likely be more fruitful.

Bollen's advice has never been more relevant. The breadth and scope of indicators regarding democracy that currently exist is unprecedented. Attending to measurement concerns is also becoming more important. Hill Jr. and Jones (2014) argue, particularly as it relates to studies of state repression and democracy, that the only reasonable way forward is to generate measures that cleanly and clearly operationalize a relatively narrow definition of democracy. Ultimately, without invoking Bollen's advice explicitly, they are arguing for precisely the same sort of care in measurement that Bollen does.

Questions will always remain in the quantitative measurement of democracy. As new indicators are collected and new theories abound, there will always be opportunities to incorporate new theoretical insights into empirical measurements.

Finally, let's go back to the original question – "What is democracy and how do we study it?" For me, studying democracy entails understanding how democratic behaviours and institutions condition the state's behaviour in other domains, like conflict or repression. To do this effectively, we must have good measures of the concepts that motivate our study. The answer to the second half of the question – "How do I study it?" – is from a quantitative, positivist perspective. Studying democracy requires defining the concept in a way that captures its important aspects relative to an outcome of interest (in my case, state repression). To study democracy is to understand the observable, real-world implications of democratic institutions and behaviour on other socio-political phenomena.

NOTES

1 As a reminder, reliability is the reproducibility of a result, akin to accuracy. Validity is the extent to which the proposed measure captures the systematic features of the object of measurement and those features alone.

2 Many in this literature suggest that autocratic regimes are likely to repress all of the time at quite high levels. Olson (2000), on the other hand, suggests that for any regime, there is an optimal amount of repression that is based on demand and may be relatively low, even in autocratic regimes. Leaders who engage in large-scale repression bear the opportunity costs of doing so.

3 Note that leaders are regularly assumed to be power- and tenure-maximizing. That is, a leader's main goal is to stay in power as long as possible, as that permits control over the resource rents, tax base, and other benefits that can be used for personal or group benefit.

4 This is the xrcomp variable from the Polity IV dataset.

5 This is the parcomp variable from the Polity IV dataset.

6 This is the xconst variable from the Polity IV dataset.

7 This is the polconiii measure from the POLCON dataset.

8 The concepts of validity and reliability are central to positivist political science. The concept of validity references the congruence or "fit" between the operational definition of a concept and the concept itself. Essentially, the question is whether the operational definition accurately reflects the features of the underlying concept and only those of the underlying concept. Relatedly, the term "reliability" references stability and consistency in measurement: Are successive applications of an operational definition of a concept measuring the concept consistently and dependably? (Singleton and Straits 2004). In this context, measurement reliability refers to the interrelationships between the indicator variables. If they are very closely related, they have high reliability (Carmines and Zeller 1979).

9 Correlation is bounded on a scale from [-1,1], with numbers increasingly distant from zero indicating a stronger relationship.

10 For example, Polity IV covers all free states from 1800 to the present (Marshall, Gurr, and Jaggers 2017).

REFERENCES

Alvarez, Michael, Jose Cheibub, Fernando Limongi, and Adam Przeworski. 1996. "Classifying Political Regimes." *Studies in Comparative International Development* 31, no. 2: 1–37. https://doi.org/10.1007/bf02719326

Armstrong, II, David A. 2009. "Measuring the Democracy-Repression Nexus." *Electoral Studies* 28, no. 3: 403–12. https://doi.org/10.1016/j.electstud .2009.05.007

– 2011. "Stability and Change in Political Rights and Civil Liberties." *Journal of Peace Research* 48, no. 5: 653–62. https://doi.org/10.1177/0022343311411744

Bernhard, Michael, Timothy Nordstrom, and Christopher Reenock. 2001. "Economic Performance, Institutional Intermediation and Democratic Breakdown." *Journal of Politics* 63, no. 3: 775–803. https://doi.org/10.1111 /0022-3816.00087

Bollen, Kenneth A. 1986. "Political Rights and Political Liberties in Nations: An Evaluation of Human Rights Measures, 1950–1984." *Human Rights Quarterly* 8, no. 4: 567–91. https://doi.org/10.2307/762193

– 1990. "Political Democracy: Conceptual and Measurement Traps." *Studies in Comparative International Development* 25, no. 1: 7–24. https://doi.org/10.1007 /bf02716903

Carmines, Edward, and Richard Zeller. 1979. *Reliability and Validity Assessment.* Thousand Oaks, CA: Sage.

Cingranelli, David L., and David L. Richards. 1999. "Measuring the Level, Pattern and Sequence of Government Respect for Physical Integrity Rights." *International Studies Quarterly* 43, no. 2: 407–18. https://doi.org/10.1111 /0020-8833.00126

Coppedge, Michael, John Gerring, Staffan I. Lindberg, Svend-Erik Skaaning, Jan Teorell, David Altman, Michael Bernhard, M. Steven Fish, Adam Glynn, Allen Hicken, Carl Henrik Knutsen, Joshua Krusell, Anna Luhrmann, Kyle L. Marquardt, Kelly McMann, Valeriya Mechkova, Moa Olin, Pamela Paxton, Daniel Pemstein, Josefine Pernes, Constanza Sanhueza Petrarca, Johannes von Romer, Laura Saxer, Brigitte Seim, Rachel Sigman, Jeffrey Staton, Natalia Stepanova, and Steven Wilson. 2017. "V-Dem Country-Year/Country-Date Dataset v7.1." https://www .v-dem.net/

Cutright, Phillips. 1963. "National Political Development: Measurement and Analysis." *American Sociological Review* 28, no. 2: 253–64. https://doi.org /10.2307/2090612

Dahl, Robert. 1971. *Polyarchy: Participation and Opposition.* New Haven, CT: Yale University Press.

Davenport, Christian. 2007. *State Repression and the Domestic Democratic Peace.* Cambridge: Cambridge University Press.

Davenport, Christian, and David A. Armstrong, II. 2004. "Democracy and the Violation of Human Rights: A Statistical Analysis from 1976–1996." *American Journal of Political Science* 48, no. 3: 538–54. https://doi.org/10.1111/j.0092 -5853.2004.00086.x

Eckstein, Harry, and Ted Robert Gurr. 1975. *Patterns of Authority: A Structural Basis for Political Inquiry.* New York: Wiley-Interscience.

Freedom House. 2017. *Freedom in the World.* New York: Freedom House.

Gastil, Raymond D. 1979. "The Comparative Study of Freedom: Nature and Purposes." In *Freedom in the World: Political Rights and Civil Liberties*, edited by Raymond D. Gastil, 3–14. New York: Freedom House.

Gates, Scott, Håvard Hegre, Mark P. Jones, and Håvard Strand. 2006. "Institutional Inconsistency and Political Instability: The Duration of Polities." *American Journal of Political Science* 50, no. 2: 893–908. https://doi.org/10.1111/j.1540-5907.2006.00222.x

Held, David. 2006. *Models of Democracy*, 3rd ed. Cambridge, MA: Polity Press.

Henisz, Witold J. 2002. "The Institutional Environment for Infrastructure Investment." *Industrial and Corporate Change* 11, no. 2: 355–89. https://doi.org/10.1093/icc/11.2.355

Hill Jr., Daniel W., and Zachary M. Jones. 2014. "An Empirical Evaluation of Explanations of State Repression." *American Political Science Review* 108, no. 3: 661–87. https://doi.org/10.1017/s0003055414000306

Keefer, Philip. 2002. "DPI2000 Database of Political Institutions: Changes and Variable Definitions." Codebook. https://datacatalog.worldbank.org/dataset/wps2283-database-political-institutions

Keefer, Philip, and David Stasavage. 2003. "The Limits of Delegation: Veto Players, Central Bank Independence and the Credibility of Monetary Policy." *American Political Science Review* 97, no. 3: 407–23. https://doi.org/10.1017/s0003055403000777

Lipset, Seymour M. 1959. "Some Social Requisites of Democracy." *American Political Science Review* 53, no. 1: 69–105. https://doi.org/10.2307/1951731

Lord, Carnes. 2013. *Aristotle's Politics*, 2nd ed. Chicago: University of Chicago Press.

Marshall, Monty G., Ted Robert Gurr, and Keith Jaggers. 2017. *Polity IV: Dataset User's Manual*. Vienna, VA: Center for Systemic Peace. http://www.systemicpeace.org/inscr/p4manualv2016.pdf

Munck, Gerardo, and Jay Verkuilen. 2002. "Conceptualizing and Measuring Democracy: Evaluating Alternative Indices." *Comparative Political Studies* 35, no. 1: 5–35. https://doi.org/10.1177/001041400203500101

Olson, Mancur. 2000. *Power and Prosperity*. New York: Basic Books.

Poe, Steven, and C. Neal Tate. 1994. "Repression of Personal Integrity Rights in the 1980's: A Global Analysis." *American Political Science Review* 88, no. 4: 853–72. https://doi.org/10.2307/2082712

PRS Group. 2009. *International Country Risk Guide Methodology*. East Syracuse, NY: PRS Group.

Przeworski, Adam, Michael Alvarez, Jose Antonio Cheibub, and Fernando Limongi. 1996. "What Makes Democracies Endure?" *Journal of Democracy* 7, no. 1: 31–55. https://doi.org/10.1353/jod.1996.0016

Quinn, Kevin. 2004. "Bayesian Factor Analysis for Mixed Ordinal and Continuous Responses." *Political Analysis* 12, no. 4: 338–53. https://doi.org/10.1093/pan/mph022

Ramsay, Kristopher W. 2011. "Revisiting the Resource Curse: Natural Disasters, the Price of Oil, and Democracy." *International Organization* 65, no. 3: 507–29. https://doi.org/10.1017/s002081831100018x

Schumpeter, Joseph A. 2003. *Capitalism Socialism and Democracy*. London: Routledge.

Singleton, Royce, and Bruce Straits. 2004. *Approaches to Social Research*, 4th ed. New York: Oxford.

Stohl, Michael, and George Lopez, eds. 1984. *The State as Terrorist: The Dynamics of Government Violence and Repression*. Westport, CT: Greenwood Press.

Treier, Shawn, and Simon Jackman. 2008. "Democracy as a Latent Variable." *American Journal of Political Science* 52, no. 1: 201–17. https://doi.org/10.1111/j.1540-5907.2007.00308.x

Vanhanen, Tatu. 2000. "A New Dataset for Measuring Democracy, 1810–1998." *Journal of Peace Research* 37, no. 2: 251–65. https://doi.org/10.1177/0022343300037002008

Weber, Max. 1978. *Economy and Society*. Berkeley: University of California Press.

CHAPTER SIX

A Democratic Continuum?

Bruce Morrison

INTRODUCTION

In 2011, a powerful wave of democratization began in Tunisia and spread across North Africa and the Middle East. And yet, the substantial initial hopes raised by the Arab Spring have by and large been dashed, certainly outside of Tunisia. Why has this been the case? According to standard approaches, the countries in question were simply not ready for the democratic openings with which they were presented, as they lacked the required level of either economic development, modern class formation, civil society organization, or state building. A country like Egypt could make an impressive democratic move, including freely electing a party previously excluded from power. But Egypt could not sustain its democratic gains. Instead, deep social and religious divisions bubbled up to the surface, stimulating a level of conflict that young democratic institutional arrangements could not manage. The resulting difficulties are held to have facilitated the emergence of a military dictatorship under General Abdel Fattah el-Sisi. Democracy was simply outmatched by the challenges of Egyptian society, and faltered as a result.

In the hands of political scientist Sheri Berman, historical institutionalism offers a helpful and satisfying alternative perspective on these important developments. When young democracies fail, in her view, it often has little to do with their own performance amidst challenging transitional circumstances, and more to do with the way in which the pre-existing authoritarian regime exploited the lines of division within society. Dictatorships have tended to play divide and rule and to deprive moderate opposition groups of the oxygen they need to develop. Post-transitional regimes are, therefore, left not just with the challenges of establishing a democracy, but also of overcoming the subversive legacies of the dictatorial era. For Berman, then, "stable liberal democracy usually emerges only at the end of long, often violent struggles, with many twists, turns, false starts, and detours" (Berman 2013, 66).

Berman gains insight by situating the struggle to democratize within the historical and institutional context of the country in question. As she applies also to France and other Western European early democratizers, the likelihood of sustainable regime change is influenced by more than just the balance of social forces in place at the point of departure. The various contending groups operate within a context that influences their path and prospects for success. This leads her to call for more attempts to democratize, as well as more patience with such attempts, as the problems encountered by democratizers are not democracy's fault and will take some time to eradicate. Undermining democracy, and thereby rewarding a new dictatorship for the sins of an earlier one is, to Berman, irrational and deeply unfortunate.

Berman's analysis serves as a helpful introduction to historical in-stitutionalism as an approach to democratization. This approach sees institutions not just as outcomes to be explained, but, as in the case of authoritarian legacies, central causal contributors as well. This approach also aims to place democratization within its context, particularly its temporal context. Important processes manifesting themselves over time, sometimes on their own and sometimes in interaction with others, are seen as capable of having a significant impact on the attempt to establish democratic institutions and practices. And this works in reverse fashion as well. Berman claims that Western European democracies, though developing in the nineteenth and early twentieth centuries, became consolidated only at the end of the Second World War. Her reasons are revealing, as they point to the ways in which Western Europe had over-come the historical conditions that imperilled democracy, thus enabling a new departure. So, for instance, the revealed cruelty of Nazism and the Holocaust undermined the legitimacy of right-wing dictatorship, the war had rendered European countries more uniform and therefore less internally divided, and organized labour had gradually acquired the ability and legitimacy to extract equalizing concessions such as welfare policies, which further reduced the degree of social conflict. Crucial institutional support came from the United States and the early stages of European integration (Berman 2016, 407–10). A series of historical causes had, therefore, prepared Western Europe for durable democratization.

QUESTIONS AND RETHINKING THE CONCEPT OF DEMOCRATIZATION

Why did some Western European countries succeed at establishing modern democracies, while others, such as Germany, suffered initial and highly consequential failure to do so? Why did Costa Rica alone among Central American countries manage a successful passage to democracy? What makes some countries as opposed to others more likely to abandon democracy during times of crisis? What explains the adoption and effects of particular electoral systems? Historical institutionalists routinely address such large and compelling questions, guided by an orientation to real-world outcomes and especially those that confound the expectations generated by existing theories. Among other things, this approach has led to the exploration of novel ways of conceptualizing as well as accounting for democratization.

Democratization is the process by which a country becomes democratic. We have, however, recently come to recognize that this is far from a straightforward thing, and historical institutionalism has played a huge role in this process of re-evaluation. So, for instance, scholars now acknowledge and factor in to their analysis the fact that democracy is a complex and multi-faceted phenomenon. It involves extensive popular participation but can't be reduced to this. It also features competition during elections by more than one political party, government by election winners, and sustained and organized opposition by the losing party or parties. Democracy also depends upon a set of civil and political liberties to make political participation meaningful and ensure that competition for office is fair and balanced. Earlier accounts too often oversimplified by either presenting democratization as of a piece, or emphasizing, for example, the acquisition of the suffrage and letting it stand for democracy as a whole.[1] Historical institutionalism is an approach that, in embracing complexity, can provide a more thorough account of democratization.

If there are several components to a passage to democracy, they may not happen simultaneously. In the British case, for instance, one might argue that a competitive two-party system had been established by the eighteenth or early nineteenth century, parliamentary government with the governing executive authority dependent upon an elected parliament by the mid-nineteenth century, and universal suffrage achieved by increments from 1832 to 1928. The sequence is often substantially different from case to case. Meanwhile, some or all aspects of democratization may be subject to significant reversals, as we saw in France's retrenchment of voting rights in 1850, and as we have seen at many points in the collapse of democratic gains in countries such as Venezuela, Russia, and Egypt. Finally, the different aspects of the broader process might influence each other in important ways.

There is, therefore, no single or straightforward transition to democracy. Through at least the 1990s, some analysts held on to an extraordinary sense of confidence that the "end of history" was upon us, and that near-universal democratization would be a key part of that. More recent developments have, however, pressed us to recognize that democratization might falter and lead to the renewal of an authoritarian regime. Another very real possibility is that significant democratic features and practices might remain within otherwise authoritarian regimes, to provide legitimacy and durability. Political scientists have therefore developed a variety of names to capture different types of hybrid regime. And historical institutionalists have enthusiastically engaged with the analysis of these messy, incomplete, and multi-directional processes of democratization. In fact, this has often involved breaking down democratization into discrete episodes of change, involving advances in some aspects of democracy but without expectations of completeness or cumulation. Historical institutionalism is therefore very much in line with the way we currently understand democratization, and has in fact contributed significantly to the process of building new and perhaps better concepts. Such innovativeness regarding the characterization of the key outcome will undoubtedly persist as part of the historical institutionalist approach to democratization.

HISTORICAL INSTITUTIONALISM: EXPLANATORY APPROACHES AND METHODOLOGICAL IMPLICATIONS

Democracy is of course an important institutional outcome, but the interest of historical institutionalists derives in large part from the sense that institutions may also play a significant role in causing democracies to come into existence. But what is an institution, and what does it do?

Our understanding of institutions has evolved over time. At an earlier point in the history of political science, institutions were understood formally, in terms of the content of official documents such as constitutions and the official arrangements associated with major organizations in public life. This older form of institutionalism tended to be more descriptive and normative than theoretically oriented. It was, however, eventually found to be insufficiently in line with the scientific study of politics. While institutions never entirely ceased to interest political scientists, in the middle decades of the twentieth century attention was directed more at individual behaviour and its sources, on the one hand, and the presumed functions of the overall political system on the other. This relative neglect of institutions was addressed first by the movement to "bring the state back in" during the 1980s, and then by a self-conscious new institutionalism that began to crystallize especially beginning in the 1990s.

This new institutionalism drew inspiration from a broader understanding of institutions. Rather than merely charting and comparing formal political organizations and documents, which may not be fully reflective of actual political experience, the aim was now also to consider the informal norms and conventions that give shape and structure to human behaviour. New institutionalists appreciate that we live in a world made up of various systems of rules that regulate our lives to varying degrees. Institutions reflect power relationships, attractive values, and sets of constraints and opportunities. Important social and political results, such as conflict and stability, will be deeply affected by the institutional context.

It is generally held that there emerged at that time three distinct versions of the new institutionalism: rational choice, sociological, and historical. For rational choice institutionalism, institutions come into existence by and large in order to resolve collective action problems as actors pursue gains through coordination. Individuals have settled preferences that they try to maximize. Institutions, as sources of information, enforcement, and lower transactions costs, represent strategic equilibria that allow actors to acquire more than they would on their own. But rational choice institutionalists often also see institutions as capable of constraining political actors, and of influencing them by making some of their strategies more successful than others.

If rational choice institutionalism conceived of institutions in terms of a "logic of instrumentalism," sociological institutionalism emphasized a "logic of appropriateness" according to which actors draw from institutions the cognitive scripts that guide them to socially acceptable forms of behaviour. There is a greater reliance here on informal institutions, including "common cultural frameworks, symbolism, and taken-for-granted cognitive schema as well as formal rule systems" (Campbell 2004, 19). This normative environment will have a profound influence not just on actor strategies, but also on how they define what is and what is not in their interest. And given that sociological institutionalism expects organizations within a society to "plug in" to the common set of values and expectations, this effect will be strongly reinforced.

Historical institutionalists tend to differ from the other two types on the basis of their heightened attention to power and conflict. In democratization studies, some rational choice scholars such as Daron Acemoglu and James A. Robinson (2006) and Carles Boix (2003) have come to see democratic institutions as reflections of a shifting social balance of power in favour of the masses. With the people protesting in the streets, and not inclined to demobilize in exchange for policy promises that could quickly be pulled back, the expanded right to vote becomes an acceptable guarantee that the policy preferences of the masses will remain in place. This is an important literature, but it is by and large historical institutionalists who present institutions as the result of political struggle, and who privilege this over co-operation or cognitive alignment. And, crucially, the institutional legacies of past conflicts build in power asymmetries that influence later power struggles. According to Paul Pierson's recent work, institutions may even undermine the potential for open conflict if the imbalance is so great as to discourage those who lose by existing institutions from even trying to take remedial action (2015). Historical institutionalists are not averse to the assumption of rationality, but they see institutions as influencing not just actor strategies, but also actor preferences. Institutions are understood as capable of affecting not just individual and group interests, but also social coalitions and the course of political contestation.

Peter A. Hall and Rosemary Taylor's classic definition holds institutions to be "formal and informal procedures, routines, norms and conventions embedded in the organizational structure of the polity or political economy" (1996, 938). Institutionalists are therefore interested not just in the formal rules, but also in the expectations pressed upon us within our institutions and, more broadly, our society. This is not to say that every rule or expectation is institutional, as this would threaten to stretch the concept beyond the point of analytical utility. Rather, historical institutionalists point to rules or expectations that are collectively enforced, either by formal sanctions or public disapproval. We do not always follow institutional rules, but we are generally aware of having failed or refused to do so, and we tend to encounter at least some consequences as a result.

Historical institutionalism represents a challenge to the general political science pursuit of constant causes, according to which an identified causal factor is presumed to have the same impact in different times and places. So, for instance, scholars have long explored the relationship between the level of economic development and democracy, based on the notion that the democratizing effects of development operate in a similar manner regardless of context. Historical institutionalism, while far from indifferent to the development-democracy relationship, is deeply interested in the prospect that a causal force differs in its impact depending on when and where it appears. Historical institutionalists explore this possibility through the application of analytical tools such as path dependence and critical junctures.

According to Margaret Levi's definition of path dependence, "once a country or region has started down a track, the costs of reversal are very high" (1997, 28). Early causal factors that make a critical contribution by selecting one among a variety of options then cease to account for the path-like character of the case. Rather, either a tight chain of events or a set of self-reinforcing dynamics lock in the outcome and make it relatively impervious to the impact of disruptive forces. For David Collier and Ruth Berins Collier (1991), as well as James Mahoney (2001), this involves reactive sequences, featuring a tightly linked chain of events that chart a clear course to a durable outcome. Paul Pierson, meanwhile, has done the most to develop the idea that path dependence works mainly on the basis of processes that sustain and reinforce a given outcome (2004).

It is, for instance, well known that the QWERTY keyboard upon which we all rely is not the most efficient way to organize the keys. And yet, its institutionalization set in motion positive feedback effects involving the creation of an expensive-to-replace infrastructure of computer keyboards and the development of typing skills based on the existing layout of the keys. Over time, factors such as these made it increasingly unlikely that attempts at change would be successful. Similarly, Pierson's influential analysis demonstrated that the causes responsible for the creation of modern welfare states cannot, in becoming weaker or disappearing, also account for their collapse. This is because the welfare state has produced supportive causes of its own, for instance by spending in ways that inspired the formation of interest groups that aim to defend that line of spending on pensions, health care, and so on (Pierson 1994). According to Pierson, politics is an area of human activity particularly vulnerable to the logic of path dependence. Making things happen in politics tends to require working together with other individuals and groups, navigating a dense institutional environment, and overcoming the power advantage possessed by those who control existing institutions (Pierson 2004, 30–40). Path dependence holds that, particularly in politics, continuity may be far more common than change.

These historical paths may be generated by relatively small-scale and contingent developments, which, through the snowballing effect of self-reinforcement, nonetheless become ever more resistant to change. But also familiar to historical institutionalism is the model whereby the periods of path dependence are punctuated by a critical juncture, during which there is an unusually high degree of openness to change. In historical institutionalism, critical junctures are defined as situations featuring the substantial relaxation of structural constraints on human action. This provides enhanced opportunity for political actors to make decisions that redirect the course of history, before the ordinary structural constraints reappear and a new set of self-reinforcing dynamics are fully set in motion.

Political scientists have just begun to explore the character of the critical juncture itself, as opposed to its contribution to a subsequent path. Giovanni Capoccia and R. Daniel Kelemen have emphasized the need for a truly critical juncture to be brief relative to the path it helps to launch. They also pursue a variety of techniques that can be used to establish that more than one outcome was indeed available during the critical juncture, as well as why one of them was selected (Capoccia and Kelemen 2007). Hillel Soifer, meanwhile, has offered the helpful distinction between permissive factors, which help to erode structural forces and thereby make the critical juncture possible, and productive factors that, if present, may translate the substantial potential for critical change into an actually transformative impact (2012). But, overall, the model of periods of path dependence punctuated by periods of openness to contingent and yet decisive change is an important expression of the structured character of historical institutionalism.

Historical institutionalism's emphasis on timing and sequencing also poses a challenge to the constant causes approach, as the same factor will have a different impact depending on when it occurs in relation to other factors. Robert Dahl, in his classic *Polyarchy: Participation and Opposition* (1971), offers the claim that democratization will be most stable and successful if the establishment of competition between two or more parties precedes the broad expansion of voting rights. Well-established habits of elite competition within well-institutionalized representative bodies will limit the potentially destabilizing effects of mass participation.

Fareed Zakaria, meanwhile, recently initiated a vibrant debate based on his sense that liberalization, including state formation and a well-established structure of law and rights, must come before mass inclusion to ensure a stable passage to a liberal rather than illiberal democracy (1997). Given what we know of Sheri Berman's position from this chapter's introduction, it should not be surprising that she rejects this particular sequencing claim. In her view, democracies will always be tasked with cleaning up a series of post-authoritarian messes before they become fully established, and so there is never a better time than the present to get started on democratization. As a good historical institutionalist, she supports her claim with a revisionist reading of Western European democratic development. Rather than smoothly extending the franchise on a securely liberal foundation, the Western European cases featured conflict, violence, and democratic reversals as well as gains before democrats scrapped their way to consolidated regime change by ultimately prevailing over anti-democratic groups, impulses, and practices. Dictators will not permit the foundations for a properly liberal democracy to be laid on their watch. Only democrats can be trusted to do so.

This analysis is a reminder that, as established earlier, democratization is itself not necessarily a short-term outcome, although scholars have often treated it in precisely these terms. Historical institutionalism has contributed by acknowledging that democratization is a complex and extended process, which has opened the door to more insightful treatments of its various stages and aspects. But historical institutionalism has also enabled us to see that causal processes may also be short- or long-term in character. Historical institutionalism therefore calls for caution in the reflexive appeal to proximate causes, which may deprive us of the ability to discern the contribution of, for example, James Mahoney's nineteenth-century policy decisions on twentieth-century regime change in Central America.

It is on these foundations that historical institutionalism is associated with tightly researched, case-based treatments, either singly or in small numbers. Historical institutionalists are not at all averse to large-N quantitative work, but their bread and butter tends to be qualitative study of cases taken as wholes with "known histories and identities" (Ragin 1987, 9). These cases are presumed more often than not to yield complex causal relationships, by which is meant that causal factors have their influence in interaction with contextual features. The aim is therefore to determine "how different conditions or parts fit together" (Ragin 1987, 26), which is precisely what may be missed if cases are examined less carefully and knowledgeably, just to the point of determining values on a limited set of variables. Historical institutionalists are inclined to keep digging, and in particular to learn enough case history in order to be able to discern complex and extended causal processes.

This has stimulated a methodological reliance on process tracing, a research technique that pursues causal mechanisms in all their complexity. The aim is certainly positivist, in the sense laid out in chapters 1 and 4 of this volume by Anderson and Stephenson. Historical institutionalists explore cases as wholes in order to develop hypotheses, but also to test these and other falsifiable hypotheses against a wide array of case-based details.[2] Certainly, they often pay close attention to how actors understand the events in which they participate,[3] but they will use these interpretive emphases primarily in order to evaluate as effectively as possible the competing approaches under consideration. And in the name of testing causal propositions and pursuing generalizations, historical institutionalism often also relies on comparative analysis, which involves the careful selection of cases based either on the most similar system design (common case features, distinct outcomes) or the most different system design (discrepant case features, common outcomes). Here the attempt is to combine the analytical leverage provided by well-structured comparative research with attentive case explorations that may or may not yield persuasive causal accounts in support of any discovered covariation. Historical institutionalists remain methodologically flexible and pluralist, and yet the heavy turn to process tracing is at the core. This derives from a sense that the method should match the shift in comparative politics "from ontologies that assume causal variables with strong, consistent, and independent effects across space and time toward ones that acknowledge more extensive endogeneity and the ubiquity of complex interaction effects" (Hall 2003, 387).

Overall, while historical institutionalism relies upon a wide array of causal dynamics, the approach can be fairly straightforwardly identified, evaluated, and even put into practice by students. It helps to set historical institutionalist accounts against the backdrop of approaches that explain political outcomes by pointing to action grounded in individual or group interests. For historical institutionalists, existing institutions may simply not match up with contemporary interests, or necessarily change as these interests change. The work of historical institutionalists also encourages scholars to think of social or political action as mediated by such factors as the institutional context, the timing of action in relation to other influential developments, or the extent to which other factors have enabled change by eroding the normally constraining structural forces. It is by reflecting on what other approaches claim actors want or are capable of accomplishing that we can detect the impact of institutions or temporality.

ALTERNATIVE APPROACHES TO INSTITUTIONAL CHANGE: INCREMENTAL, ENDOGENOUS

While many historical institutionalists have put to effective use the punctuated equilibrium model featuring periods of path dependence occasionally broken by a critical juncture during which a significant redirection may occur, others have stressed that this cannot be the only way of conceiving of institutional change. Paul Pierson did helpfully point us to sources of continuity, and historical institutionalists have in general made the case that, for instance, welfare states and varieties of capitalism represent highly interconnected and mutually reinforcing institutional orders that make continuity more likely than change. However, recent economic, social, and ideological challenges to these complex institutional systems have, in the eyes of many scholars, yielded more change than path dependence would incline us to notice. Liberal pressures, for instance, have imprinted themselves on conservative and social democratic welfare regimes, although the effects have indeed been partial and influenced by the features of the path.

The stimulus to rethink historical institutionalism's understanding of institutional development was the product also of the observation that institutionalism requires an endogenous theory of institutional change.

The reliance on path dependence made institutional continuity the routinely expected outcome, thereby rendering institutional change not just surprising but also difficult to explain. Why did path dependence break down? Did the failure of path dependence offer the strongest argument against this approach to explanation? Often, the response has been that a powerful external force, such as a war or revolution, overpowered the tendency to institutional continuity. But this may be selectively applied, and, in any case, it certainly leaves institutionalists with the problem of exogeneity. Alternatively, historical institutionalists draw back beyond the critical juncture and its relaxed structural constraints to the critical antecedents, or the causes that made the critical juncture possible. It has, however, proven difficult to draw sufficiently sharp lines between the critical antecedents and the critical juncture.

So, how might institutions generate change in their own right? Given that institutions have distributional consequences, those largely excluded from benefits associated with a given set of rules will have an interest in changing them. But whereas some scholars emphasize that institutions solidify themselves over time by shaping preferences and structuring social relations, for Kathleen Thelen, above all, institutions often lack clarity in terms of the rules they support and how they may be put into practice. This may be because institutions are the result of complex and ambiguous compromises, or because their framers failed to anticipate all possible circumstances and applications. Meanwhile, there may be a gap between rule framing and rule enforcement. The implication is that institutions provide space for the dissatisfied to push back in ways large and small against the meaning of the rules, or their enforcement or implementation, or the relationship between the two. The playing out of these tensions and struggles internal to institutions can be a source of gradual or incremental institutional change. The social coalitions supporting institutions may therefore fray for reasons other than an externally derived shift in the balance of power; rather, the institutions themselves create an opening for change. According to Mahoney and Thelen, therefore, "coalitions form not only as representatives of alternative institutions but also as movements seeking particular interpretations of the ambiguous or contested rules of a given institution" (2010, 11).

Thelen and her co-authors have identified at least four major modes of incremental institutional change, and examining them closely aids substantially in understanding the precise kind of change involved (2005).

When contention leads to the development of new rules in substitution for the old, it is called displacement. Incremental change comes about when, for instance, a new institution appears alongside an existing one and people gradually adopt the new set of rules because they find them more beneficial. A second mode, layering, is similar to displacement, but here existing institutional arrangements are amended or supplemented rather than replaced outright. If, for instance, a private option is added to an existing public pension scheme, it may prove more attractive and gradually draw adherents. Both of these modes acknowledge that change-oriented actors might not be able to completely subvert or transform an existing institution benefiting from positive feedback, but also that they may nonetheless initiate change through smaller-scale institutional innovation. Change is institutionally constrained, but potentially transformative over time.

Those not in a position to replace an institution in its entirety may also exploit opportunities to engage in institutional conversion, made possible by the fact that institutions are ambiguous and can therefore be redefined in terms of their meaning, purposes, and functions. Finally, it is now well recognized that there is no such thing as an entirely static institution. Rather, institutions find themselves in a constantly changing context, to which they must adapt in order to remain intact. If this does not happen, due either to neglect or to the active pursuit of certain outcomes, an institution may be subject to incremental change through the process of drift. Overall, incremental institutional change happens when revisionist actors can identify and cultivate the weak and uncertain spaces within otherwise sustainable institutions, and set in motion a dynamic that gradually erodes or alters these institutions. Mahoney and Thelen argue that the nature and behaviour of institutional rivals will vary based on the strength or weakness of the opportunities to veto change, and the degree of discretion available in interpreting and enforcing the institutional rules (2010).

Institutions not subject to change during a critical juncture may also undergo incremental change because they occupy a broader institutional environment where interactions are frequent and consequential. Historical institutionalism brings into play a sense that complex institutional arrangements such as liberal democracy are in fact complex collections of multiple institutions. It also combats the notion that these institutions developed together and fit together logically and straightforwardly. Rather, democracies feature institutions that emerged at different points in time and happened to link together in a process called intercurrence. These institutional components, while rendered compatible to some extent by historical processes, are also potentially in tension with each other. They may be based on principles that cannot easily or always be reconciled, such as the freedom not to participate and the dependence of the democratic order on a rather high and sustained degree of participation. Or the rule of the majority and the desire to protect the rights of certain minorities. Furthermore, historical institutionalists have led the way in taking stock of the various traditional institutions, such as the United States' Electoral College or the United Kingdom's House of Lords, both of which proved impossible to dislodge and ultimately had to be rendered at least partially compatible with the liberal democratic order.

Overall, this new work on endogenous and incremental institutional change provides researchers with clear cues as to where to look within their cases for the most telling pieces of evidence. So, for instance, they should pay attention to challengers to the status quo who attempt to prey upon the points of ambiguity within institutions, to the introduction of small and seemingly insignificant institutional arrangements that supplement without immediately challenging a much more settled institution, or to the genealogy of today's components of liberal democracy and the process of their assembly over time. The work in historical institutionalism thus continues to offer guidance as to how to tackle vast cases and come up with the most compelling material for analysis.

RESULTS TO DATE OF HISTORICAL INSTITUTIONALISM ON DEMOCRATIZATION

Historical institutionalism, in exploring cases, carefully constructed comparisons, and causal mechanisms in substantial detail, and doing so in order to sift out the influence of temporal phenomena on the development, persistence, and consequences of institutions, has made a significant contribution to political science in general, and has now begun to do the same for the study of democratization. Although still quite new to the game, historical institutionalism has shown signs of remarkable promise in making sense of the complexity of democratic change.

Brian Downing's analysis in *The Military Revolution and Political Change* (1992) can effectively demonstrate how historical institutionalism's powerful tools can be put to work in the service of a complex and compelling argument. First, whereas most accounts of modern European democracy have tended to emphasize the causal contribution of modern social forces such as economic development and the formation of the middle and working classes, Downing reaches back to medieval times to find what he considers the institutional foundations upon which modern democracy was constructed. Western medieval society was distinct in that it featured early representative bodies, a structure of law, and a society filled with at least somewhat autonomous actors bearing rights and privileges. Historical institutionalist work on democratic development often begins with such claims of regional exceptionalism, thereby setting the stage for effective case selection and appropriate generalizations.

The key for Downing is whether these institutional foundations are eliminated or rather survive during a critical juncture in the early modern period. During the critical wars of the seventeenth century, which had become more intense and consequential for state survival, the maintenance of long-standing institutions for societal negotiation and accommodation was only possible in countries that could minimize their participation in warfare. But where urgent, existential warfare could not be avoided, seventeenth-century political leaders scuttled the old constitutionalist arrangements and pursued the coercive rather than negotiated extraction of the resources required to fight effectively. Downing presents his well-selected cases in a substantially detailed and analytically astute fashion, in order to underscore the key causal mechanisms and render his accounts as persuasive as possible. While he does of necessity cast his gaze over a broad secondary literature, he pursues within it targeted evidence as to whether war-related financial pressures were linked to moves by political authorities to circumvent or even dismantle long-standing representative assemblies.

The critical juncture as a point of departure does not in this case rely heavily on contingency. Rather, the emphasis is on a powerful set of antecedent conditions in the form of a fifteenth- and sixteenth-century revolution in military technology, and a country's geographical position relative to the major wars of the era. German states, for instance, find themselves at the heart of conflict, whereas England can act as if these are "wars of choice." The critical juncture establishes the divergence of cases into different, and enduring, paths. Revealingly, England builds a model democracy securely on the foundation of a parliamentary body with deep historical experience and legitimacy. Germany lacked this opportunity, having earlier eliminated constitutionalist arrangements in key formative states such as Prussia. Modern democratizing pressures will nonetheless come, but their effects will differ from path to path. German industrialization, and class and party struggle, led elites to make significant democratic concessions beginning in the second half of the nineteenth century. But whereas in England these modern forces were channelled by the institutions of medieval constitutionalism, which in the process reworked them into the institutional bases for modern democracy, in Germany these pressures had to be integrated within brand new representative institutions that lacked historical legitimacy and stature, with instability and failure a more likely result. So, we see here the role of long-standing institutional foundations for democracy, a critical juncture separating the cases into paths based on their ability to sustain these institutional foundations, and finally modern structural developments whose impact on regime development is different depending on the path each case is on.

In James Mahoney's work on Central America, democratization depended on liberal reforms opening countries to agricultural commercialization. Where these reforms proceeded, they spurred the development of centralized states, economic modernization, and a productive clash between agrarian elites and democratic movements. Thus did "the endurance of institutions and structures over time trigger a chain of causally linked events that, once itself in motion, unfolds independently of the institutional or structural factors that initially produced it" (Mahoney 2001, 10). These reactive sequences enabled successful democratization in Costa Rica, but not in El Salvador and Guatemala, where a radical and coercive liberalization process too greatly polarized society and inspired elites to use the power of the state to repress. In Honduras and Nicaragua, the absence of liberal policy change meant also the absence of these reactive developments. As a result, the removal of American intervention in the 1930s created an opportunity for progressive change that these countries were, on historical grounds, simply not prepared to exploit. The path determines the impact of post–critical juncture forces for change. And given the importance of the critical juncture, it is significant that Mahoney establishes that his broader case selection, which includes El Salvador, Nicaragua, and Honduras, permits him to call into question Deborah Yashar's claim for a critical juncture in the 1940s and 1950s based on a paired comparison of Costa Rica and Guatemala (Mahoney 2001, 26–7; Yashar 1997).

The strengths of historical institutionalism as an approach to democratization can also be seen in relation to what is essentially a research manifesto by Capoccia and Ziblatt (2010). For these authors, an earlier generation of scholars of European political development relied too much on class analysis, in part because they tended to "read history backwards" from the standpoint of democratic outcomes, imputing democratic desires to class actors without adequate empirical support. Capoccia and Ziblatt's call to "read history forward" involves examining closely and open-mindedly the role and motivations of actors in key episodes of democratic change. They therefore emphasize the reconstruction of actors' aims, options, and encountered constraints and opportunities. Capoccia and Ziblatt claim that, while class remains significant, other social cleavages such as ethnicity and religion often served as the basis for the conflicts that caused democratic change.

On more institutionalist grounds, they also argue for the significance of political parties and partisanship. They feel the party-based drive to democratize has been neglected because parties have been treated as mere extensions and expressions of various social classes. Rather, they claim, strictly class-based parties are a rarity, and parties are generally cross-class phenomena, or rather complex social coalitions that not only organize but also shape the aims of various groups involved in democratization. Just as importantly, political parties are sources of independent incentives that may encourage party leaders to enhance voting rights, and should therefore be emphasized by those interested in explaining instances of democratization. So, for instance, British prime minister Benjamin Disraeli could be said to have driven the surprisingly ambitious democratic reform of 1867 in order to both secure his leadership role in a party that had only partially accepted this "outsider" and to beat the rival Liberals at their own reforming game and recast the electoral rules in favour of Disraeli's Conservatives.

More broadly, a new research agenda has developed premised on the notion that the establishment of a stable democracy depends on the successful integration of a conservative party willing to play by the rules of the democratic game. Edward Gibson has pursued this in the Latin American context (Gibson 1996), while Ziblatt's recent work has demonstrated persuasively that the British Conservative Party became open to engaging with and even encouraging British democratization because of the institutionalization after 1832 of competition to register voters. In striving to win this competition, the Conservative Party built up the kind of organizational capacity that gave them confidence that they could hold their own and even prevail in a competitive, mass-participation democracy. And, given the remarkable success of the British Conservatives from the late nineteenth century onward, it is hard to argue against their democratic gamble. In Germany, however, Ziblatt finds that conservative party formation was weaker, their lack of confidence leading them to resist rather than embrace democratization (Ziblatt 2016).

Capoccia and Ziblatt's insistence that we "read history forward" is also very much in line with historical institutionalism's tendency to recognize and work with the complex and extended character of the democratization process itself, to the point of reconceiving democratization as made up of distinct facets, such as participation, competition, electoral systems, and the like, or into episodes of democratic change, which may be analysed independently or interactively. Amel Ahmed, for instance, has done a wonderful job of recasting the debate over early electoral systems in Europe, capturing both Westminster-style single-member plurality and proportional representation as exploited by different sets of actors precisely for their ability to limit the full effects of mass democratization. Both systems nonetheless were later incorporated as more or less satisfying elements of a fully developed liberal democracy. These historical complexities have helped us to make better sense of the hybrid regimes of today, and more generally of addressing the difficulty of saying precisely when democracy has begun. Ahmed's analysis, meanwhile, has led us to ask somewhat different questions, in her case related to the choices made by parties to accommodate or attempt to confine the challenge from below, which has led her to consider the extent to which the parties that emerged during the critical juncture associated with the challenge of socialism were ideologically extreme and therefore threatening from the standpoint of the existing elites (Ahmed 2013).

CONCLUSION: TAKING STOCK

Historical institutionalism is both responding to contemporary changes in political development and participating in a reconsideration of the course and character of democratic regime change. We are, however, still within view of the starting line of this research agenda, and much work remains to be done. Historical institutionalists need to continue exploring the new approach to democratization based on episodes rather than a single trajectory, and to ensure that the line distinguishing what is and what is not part of the democratization process does not become so blurred as to weaken the utility of the concept. And, while historical institutionalists have revealed democracy's character as a multi-faceted institutional phenomenon, it remains an open question whether its component parts are interconnected and mutually supportive, as, say, in the case of a welfare regime or variety of capitalism. Scholars will need to discover the extent to which changing one feature of democracy creates institutional incoherence and powerful resistance. Furthermore, we need to know more about the timing of the appearance of these different elements and how much difference it makes. More generally, the democratic sequencing debate involving Zakaria, Berman, and others is young and still quite vibrant.

Meanwhile, it is only very gradually that incremental institutional change is moving from its perch in political economy over to democratization studies. Thomas Ertman recently followed the lead of Capoccia and Ziblatt in treating the British Reform Act of 1832, which extended voting rights and made some constituencies more democratic, as the product of a critical juncture opened up by conflict over the political inclusion of religious groups and the untimely deaths of key political leaders. For Ertman, the choices made during the critical juncture enabled the 1832 Act and set Britain on a path for a series of highly similar reform acts over the coming decades (Ertman 2010). My alternative approach to 1832 places more emphasis on intercurrence and antecedent conditions. Whereas popular pressure to democratize had proven unsuccessful on several previous occasions, it was effective in the 1830s because the separate assault on corruption within the British state had gradually deprived British monarchs of the resources they used to keep reforming parties out of office. Incremental institutional change within one realm, therefore, made possible critical change in the British electoral arrangements, and it did so precisely by eroding the sources of resistance to change (Morrison 2011).

More broadly, Peter A. Hall has been responding to the most fundamental institutionalist dilemma: that institutions are influential until they are no longer so. The more we acknowledge the capacity of institutions to change, and the various ways in which they do so, the less power we can claim institutions have in organizing and explaining social and political life. If self-interested actors self-consciously pursue change within them, then certainly their influence is far from complete. These concerns have led Hall to explore more deeply the bases for institutional stability and change, and to see my work and the work of others as part of an endeavour to present institutions as propped up by social coalitions, which themselves provide durability to institutions by changing only very slowly (Hall 2016). Historical institutionalists must, therefore, conduct an open-minded analysis regarding whether institutions are deserving of the central place they occupy in the approach, and to what extent. They can take comfort that the ways historical institutionalists gather evidence, define and treat cases, and pursue leads that are grounded in temporal considerations need not change as they do so. And that embracing complexity is what they do best.

NOTES

1 This of course merely scratches the surface. You may refer to chapters 2, 3, 10, and 11, among others in this textbook, for a more thorough exploration of the challenges and complexities associated with the concept of "democracy."

2 Case-based details refer to theoretically informed features of the cases being considered in an analysis. These features could include (but need not be limited to) institutional design, economic development, economic organization, and religious, racial, ethnic, and linguistic diversity.

3 Research to understand how actors conceive of events in which they participate can occur through first-hand interviews with the actors themselves, reviewing contemporaneous public pronouncements by actors (e.g., speeches, press releases, tweets) and/or by reviewing memoirs and written accounts after the fact that speak to the logics and decision criteria employed by actors in a given situation.

REFERENCES

Acemoglu, Daron, and James A. Robinson. 2006. *Economic Origins of Dictatorship and Democracy.* Cambridge: Cambridge University Press.

Ahmed, Amal. 2013. *Democracy and the Politics of Electoral System Choice: Engineering Electoral Dominance.* Cambridge: Cambridge University Press.

Berman, Sheri. 2013. "The Promise of the Arab Spring: In Political Development, No Gain without Pain." *Foreign Affairs* 92, no. 1: 64–74. https://www.foreignaffairs.com/articles/syria/2012-12-03/promise -arab-spring

– 2016. "Institutions and the Consolidation of Democracy in Western Europe." In *The Oxford Handbook of Historical Institutionalism,* edited by Orfeo Fioretos, Tulia G. Falleti, and Adam Sheingate, 403–16. Oxford: Oxford University Press.

Boix, Carles. 2003. *Democracy and Redistribution.* Cambridge: Cambridge University Press.

Campbell, John L. 2004. *Institutional Change and Globalization.* Princeton, NJ: Princeton University Press.

Capoccia, Giovanni, and R. Daniel Kelemen. 2007. "The Study of Critical Junctures: Theory, Narrative, and Counterfactuals in Historical Institutionalism." *World Politics* 59, no. 3: 341–69. https://doi.org/10.1017 /s0043887100020852

Capoccia, Giovanni, and Daniel Ziblatt. 2010. "The Historical Turn in Democratization Studies: A New Research Agenda for Europe and Beyond." *Comparative Political Studies* 43, nos. 8–9: 931–68. https://doi.org /10.1177/0010414010370431

Collier, David, and Ruth Berins Collier. 1991. *Shaping the Political Arena: Critical Junctures, the Labor Movement, and Regime Dynamics in Latin America.* Princeton, NJ: Princeton University Press.

Dahl, Robert A. 1971. *Polyarchy: Participation and Opposition.* New Haven, CT: Yale University Press.

Downing, Brian. 1993. *The Military Revolution and Political Change.* Princeton, NJ: Princeton University Press.

Ertman, Thomas. 2010. "The Great Reform Act of 1832 and British Democratization." *Comparative Political Studies* 43, nos. 8–9: 1000–22. https://doi.org/10.1177/0010414010370434

Gibson, Edward L. 1996. *Class and Conservative Parties: Argentina in Comparative Perspective.* Baltimore: Johns Hopkins University Press.

Hall, Peter A. 2003. "Aligning Ontology and Methodology in Comparative Research." In *Comparative Historical Analysis in the Social Sciences,* edited by James Mahoney and Dietrich Rueschemeyer, 373–404. Cambridge: Cambridge University Press.

– 2016. "Politics as a Process Structured in Space and Time." In *The Oxford Handbook of Historical Institutionalism,* edited by Orfeo Fioretos, Tulia G. Falleti, and Adam Sheingate, 31–50. Oxford: Oxford University Press.

Hall, Peter A., and Rosemary Taylor. 1996. "Political Science and the Three New Institutionalisms." *Political Studies* 44, no. 4: 936–57. https://doi.org /10.1111/j.1467-9248.1996.tb00343.x

Levi, Margaret. 1997. "A Model, a Method, and a Map: Rational Choice in Comparative and Historical Analysis." In *Comparative Politics: Rationality,*

Culture, and Structure, edited by Mark Irving Lichbach and Alan S. Zuckerman, 19–41. Cambridge: Cambridge University Press.

Mahoney, James, 2001. *The Legacies of Liberalism: Path Dependence and Political Regimes in Central America.* Baltimore: Johns Hopkins University Press.

Mahoney, James L., and Kathleen Thelen, eds. 2010. *Explaining Institutional Change: Ambiguity, Agency, and Power.* Cambridge: Cambridge University Press.

Morrison, Bruce. 2011. "Channeling 'the Restless Spirit of Innovation': Elites and Institutional Change in the British Reform Act of 1832." *World Politics* 63, no. 4: 678–710. https://doi.org/10.1017/s0043887111000207

Pierson, Paul. 1994. *Dismantling the Welfare State? Reagan, Thatcher, and the Politics of Retrenchment.* Cambridge: Cambridge University Press.

– 2004. *Politics in Time.* Princeton, NJ: Princeton University Press.

– 2015. "Power and Path Dependence." In *Advances in Comparative Historical Analysis*, edited by James Mahoney and Kathleen Thelen, 123–46. Cambridge: Cambridge University Press.

Ragin, Charles. 1987. *The Comparative Method.* Berkeley: University of California Press.

Soifer, Hillel. 2012. "The Causal Logic of Critical Junctures." *Comparative Political Studies* 45, no. 12: 1572–97. https://doi.org/10.1177/0010414012463902

Thelen, Kathleen, and Wolfgang Streeck. 2005. "Introduction: Institutional Change in Advanced Political Economies." In *Beyond Continuity: Institutional Change in Advanced Political Economies*, edited by Kathleen Thelen and Wolfgang Streeck, 1–39. Oxford: Oxford University Press.

Yashar, Deborah. 1997. *Demanding Democracy: Reform and Reaction in Costa Rica and Guatemala, 1870s–1950s.* Stanford, CA: Stanford University Press.

Zakaria, Fareed. 1997. "The Rise of Illiberal Democracy." *Foreign Affairs* 76, no. 6: 22–43. https://doi.org/10.2307/20048274

Ziblatt, Daniel. 2017. *Conservative Parties and the Birth of Democracy.* Cambridge: Cambridge University Press.

CHAPTER SEVEN

Membership Rules for Democratic Communities: Canada and the United States

Andrew Sancton and Christopher Alcantara[1]

If democracy is "government of the people, by the people, for the people," (Canovan 1999, 10), just who are the people? Who belongs? What criteria and procedures should democratic societies use to determine membership, which most nation-states term "citizenship"? Membership rules provide an important window into the fundamental ideas that underpin a community. They speak directly to how communities weigh and value different democratic principles such as liberty, equality, inclusiveness, and participation. Membership rules are also important because "membership has its privileges."[2] With full and formal membership in a democratic nation-state, an individual gains access to a broad range of public goods, some of which are also available to non-citizens to varying degrees. These goods include access to social services, infrastructure, and physical security. Individuals also gain political rights, such as voting and the right to run for political office. In short, membership and the rules that govern how it is bestowed matter greatly for the individuals who live within democratic communities, but of course it is only one of many ways we might evaluate their democratic nature.

This chapter does not focus on nation-states because a large and well-developed literature on membership already exists at that level of analysis (Bloemraad 2006).[3] As well, Canadian citizens belong to and participate simultaneously in a multitude of different democratic communities within Canada, such as Indigenous communities, municipalities, and voluntary associations, to name a few (Maas 2013). In other words, democracy is not a concept or practice limited to the official government of a country: it can also be located in a multitude of other communities and contexts within and beyond nation-states. In this chapter, we seek to answer the following questions as they relate to Canada and the United States. Compared to national rules, which tend to prioritize inclusiveness, to what extent are the membership rules used by democratic communities located within these countries similarly inclusive? What might explain the trends that we find and what are their consequences for how we evaluate democracy in these countries?

To answer these questions, our chapter focuses on the rules governing formal membership (as they relate to the right to vote and run for office) in Indigenous communities and municipalities. Our findings suggest that each of these communities tend to have membership rules that are either more (e.g., Indigenous communities) or less (e.g., municipalities) restrictive than the ones used at the national level. These differences exist and will likely persist due to historical factors and the absence of significant pressures (internal and external) to change them.

APPROACH AND METHOD

For the purpose of this chapter, "democracy" is defined as a system for governing organizations in which rules about decision-making (or rules about who is entitled to make decisions) treat all members equally. Our approach to studying democracy is rooted in the literature on new institutionalism. According to that literature, institutions are important because they are the rules of the game that incentivize groups and individuals to behave in certain ways (Hodgson 2006). The longer a set of institutions remains in effect, the more likely it is that it will be able to resist sudden, transformative changes that deviate significantly from the original logic underpinning it. In our view, membership rules are an important part of the rules of the game because they affect the ability of groups and individuals within a community to achieve their goals.

To analyse the membership rules developed by Indigenous governments and municipalities, we engage in two types of analysis, which Miriam Smith terms "formal-legal" and "normative" (Smith 2005). Formal-legal analyses focus on the language and meaning found in laws, regulations, constitutions, and other written documents. These are important because they shape behaviour, are directly observable, and can "encapsulate the core political norms, values, structures, relationships, and practices of their societies ... [They are] an entry-point for understanding a society's higher political ideals" (Alcantara and Whitfield 2010, 124).

Membership rules, at their core, are tools that the state, a society, or an organization uses to make individuals legible and visible.[4] They are levers of power that actors use to decide who should be included in their community and subsequently how they should behave, since membership carries with it an expectation and obligation to observe the formal rules and informal norms of the community. Most democratic communities rely on one or more of the following five criteria for membership, and we use these to analyse the rules used by Indigenous and municipal communities in Canada and the United States:

- Birth within the officially defined territory of a community;
- Naturalization resulting from migration from another territorial community;
- Ancestry/descent;
- Residency within a defined territory; and
- Property ownership/leaseholding within a defined territory.

We also engage in some normative analysis of these various membership rules. This kind of analysis involves "assessing how well political institutions work according to some defined standard. Such standards may naturally be contested and may reflect particular interests or particular conceptions of what political institutions are supposed to do and the ends they are supposed to serve" (Smith 2005, 102). The classic example that Smith points to is the literature on the ability of Canada's institutions to maintain national unity in the face of regionalist and minority nationalist pressures (Smiley 1980).

In terms of a normative framework, this chapter relies on the three main criteria used by the Canadian democratic audit team (Cross 2010):[5] inclusiveness, participation, and responsiveness. They chose these criteria because "Canadians want public institutions and decision-making processes that offer them meaningful ways of participating in their democratic life [participation], that they want this involvement to include all the communities that comprise contemporary Canada [inclusiveness], and that they expect democratic outcomes to be responsive to this inclusive participation [responsiveness]" (Cross 2010, 8). Our focus in this chapter is solely on the extent to which membership rules are inclusive, which Dahl and others suggest is a core feature of democracy (Dahl 2015).

Finally, drawing upon the insights of new institutionalism, we suggest that membership rules in general are likely to be highly resistant to change. Change can occur during critical junctures, which are moments in time when the conditions are ripe for political actors to mobilize ideas and resources to implement sudden change. Change can also occur gradually through four mechanisms: layering, in which new rules are applied "on top or alongside of existing ones"; displacement, in which existing rules are deleted and replaced with new ones; drift, in which the impact of existing rules shifts due to changing contextual conditions; and conversion, in which existing rules change due to how they are strategically deployed (Broschek 2011, 553). In the absence of these forces, membership rules will likely remain locked into the original logic that produced them in the first place. In the sections below, we focus on the extent to which the various membership rules used by Indigenous communities and municipalities in Canada promote inclusiveness.

NATION-STATES: BIRTH AND NATURALIZATION

Because our communities all exist within the territories of democratic nation-states, we begin by describing the rules governing national citizenship in Canada and the United States. Generally speaking, people become citizens of nation-states either by birth or by a process of "naturalization." As we shall see later, sometimes the naturalization process is based on considerations related to "ancestry," but for now we shall treat it as a process whereby a nation-state admits migrants from other countries to full citizenship status.

Canadian citizenship did not exist prior to 1947. Canadians were "British subjects," with the same rights as their fellow royal subjects who lived in the "mother country." The Canadian Citizenship Act of 1947 caused the British Parliament to approve the British Nationality Act of the same year. The British Act perpetuated the long-standing rights of British subjects in the colonies to enter Britain at will; hence the beginning of extensive immigration to Britain from South Asia, the Caribbean, and Africa. So extensive was this immigration that in 1968 the Commonwealth Immigrants Act eliminated the right of some "British subjects" to enter Britain, tying the "right of entry" to considerations related to physical ancestral connections to the British Isles (Heater 2006, 162–3). Given that there was no such concept of British "citizenship," being a "British subject" was the equivalent – but the possession of such a status provided no "right of entry" to Britain.

Issues relating to citizenship can be more complicated than they seem, although they are much simpler in the United States, where even residents of overseas territories such as Puerto Rico are American citizens with rights of entry to the mainland. Voting rights and citizenship in democratic nation-states are not congruent. In the United States, citizens who are residents of overseas territories cannot vote in presidential and congressional elections. Minors (however defined) cannot vote in any country; nor can non-resident citizens in many countries. For a few decades in the nineteenth century, some American states allowed recent immigrants to vote in national and state elections as long as they had formally declared that they wished to become citizens (Keyssar 2009, 136–7).

Generally speaking, nation-states such as Canada and the United States have adopted inclusive rules that rely on birth and naturalization to bestow political membership on individuals. To what extent do democratic communities within these countries rely on these same principles? Below we illustrate how Indigenous communities and municipalities have come to rely on different principles – descent, residence, and ownership – and why these principles have persisted over time.

INDIGENOUS COMMUNITIES: DESCENT

Prior to European settlement in North America, the Indigenous inhabitants governed themselves through a wide variety of political arrangements. Eventually, they were overwhelmed and colonized at different speeds in different places by French, Spanish, and British settlers. This chapter cannot recount the long and varied history of Indigenous-settler relations. Instead, we focus on the formal Indigenous governments established and recognized by the United States and Canada and that remain in place today. Unlike local governments within states and provinces, Indigenous governments are related to the concept of "nation."

The Indigenous case for self-government rests to some degree on historical claims to nationhood (Poelzer and Coates 2015), hence the use in Canada of the term "First Nation." Some may question whether small Indigenous communities with their own government-designated "reserves" are themselves "First Nations," or any other kind of nation, especially if they are clearly a part of larger national communities – Cree or Ojibway, for example. What is beyond debate, however, is whether medieval London was a nation or whether citizens of any particular municipality in the present-day United States or Canada comprise a nation: clearly, we can answer no on both counts. Related to this observation is the important fact that Indigenous communities have memberships that are mainly determined by ancestry. Municipalities have lists of residents, voters, and property owners, but we do not speak of "membership" in a municipality and we certainly do not expect our names to remain on municipal lists after we have moved away or sold property.

In the United States, Native American tribes, which is the dominant term used in that country for these kinds of communities, were determined by the Supreme Court in the 1830s to be "domestic, dependent nations" whose members living on tribal land were aliens, even if they were born within the territory of the United States (Keyssar 2009, 60). They were not guaranteed full national and state voting rights until the mid-1950s. As of 2015, there were "566 Tribal entities recognized and eligible for funding and services from the Bureau of Indian Affairs (BIA) by virtue of their status as Indian Tribes" (Bureau of Indian Affairs 2016). Prior to the 1970s there was no such legal list, only a disparate collection of treaties, laws, and administrative decrees that recognized various tribes for different purposes in different ways (Fletcher 2012, 7). Even today there are some tribes to which Indigenous people are attached that have no federal recognition, usually because they have no land (8).

Membership in the tribes is completely under the jurisdiction of each tribe, so it is difficult to generalize about official American rules for determining membership in Native American communities. Most tribes use either "blood quantum" or "lineal descent" rules or some combination of the two. Both rely on proving that at least one great-grandparent or grandparent was a "full-blooded" Indian. Fletcher has argued that it is this reliance on ancestry that justifies the use of the term "tribe" in the

United States. If these tribes developed criteria that went beyond descent, then they could be more appropriately described as "nations."[6] This might be accomplished through adoption, which some communities already do, or through "the subtle incorporation of nonmembers into the tribal polity through economic and governance measures, such as employment and housing, and government services. Over time, Indian tribes could use these contacts to establish a codified form of tribal nationalization. Nonmembers could nationalize in the same way that non-citizens can nationalize into Americans" (Fletcher 2012, 13–14).

In recent years there has been an explosion of scholarship on Indigenous peoples in Canada, much of it aimed at demonstrating how European settlers in North America almost obliterated Indigenous cultures and patterns of self-government (Alfred 2008). Indigenous and Northern Affairs Canada recognizes 618 First Nations,[7] most of which are governed by band councils established under the Indian Act, a frequent target of recent critical scholarship (Abele 2007). The argument is that these institutions were imposed by the federal government without any regard to traditional Indigenous patterns of governance. There is no similar legislation in the United States.

Not all formal Indigenous governments take the form of band councils. As the result of a process that much more closely resembles nation-to-nation negotiations than does establishing band councils under the Indian Act, the Government of Canada and the relevant provincial and territorial governments have negotiated with Indigenous peoples to establish special arrangements under the James Bay and Northern Quebec Agreement (1975) and the Sechelt Indian Band Self-Government Act (1986), among other similar documents (Poelzer and Coates 2015, 50). Most of these communities have enacted constitutions to give legal and political expression to these agreements (Alcantara and Whitfield 2010). The institutional arrangements established by these constitutions are not easy to classify. Some of them look like nascent nation-states that use a presidential or parliamentary system mixed with Indigenous traditional elements (Alcantara and Whitfield 2010).

All Indigenous governments in Canada rely primarily on ancestry for the determination of membership. Before going further, however, it is important to distinguish federal decisions about membership from Indigenous decisions. The federal government keeps a list of all those entitled to "Indian status" under the Indian Act. People on the list are entitled to various federal benefits, including extended health care, exemptions from sales and cigarette taxes, and free post-secondary education. However, since 1985, Indigenous governments created under and subject to Canadian law have had the right to determine their own membership lists, including through rules about who is eligible to vote in their elections and stand for office. They cannot, however, deprive a person of band membership if such membership had been previously acquired from the federal government. It is the band decisions about membership, rather than the federal decisions about Indian status, that are relevant for this chapter, because we are considering the right to vote within the community as the prime attribute of membership. However, most bands have been reluctant to venture very far from federal determinations of Indian status (Clatworthy 2011).

Significant disputes have arisen within band councils about the right to vote and about other policy decisions relating to membership issues. One is whether the right to vote can be restricted to band members "ordinarily resident" within the band's territory. In 1999 the Supreme Court of Canada ruled that such restrictions violated the anti-discrimination provision of section 15 of the Canadian Charter of Rights and Freedoms. The majority of status Indians now live "off-reserve."

Indigenous membership rules and criteria are highly contested and controversial sites of political conflict in Canada. Pamela D. Palmater is a Mi'kmaq scholar who in the past was denied Indian status by the federal government and by her parents' band council because her grandmother married a non-Indian.[8] She argues that few band councils have used their authority to extend membership criteria beyond those contained in the Indian Act: "where the once historic goal was to become large, powerful nations, now some bands are trying to limit numbers owing to limited resources and fears of political takeovers by new members. Communities that are using their traditions to exclude people are not allowing for the many ways in which Indigenous identities have evolved and adapted to the circumstances around them" (Palmater 2011, 195).

Palmater's prescriptions for addressing these restrictions (2011, 208) are quite similar to Fletcher's, as are the arguments put forward by Poelzer and Coates (2015), who argue that

> To base citizenship solely on blood is intolerable in a liberal democracy. There is no reason not to expand the Indian Act's definition to allow for "naturalized" Aboriginal citizens. Provision

> could be made for individuals who have resided on an Aboriginal community's territory for a continuous period of time – say ten years – and who can demonstrate a thorough knowledge of that community's customs, traditions, and (where appropriate) language. This would silence claims that Aboriginal governments are race-based, which they are under the current Indian Act. (211)

It is difficult to find intellectual justifications for membership based solely or primarily on ancestry and yet, as we suggest above, there is a vigorous debate among Indigenous academics and policy-makers about the appropriateness of different membership criteria. In the world of practical politics, however, there are many reasons – most of which have been outlined by Palmater – for Indigenous leaders to want to maintain the status quo. Unless and until there is a fundamental change in the relationship between Indigenous and non-Indigenous peoples in these countries, it seems highly likely that some variant of ancestry/blood quantum will remain central to membership in Indigenous communities.

MUNICIPALITIES: RESIDENCE AND OWNERSHIP

In the Anglo-American legal tradition, municipalities are structured as corporations, as entities apart from "the Crown" or (in the United States) "the people." Not all cities and towns have always had their own governing corporations. In Britain prior to 1835, patterns of municipal incorporation were especially chaotic (Moret 2015). Although it is true that medieval municipal charters generally freed residents from the feudal control of aristocrats and/or bishops ("city air makes people free"),[9] it was never the case that these municipal corporations were remotely inclusive or democratic, even for "free" adult males. Isin (1992) states that "citizenship was associated with membership in a craft or merchant guild (which also meant possession of property as a citizen); however, not all inhabitants of the city were free citizens of the city, and inheritance and admission practices varied across cities" (21).

From medieval times until now, Anglo-American municipalities have been especially associated with real property. Most municipal functions are directly related to real property and most municipal revenues derive from a tax on real property. Property qualifications for municipal voting in the United States have always been controversial. In colonial times, they were widespread, as in Britain. In the post-revolutionary period they came increasingly under attack and many were eliminated by the various state legislatures. Then they became more popular as a means to try to break the power of nineteenth-century "urban political machines." After the Civil War they were part of the arsenal of Jim Crow mechanisms in the southern states to prevent voting by African Americans. During the 1960s, following the passage of federal civil rights legislation, the Supreme Court effectively eliminated property qualifications for municipal voting. However, the court left open the possibility that there might be some special circumstances in which property qualifications at the local level would still be permissible, such as when "the powers and purposes of such entities [e.g., water districts] were extremely limited and ... the costs of their decisions were borne almost entirely by landowners" (Keyssar 2009, 273).

The National Conference of State Legislatures reports that three states – Connecticut, Delaware, and New Mexico – specifically allow for property-owning non-residents to vote in municipal elections. About a dozen other states allow such voting in various kinds of special single-purpose districts.[10] The situation is further complicated by the fact that "home rule" provisions in some states leave open the possibility that municipalities can determine their own voting rules, providing of course that such rules do not violate provisions of the state or US constitutions.

The Town of Mountain Village in Colorado is one such municipality. In the 1990s, some residents of Mountain Village asked both federal and state courts to overturn municipal election rules that allowed non-resident property owners to vote. Among other claims, the residents argued that the Equal Protection Clause (the 14th Amendment) of the US Constitution "bars nonresident landowner voting" (May v. Town of Mountain Village 1996, 2). The residents lost at both levels. One of their main problems was that the original municipal charter approved by resident voters in a referendum allowed for non-resident voting. More relevant for our purposes is the courts' recognition that non-resident property owners, who formed a slight majority of the town's approximately one thousand voters, had a legitimate interest in the town's municipal elections. In the initial federal court ruling in 1996, the judge stated:

> I find credible Defendants' contentions that the Town of Mountain
> Village is a unique resort community where nonresident landowners

own the majority of property and pay more than eight times the amount of property tax. Defendants further assert that without the significant revenues the nonresident landowners have contributed to the Town, the Town might never have come into existence. Moreover, the nonresidents continue to bear the weight of the financial burden for the Town. Defendants argue that providing the nonresident landowners the right to vote gives them a voice in the Town's future, including the taxes they will have to pay and how those taxes should be spent. (May v. Town of Mountain Village 1996, 4)

In 1997, the federal Tenth Circuit Court of Appeal upheld this ruling (May v. Town of Mountain Village 1997). The next year a Colorado state court, ruling exclusively on state constitutional issues, also rejected the residents' arguments. Once again, property taxes appeared to be a key issue, with the state court providing more details:

By affidavit of the Town Clerk and custodian of records, it was established that the 1995 total assessed value of real property was approximately $89 million. Residents owned approximately $3,896,918 of that total and paid approximately $279,955 in property taxes. Non-residents entitled to vote owned property valued at approximately $30,912,699 and paid approximately $2,221,038 in property taxes.[11]

It is impossible to imagine any American court accepting arguments that non-residents of a particular state should be allowed to vote in state or federal elections in that state because they pay a great deal of tax. Such arguments were accepted at the local level because some municipalities are very small and hence can have very high proportions of non-resident taxpayers (like Mountain Village) and because the property tax is such an important local revenue-generator. Municipalities are still intimately connected to real property, in a way that is at least partially analogous to the way that Indigenous governments are connected to ancestry and to their traditional lands.

Issues about non-resident voting in resort communities in the United States might seem of little general relevance to larger issues of inclusiveness and the nature of democracy. However, these same issues play out in some Canadian communities involving considerably more people, and raise much broader questions as well. In a survey of US legal cases relating to

"Nonresident Voter Dilution Claims," Amanda Mayo makes the following important point, which is crucial to the subject matter of this chapter:

> These cases are important because they explore what it means to be a member of a political community ... [C]ourts must consider what it means to be substantially interested in an election and, more fundamentally, what it means to belong to a cohesive group of voters. (2016, 2255)

In Canada there is no apparent constitutional protection for voting rights in municipal elections. Section 3 of the Canadian Charter of Rights and Freedoms states: "Every citizen of Canada has the right to vote in an election of members of the House of Commons or of a legislative assembly and to be qualified for membership therein." It does not require legal training to point out that section 3 is worded in such a way that it appears not to apply to municipal councils. Indeed, the Supreme Court has specifically noted that it does *not* apply to municipal elections:

> The wording of the section, as is immediately apparent, is quite narrow, guaranteeing only the right to vote in elections of representatives of the federal and the provincial legislative assemblies. As Professor Peter Hogg notes in *Constitutional Law of Canada* (3rd ed. 1992), vol. 2, at p. 42–2, the right does not extend to municipal elections or referenda. (Haig v. Canada 1993)

The provinces therefore have great freedom to legislate for municipal elections. An examination of provincial websites for municipal elections shows that none of the four Atlantic provinces allow non-resident municipal voting. Neither does Alberta, except in a special category of municipalities known as "summer villages." In Quebec, non-resident property owners and non-resident occupiers of business rental properties can vote in municipal elections. Non-resident property owners can vote in British Columbia, Manitoba, and Saskatchewan but in British Columbia there can only be one non-resident voter for each property, even if such property is jointly owned.

In British Columbia, all municipalities are required to belong to "regional districts," inter-municipal bodies charged with providing regional services of one kind or another. These districts are governed by boards comprised of representatives from the various member municipalities.

In calculating the voting strength of each member municipality within each district, non-resident property owners are not counted (Sancton, Cobban, and Spicer 2017a, 8) because the calculations are based on census results, which count all permanent residents, including minors and non-citizens, but not people who own a second home in the municipality. This issue is very important in Ontario, as we shall see below. It also raises important questions about how we count municipal "members."

The District Municipality of Muskoka, north of Toronto in Ontario, provides regional municipal services to six "area municipalities," all of which are represented by their mayors and other municipal councillors on the Muskoka District Council. In the 2016 federal census, the number of permanent residents in Muskoka was determined to be 60,391. But during the summer there are approximately 85,000 additional seasonal residents in Muskoka (Sancton, Cobban, and Spicer 2017a, 14). According to municipal electoral laws in Ontario, non-resident owners of property and their spouses (but not corporations or trusts) can vote in municipal elections as long as they are Canadian citizens. Such voters wield considerable political power within the area municipalities, especially in the Townships of Georgian Bay, Lake of Bays, and Muskoka Lakes.

But it is at the level of the district municipality where the issue of non-resident voters is particularly contentious. Each municipality is represented on the District Council roughly in accordance with its share of the total district population. But how should "population" be defined? For electoral purposes in most parts of Canada, including Ontario, population is determined by the federal census, which, as we have seen, counts only permanent residents. However, when the District Municipality of Muskoka was created by the Ontario provincial legislature in 1970, summer residents were also included in determining representation on the District Council, but each one was only counted for half the value of a permanent resident (Sancton, Cobban, and Spicer 2017a, 14).

In addition to summoning up images of how slaves were counted for the purposes of congressional representation in the pre–Civil War United States (the so-called Three-Fifths Compromise), this formula provoked a number of other problems. Exactly how are non-permanent residents to be counted? Determining property owners and their spouses who are

Canadian citizens is relatively easy, but what about long-term renters? What about other adult family members who spend much of the summer in Muskoka (Sancton, Cobban, and Spicer 2017b)? If these people are to be counted for representational purposes on the District Council, why not count family members of permanent residents who come back to their parents' or relatives' homes to spend the summer?[12]

These questions are difficult to answer – and yet answering them is of considerable political and financial consequence. District expenses are apportioned to each area municipality in proportion to its share of the total assessed value of all the taxable properties in Muskoka. Seasonal residents want to receive equal treatment with all permanent residents. Some even want non-Canadian citizens and family trusts to be able to vote and to be counted for district representational purposes. Such demands in turn cause permanent residents to state that, if seasonal residents are to be counted in this way, then their family members who join them in the summer time should be counted as well.

Neither the Constitution of Canada, nor the Ontario government, provides any guidance on this matter. Not surprisingly, the council of the District of Muskoka has been unable to agree on any formula for representation on the District Council other than that which was originally established. There is no way that this issue can be resolved other than by coming to some understanding, either locally or provincially, about the membership rules for local political communities. In most places in Ontario, these rules are primarily of symbolic importance only – municipal elections are determined by permanent residents who are Canadian citizens, even if a small number of non-resident property owners are also allowed to vote. But in Muskoka the rules are of great practical importance as well.

Currently, the main political leverage that non-resident property owners have in Muskoka is that they can vote in the elections for the councils of the area municipalities. Such leverage ensures that the issue of the representation of their interests becomes very important on the District Council. People who believe that it is perfectly appropriate for non-resident Canadian property owners to have a municipal vote should ask themselves if they also believe that non-resident property owners who are Americans (for example) should be able to vote in Muskoka's provincial or federal elections. If they believe that they should, then they are at least being consistent, at the cost of negating common conceptions of the meaning of citizenship in nation-states. People who believe, however, that non-resident property owners should be allowed to vote *only* at the municipal level are probably conceiving of municipalities as being more like the private corporations that govern condominiums than nation-states in which voting rights are only granted to citizens (London Free Press 2017).

CONCLUSION

Membership rules for democratic organizations are crucial. Groups use them to regulate who can belong, who should benefit, and who should have input and authority over collective decisions. They are the most profound of constitutional provisions; in fact, organizations need to have some conception of membership even before they begin to deliberate about their constitutions.

Generally speaking, democratic communities located within nation-states derive their membership rules, at least in part, from state legislation, and so while each of their membership rules may seem similar to the national ones in which they are embedded, they nonetheless vary in accordance with historical and contextual features inherent to the communities themselves. For municipalities, rules about membership in North America are more expansive, in some respects, than those used by nation-states and ultimately derive from decisions made by state constitutions and/ or state/provincial legislatures. We saw, however, in the case of the Town of Mountain Village, that American courts deferred to a "home rule" decision made originally in a referendum to grant voting rights to non-residents. In the absence of any contrary action by the Colorado legislature, non-resident property owners will be unlikely to give up their ability to control the local decision-making process in that town. In the Muskoka region of Ontario, the votes of non-resident property owners are secured by provincial law, which seems unlikely to change anytime soon. How to structure voting power within the Muskoka District Council is not currently subject to explicit provincial rules; decisions concerning the weight to be given to non-residents are solely within the authority of the District Council. Deciding on reasonable principles to guide such decisions is far from easy.

When it comes to membership, probably the most difficult issues involve Indigenous nations, whose rules are more restrictive compared to those used for Canadian citizenship. Like most nation-states (but perhaps not Canada and the United States), national identity for Indigenous peoples is based primarily on ethnicity and so the principle of descent tends to be paramount in those communities. Unlike most nation-states, First Nations in Canada and tribes in the United States are generally small in population, weak in political authority, and limited in their ability to raise revenue and generate economic prosperity, with some exceptions (see Jorgenson 2007; Flanagan, Alcantara, and Le Dressay 2010). In these circumstances it is hardly surprising that they would not want to open their membership to people who do not share their own ethnic origins. Inevitably, then, they must rely on some version of "blood quantum" or "lineal descent."

First Nations and municipalities are alike in that they are neither business corporations nor private associations. They share many – but not all – of the characteristics of nation-states and of subnational communities, such as American states and Canadian provinces (McMahon and Alcantara 2019). This is precisely what makes them so potentially interesting for students of democracy. It is too simplistic to argue that we should apply the same standards of democracy to these entities as we do to nation-states. The reasons for the existence of each of these entities are more limited and specialized than those of nation-states and we must adjust our conception of democracy to meet their special circumstances. There will be much disagreement and debate about exactly how we should do so, which is precisely why political scientists should pay attention to them.

Many Indigenous communities are relatively small and feel threatened by the larger settler societies in which they are embedded. In these circumstances it is not surprising that they would be suspicious of any proposal for more liberal membership rules that could change the nature of the communities they are aiming to protect. In most municipalities, non-resident voting by property owners (where it is allowed) is not a big issue, because almost all voters are residents. However, in this chapter we have seen municipal examples in both the United States and Canada where non-residents are so politically powerful that residents have tried to limit their political representation. Concern about membership rules is highest when people with the greatest stakes in protecting self-governing communities feel that they might be losing the ability to define the very communities that are so important to them.

NOTES

1 The authors wish to thank Tom Flanagan, Charles Jones, Graham White, and Carol Agocs for their comments on earlier versions of this manuscript.
2 This was the slogan used by the American Express Credit Card several decades ago. Membership also involves citizens having a range of duties to the state.
3 This chapter changes the unit of analysis to which the concepts of democracy and membership rules within a democratic community are applied. In this case, the unit of analysis is democratic communities, the subnational entities or objects that are under study.
4 James Scott uses the term "legibility" to refer to the process by which states impose order and organization upon the political world (see Scott 1999).
5 Some authors added additional criteria in their studies but the three listed here were the key anchors used throughout all books.
6 The word "nation" is derived from the Latin verb "natio" (to be born), which links this concept to birth. Others, of course, argue that a nation is better conceived of as an imagined community, socially constructed by human beings but no less real than nations determined by birth (see Greenfeld 1993; Anderson 2016).
7 See http://fnp-ppn.aandc-aadnc.gc.ca/fnp/Main/index.aspx?lang=eng.
8 See Ball (2012).
9 Max Weber quoted in Isin (1992, 16).
10 See http://www.ncsl.org/research/elections-and-campaigns/non-resident-and-non-citizen-voting.aspx.
11 The remaining property was owned by corporations and trusts – i.e., not by "natural persons" (see May v. Town of Mountain Village 1998, 1).
12 For some of the public's views on these matters, see the written submissions to the public consultation sessions, available at https://muskoka.civicweb.net/filepro/documents/30342.

REFERENCES

Abele, Frances. 2007. "Like an Ill-Fitting Boot: Government, Governance and Management Systems in the Contemporary Indian Act." Research Paper for the National Centre for First Nations Governance.

Alcantara, Christopher, and Greg Whitfield. 2010. "Aboriginal Self-Government through Constitutional Design." *Journal of Canadian Studies* 44, no. 2: 1222–45. https://doi.org/10.3138/jcs.44.2.122

Alfred, Taiaiake. 2008. *Peace, Power, Righteousness: An Indigenous Manifesto.* Toronto: Oxford University Press.

Anderson, Benedict. 2016. *Imagined Communities.* New York: Verso.

Ball, David P. 2012. "Palmater Dubbed a 'Wild Card' in Race for National Chief." *Windspeaker* 30, no. 4. http://www.ammsa.com/publications/windspeaker /palmater-dubbed-%E2%80%9Cwild-card%E2%80%9D-race-national-chief -afn-election

Bloemraad, Irene. 2006. *Becoming a Citizen.* Los Angeles: University of California Press.

Broschek, Jörg. 2011. "Conceptualizing and Theorizing Constitutional Change in Federal Systems." *Regional and Federal Studies* 21, nos. 4–5. https://doi.org /10.1080/13597566.2011.578949

Bureau of Indian Affairs. 2016. *Indian Entities Recognized and Eligible to Receive Status from the United States Bureau of Indian Affairs.* https://www .federalregister.gov/documents/2016/01/29/2016-01769/indian-entities -recognized-and-eligible-to-receive-services-from-the-united-states-bureau -of-indian

Canovan, Margaret. 1999. "Trust the People! Populism and the Two Faces of Democracy." *Political Studies* 47, no. 1: 2–16. https://doi.org/10.1111/1467 -9248.00184

Clatworthy, Stewart. 2011. "Indian Registration, Membership, and Population Change in First Nations Communities." In *Aboriginal Policy Research,* vol. 5, edited by Jerry P. White, Paul Maxi, and Dab Beavon, 99–120. Toronto: Thompson Educational. http://apr.thompsonbooks.com/?q=content /volume-5

Cross, William, ed. 2010. *Auditing Canadian Democracy.* Vancouver: UBC Press.

Dahl, Robert A. 2015. *On Democracy.* New Haven, CT: Yale University Press.

Flanagan, Tom, Christopher Alcantara, and Andre Le Dressay. 2010. *Beyond the Indian Act.* Montreal and Kingston: McGill-Queen's University Press.

Fletcher, Matthew L.M. 2012. "Tribal Membership and Indian Nationhood." *American Indian Law Review* 37: 1–17.

Greenfeld, Liah. 1993. *Nationalism.* Cambridge, MA: Harvard University Press.

Haig v. Canada. 1993. 2 S.C.R. 995.

Heater, Derek. 2006. *Citizenship in Britain: A History.* Edinburgh: Edinburgh University Press.

Hodgson, Geoffrey M. 2006. "What Are Institutions?" *Journal of Economic Issues* 40, no. 1: 1–25. https://doi.org/10.1080/00213624.2006.11506879

Isin, Engin. 1992. *Cities without Citizens.* Montreal: Black Rose.

Jorgenson, Miriam, ed. 2007. *Rebuilding Native Nations.* Tucson: University of Arizona Press.

Keyssar, Alexander. 2009. *The Right to Vote: The Contested History of Democracy in the United States,* rev. ed. New York: Basic Books.

London Free Press. 2017. "Infrastructure a Mess, but Tax Hike Not the Fix." *London Free Press,* 28 August.

Maas, Willem, ed. 2013. *Multilevel Citizenship*. Philadelphia: University of Pennsylvania Press.

May v. Town of Mountain Village. 1996. 944 F. Supp. 821-Dist. Court, D. Colorado.

May v. Town of Mountain Village. 1997. 132 F. 3d 576-Court of Appeals, 10th Circuit.

May v. Town of Mountain Village. 1998. 969 P. 2d 790-Colo: Court of Appeals, Div. A.

Mayo, Amanda. 2016. "Nonresident Vote Dilution Claims: Rational Basis or Strict Scrutiny Review?" *University of Chicago Law Review* 83, no. 4: 2213–55.

McMahon, Nicole, and Christopher Alcantara. 2019. "Running for Elected Office: Indigenous Candidates, Ambition and Self-Government." *Politics, Groups, and Identities*, 1 March: 1–20. https://doi.org/10.1080/21565503.2019.1584750

Moret, Frédéric. 2015. *The End of the Urban Ancient Regime in England*. Newcastle-upon-Tyne, UK: Cambridge Scholars Publishing.

Palmater, Pamela. 2011. *Beyond Blood: Rethinking Indigenous Identity*. Saskatoon: Purich.

Poelzer, Greg, and Ken S. Coates. 2015. *From Treaty Peoples to Treaty Nation*. Vancouver: UBC Press.

Sancton, Andrew, Timothy Cobban, and Zachary Spicer. 2017a. *District of Muskoka Council Composition Interim Report* (2 October). https://muskoka.civicweb.net/filepro/documents/30330?preview=30333

– 2017b. *District of Muskoka Council Composition Review Final Report* (16 October). https://muskoka.civicweb.net/document/30444

Scott, James. 1999. *Seeing Like a State*. New Haven, CT: Yale University Press.

Smiley, Donald. 1980. *Canada in Question*. Toronto: McGraw-Hill.

Smith, Miriam. 2005. "Institutionalism in the Study of Canadian Politics." In *New Institutionalism*, edited by Andre Lecours, 1010–27. Toronto: University of Toronto Press.

CHAPTER EIGHT

Representation and the Practice of Politics

Rob Leone and Josh Morgan

Political science has been preoccupied with the idea of democracy. A great number of political scientists have devoted their life's work to understanding representative democracy and to assessing whether the people's will is reflected in the government we have or whether we could have a better system if we changed some of the rules associated with democracy, elections, and governing (e.g., Mill 1861; Dahl 2015; Ajzenstat 2007). In a democracy, representatives are elected to act upon the will of the people, and being representative of the people's will should mean that our legislators are free to act on the wishes of their constituents. In this chapter, we are interested in assessing whether representatives are either free to act in a manner that represents their local constituents or whether they are constrained by the explicit and implicit rules and norms associated with legislator behaviour in Canada. Part of the appeal of this particular topic for us is that we are not only theoretically interested in the concept as knowledgeable people in political science, but we, as authors of this chapter, also have experience being elected representatives of the people. Both of us have run in elections, earned the support of people within a constituency, and have gone about representing their interests in a deliberative assembly.[1]

Representation by legislators has not had a favourable treatment in either the academic literature or the popular media in Canada. Academics talk of representatives as being too constrained by the rules and norms that govern their behaviour in a democratic assembly

(Docherty 1997, 2005). For example, some work shows that unelected staff and bureaucrats are actually controlling deliberative assemblies and making laws (Savoie 1999, 2014). In this sense, political represent-atives are relegated to being followers of the advice of the unelected, and if constituent interests dictate that they would prefer their repre-sentative to act differently, there are serious disincentives for elected representatives to speak out against the dictum from these unelected political staff in parliamentary assemblies. Occasionally, journalists will report about members being "whipped"[2] or coerced by these nameless, faceless individuals who advise and guide. And when elected members depart, organizations, such as the Samara Centre for Democracy, conduct exit interviews of former politicians that feed into this frenzy that representatives do not represent constituents' interests – they are merely there to serve and carry out the wishes of party leaders and the staff that support them. Former MP Keith Martin argues that it is not the constituents that guide legislative behaviour. He suggests in an interview that "It's poll-driven politics, and it's also driven by advisers, many of whom are quite young, highly radicalized, and driven by par-tisan interests as opposed to the public good" (Loat and MacMillan 2014, 166). Loat and MacMillan go on to suggest that "Many former MPs' comments illustrated a conviction that the leader's tight control on their parties is stifling the propagation of creative solutions to legislative problems" (166). One former politician was so aghast at the apparent mistreatment of the people who put their name on the ballot that he even wrote a book about the problem (Rathgeber 2014). The idea that representatives do not, and even cannot, represent the views of their constituents in solving public policy problems has no doubt contributed to the angst and cynicism with which some regard democracy, and particularly representative democracy.

In this chapter, we argue that while institutional norms and rules do constrain representatives, what is not captured in the dominant assessment of how well an elected individual represents the interests of the governed are different criteria that, if considered, demonstrate the opposite result. Moreover, while concepts like party discipline and whipped votes are certainly prevalent in parliamentary contexts, we argue that other aspects of influence, such as listening to and acting on constituents' interests through other means, have, with some exceptions (e.g., Blidook 2010), not been as prominently studied. We will demonstrate this by comparing two cases. In the first case, we explore representation in a non-party and non-parliamentary system – the municipal level. We do this to establish a narrative of representation absent the institutional structures that have often been deemed to be constraining of representation in the parliamentary system (e.g., party discipline and whipped votes). In the second case, we explore representation in a party-based parliamentary system to demonstrate that the very same elements of representation are present. Together, these cases demonstrate that representation of constituent concerns happens despite the institutional pressures that have traditionally been said to constrain it.

THE TRADITIONAL STORY OF REPRESENTATION

To begin, the story of democratic representation in Canadian political science has predominantly involved the idea that there is a long-term trend toward the declining relevance of both Parliament and parliamentarians. Instead, party leaders, and the appointment of political staff that support party leaders, are becoming more important and prevalent. The overarching thesis of research in this area is that democratic representation in Canada is dying, if not already dead. If people believe that their representative is not representing their interests, then this can contribute to cynicism about democracy and the democratic process.

One of the terms associated with the strengthening position of leaders in legislatures is "governing from the centre," which is part of the title of a seminal book on the subject by Donald Savoie (1999). There are a couple of factors underlying the governing from the centre thesis. The first is the idea that central agencies and line departments are becoming far more important and powerful in Canadian government and politics than Parliament itself. Central agencies are coordinating bodies that control what policies and legislation ultimately look like and ensure that the wishes of the prime minister are carried through. Two important central agencies in the Canadian context are the Prime Minister's Office, which controls the political arm, and the Privy Council Office, which controls the bureaucratic arm of government. Line departments control taxation and spending and the creation of annual budgets. Most important pieces of legislation consider taxing, spending, and the budget, and all governments in Westminster systems require passage of "money bills" in order to maintain the confidence of Parliament and continue governing. These central agencies and line departments, such as Finance and the Treasury Board, essentially control the apparatus of government. What emerges from these central agencies is coordination and control so that the governing party leader can ensure that the apparatus of government follows their direction and agenda. The decisions that are made in these central agencies are a foregone conclusion for Parliament, and thus Parliament itself acts as a rubber stamp of predetermined policy. The conclusion drawn is that parliamentarians have a diminished role as a result.

Another idea that emerges from the governing from the centre literature (Savoie 1999, 2014) is that unelected and unaccountable staffers and public servants, particular those in these central agencies, are more powerful than the people that voters send to Parliament. This culminates at the apex of power, which is the Prime Minister's Office (PMO). The PMO employs political staffers that are loyal to, and serve at the pleasure of, the prime minister. The growth of the staff and budget of the PMO over several decades has been used as evidence to show the growing influence of the central agencies and the declining influence of Parliament and parliamentarians. As the PMO has grown, Savoie argues, Parliament's importance has declined. Policy ideas, agenda-setting, and voting patterns are all determined outside Parliament. Unelected people are telling elected people what to do, what to say, and how to say it, and this is held as an example of the malaise present in Canadian democracy.

Others have looked at party discipline and have noted that it has become so strong that it has choked the individual members' ability to effectively represent their constituents (Malloy 2003; Seidle and Docherty 2003). The principal evidence used to demonstrate this is voting patterns of members in the House of Commons. The idea is that the number of free votes, which permit a member to independently vote on a law regardless of the party leadership's position, has diminished and that whipped votes are all too common. The job of the whip is to ensure that members show up and vote according to the wishes of their party leader. The narrative that parliamentarians cannot vote opposite to their party – which may go against the wishes of the MP's constituents – contributes to the idea that the concept of democratic representation is in a downward spiral (Rathgerber 2014). In addition to this idea, the concept of parliamentary career paths is important to underscore (Docherty 2005,

1997). In this case, conformity and discipline are the key ingredients of promotion from the backbenches to a position of influence in cabinet. The lack of alternative career paths for parliamentarians has contributed to the idea that the whips, House leaders, and party leaders wield extraordinary powers over MPs as these offices determine whether or not an MP advances.

Not only have these ideas of a democratic deficit been reduced to an academic exercise, but parliamentarians have even advocated for reform. As Aucoin and Turnbull (2003) explain, this even caught the attention of an aspiring prime minister who advocated for an agenda to rid the country of a democratic deficit. In his proposals for parliamentary reform, Paul Martin argued for returning democracy back to the House of Commons and away from the shackles of prime ministerial government. It was an interesting plot twist. It attempted to address the cynicism in politics that had been growing for some time, and it also implicitly suggested that stating democratic reform as a major policy objective was a top-of-mind issue for voters. In other words, it suggested that Parliament would do a better job helping citizens by empowering politicians to do their job better. Of course, Paul Martin's term as prime minister was brief, and while we cannot blame his defeat on the lack of popular appeal of his democratic reforms, we can certainly say that voters had other preferences in mind.

Nevertheless, exit interviews of MPs, which are conducted in their post-political life, shine a bright light on a pressing democratic malaise (Loat and MacMillan 2014). MPs feel shackled and constrained when it comes to doing their work. They feel as if they do not have a voice and cannot freely speak on behalf of their constituents' needs. In a familiar tune, they nearly exclusively say that they cannot communicate what they want or vote the way they want. As Loat and MacMillan write, "What we found surprising from the exit interviews was not only how often the MPs emphasized these disagreements [with their party leadership], particularly since they voted nearly all the time with their parties, but also how their parties lacked a transparent and openly agreed-upon mechanism, beyond the confines of committee or caucus, for them to voice that dissent" (2014, 138). In other words, while MPs express that there is often dissent within their parties, they feel constrained in expressing that dissent. Speak out, they say, and the MP will not be able to ask a question. Vote against the party and the MP will get dismissed from caucus. If politicians feel this way, as Loat and MacMillan (2014) detail, then it is natural for citizens to be concerned as well.

Research Design and the Democratic Dilemma

As students of politics, we often read about "the way it works." However, good students of politics must always find these peculiar situations and ask questions. Why is it that leaders in their communities decide to get involved in politics when their influence on policy is at best minimal and indirect (Blidook 2010)? Speaking from experience, we can tell you that public life is all-encompassing; politicians sacrifice their professional careers, time with families, dates with their spouses, and so on, to get paid a little bit to do a whole lot. Again, even knowing that the romanticized version of politics does not exist, why are professionals and community activists getting involved if serving the public that they seek to represent is no longer part of the job description? As one current and one former politician, we often get asked questions such as this. Having lived and breathed it, we have a different conception of democracy than that described above. In what follows, we provide a glimpse of democracy from a representative's "insider" perspective, and challenge some of the conventional wisdom.

While our experiences have allowed us to reach a countervailing conclusion about the practice of democracy compared to those outlined above, in order for us to effectively express our view to a standard that other academics have set in the past, we must appeal to research methods. For this reason, we will utilize principles of the comparative method (Lijphart 1971, 1975), initially designed to assess and draw conclusions about causality based on the similarities or differences of systems analysed. In this chapter we will use a comparative method – known as a most different systems design (MDSD) – for more exploratory and descriptive purposes. The MDSD allows political scientists to study different political systems that produce similar outcomes and see if similar independent factors can be identified. In other words, if two political systems are different, yet they produce similar tendencies, a stronger conclusion can be drawn that the variable held in common contributes to that outcome.

Our method of evaluating whether democratic representation of constituents is as constrained as the literature claims is to approach the question from an alternative perspective. Instead of evaluating representation quantitatively, relying on observable, behaviour-related markers of representation, we take an ethnographic approach. We focus on in-depth case studies of the activity of legislators in two very different contexts that produced similar legislative outcomes. The question to consider is whether the degree to which the legislator was involved in representing their constituents (and in turn influencing the observed outcomes) varied. If yes, then arguments about legislator representativeness need to be tempered. If no, then we have evidence to suggest that democratic representativeness carries across systems.

In this chapter, we investigate policy development in two different types of democratic government found within the Canadian federation – one from the municipal level and the other from the provincial level – to draw our conclusion that legislator representation is remarkably similar. We call these two examples "different" for several reasons. The first is that the governing structure of the Ontario provincial legislature follows Westminster parliamentary rules. At its most basic understanding, this involves a first minister and a cabinet who are elected members of that assembly and who serve the dual role of being a member of the Executive Council as well. The City of London is not structured that way. It has a mayor that serves as the chair of council, but there is no executive-style office that goes along with it. As we have previously discussed, the literature points to the fact that leaders could utilize the promise of being part of cabinet as a way of maintaining influence over MP behaviour. This is a key difference between parliamentary and municipal systems, as the council's mayor does not act like a leader in the Westminster sense by offering a potential inducement to help sway the behaviour of local councillors.

Another key difference is what Savoie (1999) calls the intense growth of the PMO and other central agencies – which has diminished Parliament's relevance. Since line agencies do not exist at the municipal level of government, this points to another key difference between the two systems. In addition, political parties do not exist in the Ontario municipal context, while they are very prevalent in the parliamentary context. The literature points to the dominating influence of parties as a constraint on a member's ability to think and act on the issues of his or her constituency. Thus, municipal politicians are not constrained by the same kind of discipline from a group of party activists that demand some cohesion and uniformity in communications, messages, and approach. These are among the defining aspects of the idea that MPs in a parliamentary context are shackled from truly representing their constituents' interests due to the existence of institutional rules and norms.

Before we begin to discuss the cases, which are developed with reference to our own experiences within them, it is important to elaborate why we are, in fact, choosing them. The first case we are comparing is drawn from an Ontario municipal perspective. What is interesting about the case is that the evaluation of representation – free from a carrot-wielding leader, the nameless, faceless advisers to leaders, and the shackles of party discipline – is an expression of representative politics in its rawest form. It builds the case for representative democracy working without the power superstructures we know exist from our understanding of parliamentary systems. Local government also deals with issues that most directly affect people. Councillors are also more likely to represent fewer people, and are thus more able to have their ear to local concerns. The second case deals with the provincial context and applies the democracy of municipalities to the parliamentary context. Here, as we have explained, there are the phenomena of powerful, incentive-bearing leaders and party discipline that are supposed to constrain independence among the parliamentary caucus. If a similar level of legislator representativeness is observed in both of these different systems, as we intend to demonstrate, then our assessment that our proud tradition of representative democracy is alive and well will be borne out by our use of the MDSD comparative method.

Our experience as politicians draw us to the conclusions that we are advancing in this chapter. In many ways, we are presenting here an ethnography of what happens in deliberative legislatures. Ethnographic research situates the observer within the social setting that they are exploring (Sarsby 1984). The comparative cases we speak of put us, as researchers, at the very centre of the social setting that we are exploring in ways that other researchers simply could not replicate without having the benefit of being elected or at least serving in some capacity very close to elected officials. The value of an ethnographic approach is that the researcher is able to understand the context of social interaction and human behaviour in order to provide a fuller appreciation of the subject matter being studied. Among the categories of researcher immersion into a social setting, we are considered covert participant researchers (Spiker 2011). Our roles were those of politicians and others in the social setting in which we operated did not know that we were eventually going to write about what we discovered.

Together, these methodological considerations help us draw conclusions about representative democracy that differ from those put forth in the dominant literature in Canadian political science. We argue that representative democracy is alive and well, contrary to what the media, academics, and indeed most politicians might seem to think. To establish the point, we turn to our two comparative cases, which will then be followed by analysis.

THE CASE OF A TRAFFIC LIGHT IN LONDON, ONTARIO

Our first case study deals with an issue at the municipal level. Prior to the 2014 municipal election, the residents of Hyde Park, which is located in the northwest corner of London, Ontario, wanted a traffic light installed at the corner of South Carriage Road and Hyde Park Road. These residents organized a petition with 616 signatures from local ratepayers. The local Hyde Park Business Association joined in support and rallied area businesses and community members. The petition was submitted to council, which then passed a motion to refer the matter to London civic administration to provide a report back to council after the completion of a road-widening project that impacted the intersection. During the 2014 municipal election, Morgan was asked his views on the project and suggested that he would take up the residents' concerns should he be elected to council. He subsequently won the election.

In November of 2016, a staff report was presented to the Civic Works Committee that indicated that the traffic light was not warranted (according to the process used to determine traffic light installations and the professional opinion of the Transportation Division staff). Indeed, the metrics were clear, but the report also produced data that showed the speed at which those metrics were changing at the intersection. There was also a new French immersion Catholic elementary school being constructed in the area; as the school would have a regional catchment, it was anticipated that it would have about twenty buses and a large volume of vehicle drop-offs. This, in combination with the significant residential development in the area and the support of hundreds of residents in the neighbourhood, prompted Morgan to move a motion that, notwithstanding the direction of the city engineer, civic administration be directed to proceed with the installation of a traffic signal. That motion lost at committee by a 2–3 vote and then again at council by a 6–7 vote.

After the council decision, Morgan worked with community members and city staff to develop next steps. Morgan convinced staff to commit to conducting a new traffic study that would be completed after the new school opened. In the community, Morgan updated the residents on the results of the vote and kept a database of the residents who initially raised the concern. He also added people to the list as they contacted him about the traffic light issue over the next year. Morgan also started working with the new school community and the parents who had immediate concerns after the school opened. He continued to communicate with interested residents, businesses, and stakeholders and kept them up to speed on the process and indicated that they would be informed when the matter could be raised again.

During the summer of 2018, Morgan drafted a new letter to the Civic Works Committee asking that the traffic light be installed. Civic administration presented the new traffic study, which showed a significant increase in the installation metrics but indicated that it still did not meet the threshold for installation. The community rallied, and hundreds of residents drafted emails to members of council asking them to support Morgan's call for a traffic light. These efforts were effective, and the committee voted 4–0 to recommend the installation. In the days leading up to the council meeting, council members who were opposed to the installation of the traffic light asked civic administration for data showing the other traffic lights that did not meet the warrants. The list showed that there were other intersections, located in various wards across the city, that were closer to meeting the warrants than the Hyde Park intersection. The debate quickly turned into a discussion about "queue-jumping" and "moving this ahead of an intersection in my ward." The debate was prolonged, and as councillors spoke it was clear that this would be a very close vote.

When Morgan's opportunity to speak came about, he discussed the need to listen to the community and spoke about the level of engagement on this issue. He stated that it is the right of the elected municipal council to make this decision regardless of the advice from the staff. Morgan argued that given the nine-month timeline for installing the lights, the thresholds for doing so may be met by the time the lights are in place. For the councillors concerned about queue-jumping, Morgan worked to find a source of financing that ensured other intersections would not be bumped down the list. In effect, he used every tool in his toolbox to represent his constituents. At the same time, he supported and encouraged the democratic activation of those constituents, a process that occurred independent of the results of the outcome.

Analysing representation simply by counting winning and losing votes would have meant that Morgan was less successful at representing his constituents with the first motion he posed, and if we were limiting our study to a short time frame, we would not have caught the fact that he was more successful the second time around. However, this qualitative account demonstrates the various steps that Morgan utilized to rally support and to advocate on behalf of his constituents. Neither a staff recommendation nor a negative vote stopped Morgan from representing his constituents. It motivated him to work harder to the point that his constituents knew he was working on their behalf. The persistence of his advocacy prompted a new motion to approve the lights, which was successful. Further, and irrespective of the vote result, the process supported and encouraged civic engagement in the community. This involvement and activation may be of inherent value to democracy itself. Morgan observed that by being an active and accessible representative, the community was supportive of his efforts despite the initial legislative defeat.

We now turn to our next case study to see if we can establish the same kind of representative pattern.

THE CASE OF SAVING LOCAL CHILD-CARE CENTRES

The purpose of beginning with the Morgan example is to highlight the exercise of representative democracy unconstrained from the institutional forces that we see in parliamentary systems – namely, centralized party control where politicians are simply rubber-stamping the views of the party leader and his or her advisers. This centralized form of power does not exist in municipalities. Unelected public servants are still present and provide regular advice to council, but they do not have strong first ministers and executive councils to drive policy. Neither is there a party system in municipal politics in Ontario. It is on this basis that we applied the MDSD comparative method. Drawing on the two cases presented in this chapter helps us evaluate the question of whether we have an effective representative democracy that is responsive to the wishes of local citizens. If we find examples in which a politician listens to constituents and tries to fix their problems, much like Morgan did in London, then we must ultimately conclude that the same possibilities for representation exist in parliamentary systems as they do in local governments. Using a MDSD comparative method gives that conclusion added support, as we mentioned earlier.

We shift to the context of child-care policy in Waterloo region, the southern part of which overlaps with the constituency of Cambridge, held by Leone as an Opposition member in Ontario's 40th Parliament. Soon after the 2011 general election, Leone's office learned of a child-care-themed town hall meeting, which was to review the issues related to the Province's implementation of full-day kindergarten and the local school boards' interpretation of the implementation. Leone attended the town hall as an observer. To summarize the challenges discussed at the meeting, the public and Catholic school boards had decreed that they alone were going to offer before- and after-school care in schools, and thus effectively put all non-profit child-care centres co-located with schools in jeopardy, including likely bankruptcy. During the town hall meeting at which a representative from the public school board was present, parents grew increasingly angry, and when they noticed that Leone was in the audience observing the proceedings in an unofficial capacity, they started pleading with him to intervene. Parent after parent went to the microphone and demanded that the public school board change course, and most of these parents ended their comments by asking Leone to fix the situation at the provincial legislature, even though he was not a formal part of the meeting, nor, as Opposition member, was he in a position in the legislature that would allow him to compel the government to act.

Fresh out of an election, Leone knew that child care was not among the priorities of his parliamentary caucus. This created a challenge because the Official Opposition would need to be convinced that it should back the protection of non-profit child-care centres. Yet it also created an opportunity in the sense that, whatever the solution to the child-care problem would be, it did not fly in the face of any other promises the party had made during the election. Thus, Leone went to his caucus to present a potential solution to the problem. The caucus agreed to give Leone the ability to find a way to craft legislation around the situation, which he did. Leone then tabled this legislation and held a press conference to discuss the bill, which received significant local media coverage. This prompted parents to hold roadside rallies and increase their political pressure on the government and school boards to change their approach.

Institutionally, a lottery determines when members of Ontario's provincial parliament are able to debate their legislation or motions; it is typically conducted through a draw of ballot numbers. By the time he tabled his child-care protection bill, however, Leone had already used his private member's ballot on another motion, so there was no way he could debate the bill until he could draw a number again, which was likely more than a calendar year away. This did not deter him from tabling the legislation. Leone then met with both Catholic and public school board trustees and officials, who granted a meeting with him. Everyone Leone met with at the Catholic and public school boards in the Waterloo district continued to say that the rollout of full-day kindergarten would absolutely not change, and the desire for the board to be the sole provider of the early years program was consistent with government policy, even though the Waterloo district boards were the only ones in the province taking such a stance. In subsequent meetings, the local cabinet ministers were drawn into the debate. They did not appreciate the attention being drawn to the issue by the bill, meetings, and rallies. It was clear that the government would not be providing a solution to the problem.

Despite the insistence at the boards of education that people were not willing to have their minds changed with regard to the boards' status as the sole provider of child-care facilities co-located in schools, and the government's unwillingness to intervene, Leone continued to drum up support in interviews with the local press, in open letters, and at meetings. Opposition colleagues that were reluctant to join could not avoid the issue either. Within two months of tabling the legislation, the Catholic school board buckled under pressure and modified its policy to allow child-care facilities to operate in schools. This was followed by the public school board's decision to reverse its policy as well. Families, especially the ones that did not want to see their trusted child-care worker lose their job, won the day, thanks in large part to the political pressure initiated by Leone on behalf of concerned parents.

It should be noted that the child-care legislation that Leone tabled in the legislature, which is part of any parliamentarian's formal toolbox, did not need to be debated and voted upon in the legislature itself – two avenues that have traditionally been used to assess representation in parliamentary systems. In fact, the traditional assessment of voting for legislation would not have captured the real representation that took place on this issue. A vote was not even possible on the bill for at least a year; instead, resolution of this issue resulted from all the other activity that allowed Leone to represent his constituents, which traditional treatments of political representation have tended to ignore.

ANALYSIS

What do these two cases teach us? The first lesson is that there is more to assessing political representation than examining legislation or bylaws that have been passed and who voted for or against those provisions. Quite importantly, there are a number of other things politicians have at their disposal to effectively represent their constituents. When voters send their representative to work in a deliberative chamber, the representative arrives to a desk with a microphone attached. That microphone and desk command attention both inside the chamber and outside. These two case studies highlight all the work that goes on both inside the chamber and outside to effectively represent constituents. Focusing simply on the formal aspects, such as voting patterns on legislation, or the number of private member's bills that are enacted into law, do not capture the range of pathways to democratic representation. Elected officials supporting and encouraging community engagement and activation has democratic value in itself.

The second lesson is that the informal aspects of a legislator's influence have not received sufficient attention in the academic literature. We do not challenge the idea that central agencies are powerful, or that bureaucratic and political staff play an influential role in terms of what happens in deliberative assemblies, but we equally believe that the informal aspects of influence are under-reported, when they really must be examined as well. Of course, the limitation of the case-study method is that we are only talking about two cases. But Lijphart (1975) argues that this limitation can be overcome either by increasing the number of cases or by keeping the number of variables small. Both authors can point to dozens of similar examples where we have used informal aspects of influence to effect change. From an experiential perspective, we also know that many of our colleagues who sit, and have sat, in deliberative assemblies have similar examples. Our representatives' ability to effect change for constituents has not been hampered by the control we have seen from leaders and central agencies. They simply use other means to express that representation. We used the comparative method to go into further detail about how, despite the two different approaches to governing and governance at the provincial and municipal level in Ontario, the informal aspects of a politician's power are similar, and this conclusion is virtually ignored in the dominant literature describing a democratic deficit in Canada.

The third lesson implicit in our case studies, but which we will make explicit here, is that a legislator has more than one place of work. Our parliamentary system requires that legislators spend time in the chamber and time in their communities when they are not in the legislative chamber. This happens because our elected politicians have to abide by the laws that they pass. However, from an academic perspective, the literature tends to focus, with only some exceptions, on the one place of work with respect to representation (i.e., legislative chambers) and not the other (i.e., representatives' constituencies or wards). The literature tends to cover the work done inside the deliberative chamber extremely thoroughly, but the opposite is true for the informal aspects. Periods of recess, which the media likes to call "vacation" or "break week," are known as constituency time to a politician. That time is used to attend events, deal with casework, and meet with stakeholders. We know that these aspects of representation exist, but we do not study the effects of this representation, even though it is vitally important that we do so. One of the reasons for this is that it is much harder to conceptualize and systematically measure these processes of representation. This is why it is important to consider applying varying research methods to the study of representative democracy, which we do from a qualitative perspective in this chapter. It is necessary to develop a fuller appreciation of the range and scope of a representative's work. If more people understood what their representatives do and how they go about their work – particularly the non-partisan work that goes on in the constituency – then it may be possible to be less cynical about the state of our politics and democracy.

CONCLUSION

This chapter has sought to provide some background on a dominant theme in the study of Canadian parliamentary democracy – namely, the claim that our representative democracy is being challenged by the fact that certain figures and structures in the system (e.g., leaders, political staff, party caucuses, bureaucrats) seem to be growing more powerful than the politicians we elect to represent us in a deliberative chamber. If politicians only rubber-stamp legislation from the centre, then why do so many people want to leave their jobs only to become a robot in Parliament? The point that we have been making in this chapter is that there is real representation, but that real representation might not always be physically seen in legislative assemblies. The problem is that we are not capturing some of the real representation that happens outside legislatures. Using an ethnographic, qualitative approach to building these cases, we are able to conclude that, despite different institutional designs of democratic legislative assemblies, the informal approaches to representation demonstrate that legislators are quite effective at responding to their constituents' concerns.

Through the use of case studies and our ethnographic participation in the research project, we were able to advance the argument that there are a variety of tools in a politician's toolbox with which they can effectively represent his or her constituents, such as listening to voters, advocating for policy change through formal challenges, and rallying support. These are aspects of the job that have not been sufficiently addressed in the academic literature, but they are aspects of the job that are apparent to us, two covert participant researchers. The case study method, combined with the MDSD comparative method, allowed us to explore whether representation of this type held across systems. Similar forms of representation occurred in both, which adds strength to the conclusions that this chapter has advanced – namely, that representative democracy is still alive and well despite the central agencies that have dominated the literature on Canadian representation to date.

In the end, methodological considerations are most useful in both challenging conventional orthodoxy and providing a pathway for advancing a competing conclusion. There is, of course, more that can be done to further contribute to different ways of thinking about political representation. First, more cases can be added to provide further evidence in favour of the findings. Second, when exit interviews are taking place, perhaps the questions posed to outgoing politicians could reflect the conclusions drawn from this study. Third, some consideration of how we can quantify a parliamentarian's work could be considered. While these are difficult to quantify, this chapter makes the case that we should broaden our appreciation of a politician's work to include rallies organized, town hall meetings held, and so on, all of which lead to positive change through policies and regulations. We made the case in this chapter that we can gain a better understanding of our representative democracy by thinking about the topic in different ways, and studying it through different methods.

NOTES

1 Rob Leone was elected to the Ontario Legislative Assembly as the MPP for Cambridge in October 2011 and served until June 2014. Josh Morgan was elected as a city councillor in London, Ontario, on 27 October 2014, and re-elected to the same office on 22 October 2018.
2 Many deliberative assemblies have party caucus whips, which are positions members of that assembly hold. Whips are responsible for ensuring that enough members of the party caucus vote according to the wishes of the party caucus in the legislature. Whips are one of the central enforcers of party discipline and are present in both Westminster parliamentary systems and American congressional systems.

REFERENCES

Ajzenstat, Janet. 2007. *The Canadian Founding: John Locke and Parliament.* Montreal and Kingston: McGill-Queen's University Press.
Aucoin, Peter, and Lori Turnbull. 2003. "The Democratic Deficit: Paul Martin and Parliamentary Reform." *Canadian Public Administration* 46, no. 4: 427–49. https://doi.org/10.1111/j.1754-7121.2003.tb01586.x
Blidook, Kelly. 2010. "Exploring the Role of 'Legislators' in Canada: Do Members of Parliament Influence Policy?" *Journal of Legislative Studies* 16, no. 1: 32–56. https://doi.org/10.1080/13572330903541979
Dahl, Robert. 2015. *On Democracy,* 2nd ed. New Haven, CT: Yale University Press.
Docherty, David. 1997. *Mr. Smith Goes to Ottawa: Life in the House of Commons.* Vancouver: UBC Press.
– 2005. *Legislatures.* Vancouver: UBC Press.

Lijphart, Arend, 1971. "Comparative Politics and the Comparative Method." *American Political Science Review* 65, no. 3: 682–93. https://doi.org/10.2307/1955513

– 1975. "The Comparable Cases Strategy in Comparative Research." *Comparative Political Studies* 8, no. 2: 158–77. https://doi.org/10.1177/001041407500800203

Loat, Allison, and Michael MacMillan. 2014. *Tragedy in the Commons: Former Members of Parliament Speak Out about Canada's Failing Democracy.* Toronto: Random House.

Malloy, Jonathan. 2003. "High Discipline, Low Cohesion? The Uncertain Patterns of Canadian Parliamentary Party Groups." *Journal of Legislative Studies* 9, no. 4: 116–29.

Mill, John Stuart. 1861. *Considerations on Representative Democracy.* Cambridge: Cambridge University Press.

Rathgeber, Brent. 2014. *Irresponsible Government: The Decline of Parliamentary Democracy in Canada.* Toronto: Dundurn Press.

Sarsby, Jacquie. 1984. "The Field Work Experience." In *Ethnographic Research: A Guide to General Conduct,* edited by R.F. Ellen, 87–130. New York: Academic Press.

Savoie, Donald. 1999. *Governing from the Centre: The Concentration of Power in Canadian Politics.* Toronto: University of Toronto Press.

– 2014. *Power: Where Is It?* Montreal and Kingston: McGill-Queen's University Press.

Seidle, F. Leslie, and David Docherty. 2003. *Reforming Parliamentary Democracy.* Montreal and Kingston: McGill-Queen's University Press.

Spiker, Paul. 2011. "Ethical Covert Research." *Sociology* 45, no. 1: 1–16. https://doi.org/10.1177/0038038510387195

CHAPTER NINE

The Democratic Dimensions of Specialized Governments

Joseph Lyons

INTRODUCTION

When most of us think about democratic governments, we think about general-purpose governments. These are local, subnational, and national governments that perform many functions and are based on cultural and geographic communities. There is another type of government, however: specialized jurisdictions that perform only a single or limited number of functions and are designed around the "geography of the problem" that they are intended to address (Hooghe and Marks 2003; Frey and Eichenberger 1999). Many important services, that people could be forgiven for assuming are delivered by general-purpose governments, are in fact provided by specialized jurisdictions. Citizens need to be informed for democracy to function properly, so the relative obscurity of specialized jurisdictions raises important questions.

Specialized jurisdictions exist at all scales, but they are especially prevalent at the local level. This chapter focuses on local specialized juris-dictions in Canada, commonly known as special-purpose bodies (SPBs). It relies on existing research to evaluate the democratic consequences of delivering services through SPBs by comparing them with municipal governments, their general-purpose equivalents, across common, gener-ally accepted criteria for democracies.[1] Because the literature on SPBs is in its early stages, these comparisons are supplemented by key findings related to American special districts (more on these below) and they borrow some concepts from related European literature. Taken together, existing evidence indicates that SPBs are less democratic than municipal governments. The democratic performance of SPBs can be improved, however, by increasing opportunities for citizen input and oversight.

Because so little is known about SPBs, some contextual background on them is needed before getting deeper into the approach and methods used in this chapter. As mentioned above, SPBs are autonomous juris-dictions that perform only a single or limited number of functions. This definition casts a wide net, but because there is considerable variation in terms of authority, governing structures, revenue sources, and size, it is difficult to be more precise (see Sancton 2015). A better way to get familiarized with SPBs is to think about specific examples.

Consider the morning routine of a student on her way to class at Western University in London, Ontario (the university where all the contributing authors of this volume have worked). She wakes, showers, and catches the bus to campus. Along the way, the bus is slowed momentarily because a police officer, having just pulled someone over for speeding in a school zone, is blocking a lane of traffic. As the bus enters campus, it crosses a bridge over the Thames River. The student notices that the water level is high and wonders if it might spill its banks. Off the bus, with time to spare, she decides to grab something to eat before class. While waiting in line, she is comforted by the sight of a green notice pinned to the wall indicating that the campus eatery passed its most recent food premises inspection. She probably didn't think too much about how the services and resources she encountered along her travels were provided and/or managed – unless she was on her way to a class about local government service delivery – but many are, in fact, provided by local SPBs. Let's quickly identify each of the SPBs she encountered.

Water makes its way to London through two water-treatment systems, one drawing from Lake Erie and one drawing from Lake Huron. These systems are jointly owned and governed by the municipalities along each line. The City of London wholesales the water to the partner municipal-ities and retails it to water users in the city. The bus service in London is provided by the London Transit Commission and policing is provided by London Police Services. These agencies operate within city boundaries but are independent from the municipality. Likewise, the school that the police officer pulled the speeder over in front of is part of the Thames Valley District School Board (Catholic schools in the area are provided by the London District Catholic School Board and there are also separate public and Catholic French boards); the Thames River watershed is managed by the Upper Thames River Conservation Authority; and the food-premise inspection was done by an employee of the Middlesex-London Health Unit. All these agencies have jurisdictions that include the City of London as well as other municipalities in the region.

The point of this scenario is to highlight some of the important services provided by SPBs and to give readers a sense of just how many of them exist and affect their daily lives. The scenario mentions ten, but it is possible to identify at least ten other service areas where an SPB is the lead in London and the surrounding area (see Lyons and Spicer 2018). London likely makes more use of SPBs than most other municipalities – it is a separated city rather than an amalgamated, single-tier municipality or part of a regional government – but there are 444 municipalities in Ontario and approximately 3,653 municipalities in Canada. Even if we make a conservative estimate and say that SPBs outnumber municipalities by about two to one, that means that there are around 8,000 SPBs in Canada (Richmond and Siegel 1994; Tindal and Tindal 2004; Sancton 2015).

For those in Canada used to thinking mainly about the federal, provincial, and territorial governments, 8,000 is a big number. But it pales in comparison to the number of specialized jurisdictions in the United States, where approximately 35,000 of the country's 90,000 governments are classified as special districts – this number climbs to over 50,000 if you include school districts. Indeed, much of the theoretical and empirical work on specialized jurisdictions has been based on US examples. There are key differences between US special districts and Canadian SPBs, however. Most special districts in the United States have directly elected boards and the authority to levy taxes (Berry 2009). Thus, they are characterized by direct democratic representation and direct fee-for-service charges to citizens, two important characteristics when thinking about democratic service delivery. Furthermore, citizens and other local actors in the United States can create local governments through home-rule provisions and through initiatives and referendums (Burns 1994; Foster 1997).

In Canada, most SPB boards, except for school boards and the Vancouver Park Board, are made up of appointed representatives, often a mix of elected municipal councillors and local residents, some of whom have subject matter expertise. Rather than having taxation power, they rely on fees levied on member municipalities, intergovernmental transfers, and user fees. General-purpose governments such as the federal and provincial governments and municipalities also maintain authority over the formation of most SPBs (Magnusson 1985; Richmond and Siegel 1994; Tindal and Tindal 2004; Lyons 2015a; Sancton 2015; Furlong 2016; Lucas 2016).

So, with this background information in mind, we now turn to the task of evaluating the democratic credentials of Canadian SPBs.

APPROACH AND METHODS

This book is guided by the question, What is democracy and how do we study it? The specific focus of this chapter is local democracy and the democratic dimensions of Canadian SPBs. This approach is rooted in the institutionalist perspective. This perspective assumes that institutional structure affects behavioural and performance outcomes (Frederickson et al. 2012; Peters et al. 2016). As mentioned above, local institutions can be grouped into two categories: general purpose and specialized. Both types provide similar services but have different institutional features.

This chapter relies on pre-existing academic research to assess how these institutional differences affect democratic performance. The review article is a common method used in political science, public administration, and public policy. Review articles go beyond a mere literature review, which is a common element of most research, by compiling and analysing existing research on a topic and using it as evidence. These reviews provide a useful function by synthesizing and assessing research findings around important questions and key themes (see, for example, Fernandez and Rainey 2006; Carr 2015). Because they distil a lot of information into a more digestible format, review articles are useful for both researchers and practitioners. Review articles can come at various points during the lifespan of an area of research. For more developed lines of inquiry, the number of relevant publications may be well into the hundreds. Reviews of this nature may allow for coding based on key topics and variables (see Christenson, Paarlberg, and Perry 2017) and contributions can even be grouped by journal (see Baumgartner, Jones, and Mortenson 2018). There is value in review articles earlier on in the lifespan of a research area as well, as this can help to set the stage for future research. The literature on specialized jurisdictions in Canada is in its infancy and falls into this category.

The first step in writing this chapter was to collect relevant sources. As someone who researches in this area (Lyons 2015a, 2015b, 2016; Lyons and Spicer 2018), I relied on my own working bibliography of publications on specialized jurisdictions and supplemented this with several Google Scholar searches using keywords such as "special districts," "special purpose bodies," "local government," "Canada," and "democracy" in various combinations (Christensen, Paarlberg, and Perry [2017] use similar methods). To ensure comprehensiveness, Google Scholar's "cited by" function was used on key contributions and the reference list was reviewed by another expert in the field.[2] This review draws mostly from peer-reviewed publications. Conference papers, dissertations, and government publications were excluded, but I did include publications from think tanks and research institutions. Not all research on specialized jurisdictions focuses on democratic performance either. As such, not all the important contributions (e.g., Lucas 2016, 2017a, 2017b) figure as prominently in this review as they might have in a more general undertaking.

Because the research on Canadian SPBs is limited, this review chapter has several unique features. First, the literature on US special districts will also be surveyed as a way of considering the democratic side effects of bestowing on SPBs certain institutional characteristics. Second, for conceptual consistency and clarity, some terms from European research on multi-level governance and specialized jurisdictions are employed. And finally, because so little is known about SPBs, examples are used quite extensively.

With the collection of articles complete, the next step is to come up with the criteria to measure and compare the democratic performance of SPBs.

Most other contributions to this volume spend considerable time and energy thinking about democracy and what it means. This chapter takes a lot of that for granted by relying on generally accepted evaluation criteria. This methodological choice is helpful in two ways: it grounds the review in existing literature and is a more efficient route to the main point of the analysis – using existing research to assess the democratic credentials of SPBs. Assumptions about what constitutes democracy – or more specifically, representative democracy – are open to critique, but drawing upon pre-existing definitions and criteria and applying them in other areas can contribute to a stronger and more robust literature by broadening its reach.

Most conceptualizations of democracy include elements of both popular control and political equity (Achen 1978; Beetham 1996; Dahl

1998). From these two main elements come intermediate concepts (Beetham 1996) or component elements (Trounstine 2010), which are used in combination or in isolation, depending on the purpose of the study. There is variation but also consistency between different lists of democratic criteria. There is also some overlap within specific lists themselves. Dahl (1998), for example, uses effective participation, equality in voting, gaining enlightened understanding, exercising final control over the agenda, and inclusion of results, whereas the Canadian Democratic Audit team, led by William Cross, uses inclusiveness, participation, and responsiveness (see Sancton and Alcantara, this volume). This chapter borrows from Trounstine (2010) and uses authorization, responsiveness, and accountability. Trounstine is mostly concerned with municipal governments, which are the comparative benchmarks used in this chapter. This list also aligns with the democratic criteria often used in the local government literature and is particularly useful in highlighting the structural differences between general-purpose and specialized governments (see Tiebout 1956; Ostrom et al. 1961; Lyons and Lowery 1989; Beetham 1996; Skelcher 2006; Berry 2009; Mullin 2009; Zeemering 2012; Tausanovitch and Warshaw 2014).

So now we can go about organizing and assessing the existing literature on specialized jurisdictions according to these criteria and compare the democratic performance of SPBs and municipal governments.

COMPARING SPECIAL-PURPOSE BODIES AND MUNICIPAL GOVERNMENTS

Authorization

Authorization, through election of political decision-makers by citizens, is a cornerstone of representative democracy. It is through elections that citizens authorize democratic representatives to act on their behalf (Beetham 1996; Trounstine 2010). In Canada, we elect politicians at three levels of government: local, provincial, and national. When it comes to the three democratic criteria used in this chapter, Canadian SPBs fare the worst on authorization. In comparison with their municipal counterparts, and many US special districts, Canadian SPBs score poorly on this criterion. As mentioned earlier, apart from school boards and the Vancouver Park Board, the decision-making bodies of SPBs are not directly elected. So, we can say that SPB board members are at least one step removed from the electoral process (Sancton 2015; Lucas 2013).[3]

Canadian SPBs are not without any sort of "democratic anchorage" (Sorenson and Torfing 2005), however. This is because they are nested within general-purpose jurisdictions (Magnusson 1985; Richmond and Siegel 1994; Lyons 2015a, 2015b; Sancton 2015; Lucas 2016, 2017a, 2017b). Rather than being authorized by citizens to act on their behalf, SPBs receive authorization to govern by general-purpose jurisdictions. SPBs are created through legislation (federal, provincial, or municipal), which gives them some democratic legitimacy. Moreover, elected municipal politicians, who are appointed by their respective councils, figure prominently on many SPB boards. Other board members are often citizens appointed either by a municipality or the provincial or federal governments. Who makes the appointments depends upon the enabling legislation. If citizens and elected politicians are extremely unhappy with the performance of a specific SPB, its enabling legislation can be changed, or it could be dissolved entirely. Both are easier said than done, however. Once created, SPBs develop beneficiaries and political support and can be difficult to get rid of (see Filion and Sanderson 2014; Lyons 2015b).

Municipal governments score better than SPBs when it comes to authorization, but they are not without their own problems. Most municipal politicians are directly elected, but municipal elections are, for the most part, low-information elections (Taylor and McEleny 2017; see also Anderson and Stephenson, chapter 4, this volume). Turnout is low, often in the range of 30 to 40 per cent (Sancton 2015; Breaux et al. 2017). Incumbents also enjoy a strong advantage. Unless they are extremely unpopular or behave badly, they tend to get re-elected (Moore et al. 2015; Sayers and Lucas, 2017; Taylor and McEleny 2017). Moreover, municipal parties only exist in large cities in British Columbia and Quebec. The absence of political parties makes it difficult for voters to know what candidates will actually be able to accomplish once in office (Breux et al. 2017).

Turnout is even lower when it comes to US special districts, often in the 2–10 per cent range. So even though US special districts are authorized through elections, only a small percentage of the population votes in special-district elections, often those who have an interest in the service being provided (Berry 2009). Moreover, some special districts still have property ownership as a requirement to vote (Burns 1994). The way that

US special districts are created is also a concern. Permissive enabling legislation in many states allows local entrepreneurs such as property owners, local manufacturers, or real estate developers to create special districts to finance the provision of services and prevent annexation from neighbouring municipalities (Burns 1994; Foster 1997; Carr and Farmer 2011).

In sum, Canadian SPBs score poorly when it comes to authorization. Their embeddedness within general-purpose jurisdictions gives them some democratic anchorage, but they are at least one step removed from the electoral process. Canadian municipalities score better on this criterion. There are some problems with the way that they are authorized to act, but Canadian SPBs are afflicted by these problems as well since municipal councillors often serve on their boards. The problems with US special districts highlight some of the negative consequences associated with moving toward direct elections for specialized jurisdictions. If municipal elections are considered low-information elections, most voters are even less informed when it comes to specialized jurisdiction elections.

Responsiveness

Responsiveness is about whether governments act in accordance with citizens' preferences. In other words, are governments doing what citizens want? This is a key criterion in debates about specialized governments. Opponents of specialized jurisdictions argue that specialized jurisdictions confuse citizens and are more susceptible to the influence of private or special interests, thereby reducing responsiveness (Lyons and Lowery 1989). Supporters of specialized jurisdictions, on the other hand, argue that their singular focus allows them to be more responsive to citizen preferences (Ostrom et al. 1961; Frey and Eichenberger 1999). This is because service demands vary across service areas: people in one community might want more parks, whereas people in another nearby community might want a gold-plated fire service. If these two communities were part of the same general-purpose government, service levels for these services would likely be harmonized across the entire municipality and neither community would be entirely satisfied.

Theoretically, it is also easier for well-informed citizens to evaluate and compare the performance of specialized governments. Two specialized jurisdictions, providing the same service at the same scale, can

be compared relatively easily. Comparing two general-purpose governments is more of a challenge because of the range of services provided.
Consider the example of local school boards. If there are two separate
school boards operating near each other, parents could decide where to
send their children based on their relative performance. Overlapping
specialized jurisdictions like this also allow for the possibility of exit
(Frey and Eichenberger 1999). If parents are unhappy with how the
school board governing their children's school is being run, they could
send them to another nearby school governed by a different board. This
situation exists in Ontario, for example, where there are separate public
and Catholic school boards. Catholic schools are increasingly enrolling
non-Catholic students and opting out of religion classes is becoming
easier (McQuigge 2017; Alphonso 2018). These practices vary between
boards, but in many places non-Catholic parents essentially have the
choice of sending their child to a Catholic school or a public school. In
this case, exiting from a school board is a lot less onerous than exiting
from a municipality because you can exit without moving. Many neigh-
bourhoods are near both public and Catholic schools, so changing
schools comes with minimal transaction costs.

Comparisons of the policy responsiveness of special districts and municipal governments from the United States have had mixed results. In
her study of local drinking water policy in the United States, for example,
Mullin (2009) compares the responsiveness of general-purpose governments and special districts. Her findings indicate that the salience of the
service or public good in question influences the level of responsiveness
to the median voter. Specialized governing units, especially those with
elected boards, are more likely to respond to the preferences of the
median voter where problem severity is low, with the gap gradually
closing and general-purpose governments becoming more responsive
as problem severity rises.

In direct contrast, Berry (2009) explores what he considers to be the
two defining characteristics of special districts – territorial overlap and
concurrent taxation. These, he argues, produce a fiscal common pool
that specialized governing boards can draw on to appease policy-relevant
interest groups. In other words, everyone's tax bill increases because of
the service demands of those who actually vote in, and pay attention
to, special district elections. Berry finds strong evidence to support his
claim that the jurisdictional overlap of special purpose districts results

in higher spending than is the case when the same services are delivered by general-purpose governments.

A key difference between these two studies, which may explain the divergent results, is that Mullin studied water, which is priced on a user-fee basis, whereas Berry focused on special districts that levied a property-based tax. People may pay less attention to the various levies included on their property tax bill than they would their water bill, which they have some control over. Thus, special district politicians may face different incentives, depending on the characteristics of the service being provided.

The responsiveness of Canadian SPBs is also difficult to unpack. SPBs are obligated to fulfill their mandate, which is embedded in their enabling legislation and associated regulations. To the extent that their enabling legislation reflects the public interest or is in the interests of the median voter, SPBs may be more or less responsive. The limited research that has been done on the responsiveness of Canadian SPBs demonstrates that their responsiveness varies by policy area and by level of autonomy (Frisken 1991; Horak 2012; Eidelman 2013, 2018; Sanderson and Filion 2013; Filion and Sanderson 2014; Lyons 2015a, 2015b, 2016 – not all of these sources use the term "responsiveness," but they all speak to mandate adherence and fulfillment). Much like in Mullin's work, we are likely to see differences not only between SPBs and municipalities, but also between SPBs themselves. The concept of decision significance is also instructive. In multi-level systems, a decision is significant if actors at different levels abide by the decision (van Popering-Verkerk and van Buuren 2016). Using this language, policies originating at the federal or provincial level and requiring local adherence are more likely to be significant if they are implemented by SPBs with autonomy from their municipal members.

In the case of Ontario's conservation authorities, for example, insofar as the provincial policies around watershed management are in the interest of the median voter – wisely managing resources and protecting public health and safety – conservation authorities with jurisdictions that include multiple municipalities are more likely to abide by them. Conservation authorities that include fewer municipalities, however, are more likely to neglect them. Spanning multiple municipalities fragments board membership, thereby reducing the control that any one single municipality has over a conservation authority. Thus, even if these policies do not necessarily match the preferences of individual homeowners, developers, and municipal politicians who may be supportive of development in and around natural areas, they do reflect majority preferences (Lyons 2015a). So here we have a curious situation where specialized jurisdictions, which are more insulated from municipal control, may be more responsive to the public interest because they are more likely to abide by provincial policies. In short, lack of elections notwithstanding, the legislative mandate and autonomy of SPBs may affect responsiveness.

In reference to municipalities, the discussion above has already identified some of the key influences over municipal decision-making: federal and provincial governments, local developers and business people, and local citizens (see also Sancton 2015). Municipalities are generally thought of as being responsive because they are dealing with smaller, more homogenous populations than higher levels of government. However, they face institutional and economic constraints that higher levels of government do not, thereby reducing their capacity for autonomous decision-making (see Smith and Spicer 2017).

The issue of responsiveness to federal and provincial governments has been addressed to some extent above. It has been demonstrated that greater municipal control over SPBs might increase the likelihood that the policy decisions of upper-level governments are neglected where there is room for local discretion. But there are other, mostly provincial policies that give municipal governments less room to manoeuvre. Recent changes to the Ontario Municipal Act, for example, require all municipalities to appoint an integrity commissioner and adopt a code of conduct. To the extent that municipal agendas are bogged down by requirements issued by higher-level governments, their ability to respond to local preferences will be limited.

Development and business interests are very influential when it comes to municipal politics (Logan and Molotch 1987; Horak and Young 2012). It is not so much that these interests always carry the day, but that porous municipal borders and a strong reliance on the property tax incentivizes municipalities to create favourable business environments. The competition for investment and development that this engenders sometimes means that good planning or citizen concerns are ignored (Leo 2002). As was demonstrated above, autonomous SPBs – like conservation authorities, which are less reliant on the property tax base – can play an important role in controlling some of the more negative aspects of urban development. Things can also go the other way, however, if a specialized jurisdiction is given responsibility over economic development (Lyons 2015b).

Most municipal councillors want to be re-elected, so they cannot be totally beholden to business interests. They also need to be responsive to local residents. Municipal councillors tend to respond to organized groups of citizens, especially if what they are proposing is not overly costly or can be responded to symbolically (Sancton 2015). A problem with municipal politics, and indeed politics at all levels, is that not all groups are equally well-organized. And, sometimes the loudest voices push for policies that are not in the best interests of the entire community. This phenomenon takes on a unique dynamic at the municipal level. Because much of what municipalities do relates to the built environment, homeowners tend to pay the most attention to local politics and are an influential group. Homeowners are referred to as "homevoters" in the local government literature because they care about how municipal policies affect the value of their property, and they participate more in local politics than renters (Fischel 2001). The influence and preferences of homevoters has been observed in Canada as well. Canadian homevoters, for example, are more likely to vote in municipal elections and are less supportive of social housing than renters (McGregor and Spicer 2016).

In sum, the responsiveness of Canadian SPBs varies by policy area and level of autonomy. SPBs are faithful to their mandates. If those mandates reflect majority preferences, SPBs have the potential to be more responsive than municipal governments. The responsiveness of municipal governments is contingent as well. Municipal politicians seeking re-election need to be responsive to citizens, but they are constrained in their decision-making. A lot of what they do involves responding to the policies of upper-level governments. In policy areas where municipalities do have more freedom to act, business interests and homevoters exert strong influences due to the nature of local politics.

Accountability

Now we are at the point where local officials have been authorized to act, and they have acted, so how are they held accountable for those actions? Accountability is often conceptualized in the literature as a principal-agent relationship – or perhaps more accurately as a series of principal-agent relationships. In the cleanest models, voters are principals who delegate authority to their representatives, who in turn delegate authority to administrative officials. All accountability relationships involve similar components: information (agent accounts for conduct), discussion (principal assesses agent's account), and consequences (principal punishes, corrects, or rewards agent) (see Brandsma and Schillemans 2012). This last step is especially important for our purposes. Accountability is an empty shell unless it is connected to a system of rewards and punishments. This system might include governments suffering defeat at the polls, a cabinet member resigning or being demoted, and public servants receiving raises and promotions for good work or reprimand, suspension, and/or dismissal for poor work.

The accountability relationships of SPBs are complicated (see Martin [2007] regarding the accountability relationships of police services boards in Ontario). The concept of democratic anchorage, introduced earlier, is useful in helping to unpack these relationships. As mentioned above, SPBs are created through enabling legislation originating from general-purpose governments and elected politicians often serve as board members. This creates opportunities for elected politicians to hold SPB administrators to account. Moreover, many SPBs provide a lot of information about their activities and hold open meetings, thereby creating opportunities for citizens to contribute to and scrutinize their decision-making (see Lyons and Spicer 2018). SPBs do tend to be less visible than municipal governments, though, and there are more of them, making it hard for citizens to keep track of their activities (Kitchen 1975; Del Guidice and Zacks 1976; Lucas 2013). The sanctioning ability of citizens is also reduced without direct elections. Symptoms associated with these characteristics might include higher levels of spending and more generous salaries for employees compared to what a municipality might be able to afford or justify (Furlong 2016).

SPBs are also often accountable to multiple principals – often municipal governments (sometimes more than one) as well as one or more higher-level governments (Martin 2007; Krawchenko 2011; Lyons 2015a, 2016). Given this context, an interesting question to consider is what do SPBs do when the goals of their different principals conflict?

Health units in Ontario provide a good testing ground for this question. This is because the mandate for all public health units is rooted in the same provincial legislation – the Health Protection and Promotion Act – yet governing structures vary. Most health units can be neatly grouped into two categories: autonomous and integrated. The jurisdictions of autonomous health units encompass multiple municipalities. Their boards consist of representatives from these different municipalities as well as provincial appointees. The jurisdictions of integrated health units encompass either a single-tier municipality or a regional government. The municipal council acts as the board of health. In the wake of two public health emergencies in the early 2000s, this policy area provided an opportunity to observe a natural experiment with institutional variation and the changing expectations of a principal. During this period, the Province increased its contribution to public health funding and clearly communicated to boards of health and municipalities that it did not want to see municipal funding reduced, as its goal was to increase the capacity of the public health system. Research comparing the different responses of an autonomous and an integrated health unit to this policy change found that the autonomous health unit behaved more in accordance with provincial expectations than a health unit incorporated into the administrative structure of a municipality. The autonomous health unit acted more as an agent of the provincial government and negotiated an agreement with its municipal funders to keep contribution levels stable, whereas the integrated health unit acted more as an agent of the municipality: its municipal contribution was reduced to free up money for other municipal priorities (Lyons 2016). This example can also be interpreted using the concept of decision significance introduced earlier. The provincial decision was more significant in the hands of an autonomous health unit than an integrated one.

When it comes to municipalities, their accountability relationships are generally cleaner and more straightforward. Most municipal councillors are elected, meaning that voters can punish them for poor performance at the ballot box. Some of the problems mentioned above remain relevant – low voter turnout, incumbency advantage, lack of political parties – but all things being equal, it is easier for citizens to sanction municipal politicians than it is for them to do the same for SPB board members.

On-the-ground realities can complicate municipal accountability, however. For example, most municipalities are party to one or more inter-municipal agreements, whereby neighbouring municipalities share or jointly provide certain services. But inter-municipal agreements tend to be less transparent and accountable than SPBs. This is because inter-municipal agreements usually do not include provisions requiring the partners to prepare public reports, nor are there usually scheduled meetings where officials can be questioned about the performance of these agreements (see Lyons and Spicer 2018).

The debate over the accountability track record of US special districts is far from settled. Supporters of special districts maintain that increasing the number of governments within a metropolitan area – through both geographical fragmentation and functional specialization – is good for accountability because it increases competition and opportunities for citizen participation (Ostrom 1972; Bish 2001). Opponents of specialization counter that it is bad for accountability because citizens are less informed and less satisfied in more fragmented systems (Lowery 2001). Most of the US empirical work is focused on responsiveness, rather than accountability per se. Nonetheless, as Berry notes, the likelihood of interest-group mischief is high when voting rates are so low (Berry 2009). The European literature on specialized jurisdictions tends to focus more on accountability (Skelcher, Mathur, and Smith 2005; Skelcher 2006). Much of this work translates nicely to the Canadian context (see Spicer and Lyons 2018).

In sum, Canadian SPBs are embedded in complex accountability relationships. Democratic sanction is made possible through changes to enabling legislation, by the role played by elected politicians, and citizen input and scrutiny. Compared to municipalities, however, lack of elections and their reduced visibility makes it more difficult for citizens to hold them to account. Reduced visibility is also a problem for US special districts, most of which do have elections.

DISCUSSION OF RESULTS

Democratic performance is a theme in the fledgling literature on specialized jurisdictions. This chapter contributes by assessing and synthesizing research related to the democratic dimensions of specialized service delivery. The main takeaway is that the democratic track record of Canadian SPBs is far from straightforward. In terms of the criteria selected for this chapter, the results are clearest when it comes to authorization. Most SPBs do not have elections. Municipalities do. So, municipalities win on this score. Even here some nuance is necessary, though. SPBs are authorized to act by general-purpose jurisdictions and elected politicians serve on their boards, meaning they are not completely lacking democratic anchorage.

The results for the criterion of responsiveness are difficult to interpret. A responsive government acts in accordance with citizen preferences. Municipalities are generally thought of as being responsive insofar as they can deliver a tax and service package that aligns with the preferences of citizens in defined geographic communities. However, the disproportionate influence of homevoters and business interests over municipal politics is well-documented in the literature. The conservation authority example illustrates how some insulation from municipal control might lead to policies that better reflect majority preferences. But the opposite has been observed in other policy areas. The most definitive statement that can be made is that autonomous SPBs with mandates reflecting public preferences have the potential to be more responsive than less autonomous SPBs or municipal governments delivering the same service.

For the accountability criterion, SPBs can be considered agents of general-purpose governments, often more than one. This creates opportunities for democratically elected governments and politicians to sanction SPBs if necessary. Many SPBs are also transparent in their activities, thereby providing opportunities for citizen oversight and input. They are one step removed from the electoral process, however. In comparison with municipalities, they are less accountable to citizens.

In short, Canadian SPBs are less democratic than Canadian municipalities but are not entirely lacking in democratic credentials. SPBs are often created to solve particular public policy challenges, usually those that span beyond the mandates and capabilities of a single general-purpose government department. Because of this functional orientation, democratic characteristics are not always incorporated during institutional design. But where they have been, positive democratic outcomes have been observed. US special districts also provide a cautionary tale when considering direct elections and taxing authority for specialized jurisdictions. These institutional features appear to tilt the playing field in favour of special interest groups. Given low voter turnout in special-district elections, the embeddedness of Canadian SPBs might serve as a better check against bad behaviour. Inasmuch as general-purpose governments in Canada continue to establish specialized jurisdictions, it is important that citizens, like the student in our original example, have the opportunity to be informed about and scrutinize their activities. SPBs may never be as democratic as general-purpose jurisdictions, but the closer they can get, the better. SPBs also appear to be a more democratic alternative to purely administrative forms of inter-jurisdictional co-operation, such as inter-municipal agreements. Thus, for local services that transcend municipal boundaries, creating an SPB could increase the quality of local democracy.

AVENUES FOR FUTURE RESEARCH

More research is needed on the democratic performance of SPBs. A lot of the existing literature on specialized jurisdictions compares similar general-purpose and specialized jurisdictions. Cases are selected on the explanatory variable (institutional structure) to see if there is variation in outcomes. This methodology could be used to further probe the democratic dimensions of SPBs, as it is well-suited to qualitative, quantitative, and mixed-methods approaches. Most of the findings reviewed in this chapter are preliminary. They should be tested and retested. This is the path toward developing more robust hypotheses and theories. Given the differences between Canadian SPBs and US special districts, more research related to the responsiveness and accountability of SPBs is warranted. The embeddedness of Canadian SPBs in general-purpose jurisdictions provides opportunities to grapple with and confront existing assumptions related to these criteria. Concepts from the European literature surveyed in this chapter may prove useful in these endeavours, especially decision significance and democratic anchorage. The comparative approach could be used for other criteria as well. While this chapter was about democracy, it made no reference to coordination, efficiency, and effectiveness, for example, which are all important performance indicators for specialized jurisdictions.

NOTES

1 Much of the existing research on Canadian SPBs draws case material from Ontario; as this chapter relies on existing research, the empirical content is reflective of this.
2 Any errors or omissions remain my own.

3 The 2015 plebiscite on the Metro Vancouver Congestion Tax is an interesting exception when it comes to authorization. Though not about electing board members, the plebiscite asked residents in the commuter shed served by TransLink – an SPB that provides transit and transportation-related services in BC's Lower Mainland – if they would support a 0.5 per cent sales tax increase to pay for improvements to the region's transportation network. Unfortunately for TransLink and the group of local mayors behind the proposal, the majority voted in opposition. Observers pointed to a loss of public confidence in TransLink as a possible explanation for the plebiscite's defeat (Bula 2015).

REFERENCES

Achen, Christopher. 1978. "Measuring Representation." *American Journal of Political Science* 22, no. 3: 475–510. https://doi.org/10.2307/2110458

Alphonso, Caroline. 2018. "In Push for Funding, Ontario's Catholic School Boards Enrolling More Non-Catholics." *Globe and Mail,* February 13.

Baumgartner, Frank, Bryan Jones, and Peter Mortenson. 2018. "Punctuated Equilibrium Theory: Explaining Stability and Change in Policymaking." In *Theories of the Policy Process,* 4th ed., edited by Christopher Weible and Paul Sabatier, 55–101. New York: Westview Press.

Beetham, David. 1996. "Theorising Democracy and Local Government." In *Rethinking Local Democracy,* edited by Desmond King and Gerry Stoker, 28–49. London: Macmillan.

Berry, Christopher R. 2009. *Imperfect Union: Representation and Taxation in Multilevel Governments.* New York: Cambridge University Press.

Bish, Robert. 2001. *Local Government Amalgamations: Discredited Nineteenth-Century Ideals Alive in the Twenty-First.* C.D. Howe Institute Commentary No. 150.

Brandsma, Gijs Jan, and Thomas Schillemans. 2012. "The Accountability Cube: Measuring Accountability." *Journal of Public Administration Research and Theory* 23, no. 4: 953–75. https://doi.org/10.1093/jopart/mus034

Breux, Sandra, Jerome Couture, and Royce Koop. 2017. "Turnout in Local Election: Evidence from Canadian Cities, 2004–2014." *Canadian Journal of Political Science* 50, no. 3: 699–722. https://doi.org/10.1017/s000842391700018x

Bula, Frances. 2015. "Vancouver-Region Voters Reject Sales-Tax Hike to Fund Transit Projects." *Globe and Mail,* July 2. https://www.theglobeandmail.com/news/british-columbia/transit-results/article25228292

Burns, Nancy. 1994. *The Formation of American Local Governments: Private Values in Public Institutions.* New York: Oxford University Press.

Carr, Jered. 2015. "What Have We Learned about the Performance of Council-Manager Government? A Review and Synthesis of the Research." *Public Administration Review* 75, no. 5: 673–89. https://doi.org/10.1111/puar.12415

Carr, Jered, and Jayce Farmer. 2011. "Contingent Effects of Municipal and County TELs on Special District Usage in the United States." *Publius* 41, no. 4: 709–33. https://doi.org/10.1093/publius/pjr031

Christensen, Robert, Laurie Paarlberg, and James Perry. 2017. "Public Service Motivation Research: Lessons for Practice." *Public Administration Review* 77, no. 4: 529–42. https://doi.org/10.1111/puar.12796

Dahl, Robert. 1998. *On Democracy*. New Haven, CT: Yale University Press.

Del Guidice, Dominic, and Stephen M. Zachs. "The 101 Governments of Metro Toronto." In *Politics and Government of Urban Canada: Selected Readings*, 3rd ed., edited by Lionel D. Feldman and Michael D. Goldrick, 285–95. Toronto: Methuen Publications.

Eidelman, Gabriel. 2013. *Three's Company: A Review of Waterfront Toronto's Tri-government Approach to Waterfront Revitalization*. Toronto: Mowat Centre.

– 2018. "Failure When Fragmented: Public Land Ownership and Waterfront Redevelopment in Chicago, Vancouver, and Toronto." *Urban Affairs Review* 54, no. 4: 697–731. https://doi.org/10.1177/1078087416671429

Fernandez, Sergio, and Hal Rainey. 2006. "Managing Successful Organizational Change in the Public Sector." *Public Administration Review* 66, no. 2: 168–76. https://doi.org/10.1111/j.1540-6210.2006.00570.x

Filion, Pierre, and Christopher Sanderson. 2014. "Institutional Arrangements and Planning Outcomes: Inter-agency Competition on the Toronto Waterfront." In *Canada in Cities: The Politics and Policy of Federal-Local Governance*, edited by Katherine Graham and Caroline Andrew, 131–63. Montreal and Kingston: McGill-Queen's University Press.

Fischel, William. 2001. *The Homevoter Hypothesis: How Home Values Influence Local Government Taxation, School Finance, and Land-Use Policies*. Cambridge, MA: Harvard University Press.

Foster, Kathryn A. 1997. *The Political Economy of Special-Purpose Government*. Washington, DC: Georgetown University Press.

Frederickson, George, Kevin Smith, Christopher Larimer, and Michael Licari. 2012. *The Public Administration Theory Primer*, 2nd ed. Boulder, CO: Westview Press.

Frey, Bruno, and Reiner Eichenberger. 1999. *The New Democratic Federalism for Europe: Functional, Overlapping, and Competing Jurisdictions*. Cheltenham, UK: Edward Elgar.

Frisken, Frances. 1991. "The Contributions of Metropolitan Government to the Success of Toronto's Public Transit System: An Empirical Dissent from the Public-Choice Paradigm." *Urban Affairs Review* 27, no. 2: 268–92. https://doi.org/10.1177/004208169102700208

Furlong, Kathryn. 2016. *Leaky Governance: Alternative Service Delivery and the Myth of Water Utility Independence*. Vancouver: UBC Press.

Hooghe, Liesbet, and Gary Marks. 2003. "Unraveling the Central State, but How? Types of Multi-Level Governance." *American Political Science Review* 97, no. 2: 233–43. https://doi.org/10.1017/s0003055403000649

Horak, Martin. 2012. "Multilevel Governance in Toronto: Success and Failure in Canada's Largest City." In *Sites of Governance: Multilevel Governance and Policy Making in Canada's Big Cities*, edited by Martin Horak and Robert Young, 228–62 Montreal and Kingston: McGill-Queen's University Press.

Horak, Martin, and Robert Young, eds. 2012. *Sites of Governance: Multilevel Governance and Policy Making in Canada's Big Cities*. Montreal and Kingston: McGill-Queen's University Press.

Kitchen, Harry. 1975. "Some Organizational Implications of Providing an Urban Service: The Case of Water." *Canadian Public Administration* 18, no. 2: 297–308. https://doi.org/10.1111/j.1754-7121.1975.tb01942.x

Krawchenko, Tamara. 2011. "Regional Special Purpose Bodies for Transportation and Transit in Canada: Case Studies of Translink and Metrolinx." *Canadian Journal of Regional Sciences* 34, no. 1: 1–8. http://www.cjrs-rcsr.org/V34/1/CJRS-RCSR-34-1-01.pdf

Leo, Christopher. 2002. "Urban Development: Planning Aspirations and Political Realities." In *Urban Policy Issues: Canadian Perspectives*, 2nd ed., edited by Edmund Fowler and David Siegel, 215–36. Toronto: Oxford University Press.

Logan, John, and Harvey Molotch. 1987. *Urban Fortunes: The Political Economy of Place*. Berkeley: University of California Press.

Lowery, David. 2001. "Metropolitan Governance from a Neoprogressive Perspective." *Swiss Political Science Review* 7, no. 3: SS11–16.

Lucas, Jack. 2013. "Hidden in Plain View: Local Agencies, Boards, and Commissions in Canada." *IMFG Perspectives* 4: 1–7. https://tspace.library.utoronto.ca/bitstream/1807/82711/1/imfg_perspectives_4_hidden_in_plain_view_lucas_2013.pdf

– 2016. *Fields of Authority: Special Purpose Governance in Ontario, 1815–2015*. Toronto: University of Toronto Press.

– 2017a. "Patterns of Urban Governance: A Sequence Analysis of Long-Term Institutional Change in Six Canadian Cities." *Journal of Urban Affairs* 39, no. 1: 68–90. https://doi.org/10.1111/juaf.12291

– 2017b. "Urban Governance and the American Political Development Approach." *Urban Affairs Review* 53, no. 2: 338–61. https://doi.org/10.1177/1078087415620054

Lyons, Joseph. 2015a. "Conservation Authority Board Composition and Watershed Management in Ontario." *Canadian Public Administration* 58, no. 2: 315–32. https://doi.org/10.1111/capa.12113

– 2015b. "Local Government Structure and the Co-ordination of Economic Development Policy." *Canadian Journal of Political Science* 48, no. 1: 173–93. https://doi.org/10.1017/s0008423915000220

– 2016. "The Independence of Ontario's Public Health Units: Does Governing Structure Matter?" *Healthcare Policy* 12, no. 1: 71–83. https://doi.org/10.12927/hcpol.2016.24777

Lyons, Joseph, and Zachary Spicer. 2018. "Accountability and Local Collaborative Governance." In *Accountability and Responsiveness at the*

Municipal Level: Views from Canada, edited by Sandra Breaux and Jérôme Couture, 197–220. Montreal and Kingston: McGill-Queen's University Press.

Lyons, W.E., and David Lowery. 1989. "Governmental Fragmentation versus Consolidation: Five Public-Choice Myths about How to Create Informed, Involved, and Happy Citizens." *Public Administration Review* 49, no. 6: 533–43. https://doi.org/10.2307/976575

Magnusson, Warren. 1985. "The Local State in Canada: Theoretical Perspectives." *Canadian Public Administration* 28, no. 4: 575–99. https://doi.org/10.1111/j.1754-7121.1985.tb00385.x

Martin, Dianne. 2007. "Accountability Mechanisms: Legal Sites of Executive-Police Relations – Core Principles in a Canadian Context." In *Police and Government Relations: Who's Calling the Shots?*, edited by Margaret Beare and Tonita Murray, 257–312. Toronto: University of Toronto Press.

McGregor, Michael, and Zachary Spicer. 2016. "The Canadian Homevoter: Property Values and Municipal Politics in Canada." *Journal of Urban Affairs* 38, no. 1: 123–39. https://doi.org/10.1111/juaf.12178

McQuigge, Michelle. 2017. "Students Can Opt Out of Religious Classes at Catholic School After Complaint Settled." *Toronto Star*, June 13.

Moore, Aaron, Michael McGregor, and Laura Stephenson. 2015. "Paying Attention and the Incumbency Effect: Voting Behavior in the 2014 Toronto Municipal Election." *International Political Science Review* 38, no. 1: 85–98. https://doi.org/10.1177/0192512115616268

Mullin, Megan. 2009. *Governing the Tap: Special District Governance and the New Local Politics of Water*. Cambridge, MA: MIT Press.

Ostrom, Elinor. 1972. "Metropolitan Reform: Propositions Derived from Two Traditions." *Social Science Quarterly* 53, no. 3: 474–93.

Ostrom, Vincent, Charles M. Tiebout, and Robert Warren. 1961. "The Organization of Government in Metropolitan Areas: A Theoretical Inquiry." *American Political Science Review* 55, no. 4: 831–42. https://doi.org/10.1017/s0003055400125973

Peters, Guy, Tero Erkkila, and Patric von Maravic. 2016. *Public Administration: Research Strategies, Concepts, and Methods*. New York: Routledge.

Richmond, Dale, and David Siegel, eds. 1994. *Agencies, Boards, and Commissions in Canadian Local Government*. Toronto: Institute of Public Administration Canada.

Sancton, Andrew. 2015. *Canadian Local Government: An Urban Perspective*, 2nd ed. Toronto: Oxford University Press.

Sanderson, Christopher, and Pierre Filion. 2013. "The Development of the Toronto Waterfront: Federal Presence, Institutional Complexity and Planning Outcomes." In *Federal Property and Policy in Canadian Municipalities*, edited by Michael Ircha and Robert Young, 110–56. Montreal and Kingston: McGill-Queen's University Press.

Sayers, Anthony, and Jack Lucas. 2017. "Policy Responsiveness and Political Accountability in City Politics." *University of Calgary School of Public Policy SPP*

Research Papers 10, no. 4, https://www.policyschool.ca/wp-content
/uploads/2017/03/Policy-Responsiveness-Sayers-Lucas.pdf

Skelcher, Chris. 2006. "Does Democracy Matter? A Transatlantic Research
Design on Democratic Performance and Special Purpose Governments."
Journal of Public Administration Theory and Research 17: 61–76. https://doi
.org/10.1093/jopart/muj014

Skelcher, Chris, Navdeep Mathur, and Mike Smith. 2005. "The Public
Governance of Collaborative Spaces: Discourse, Design and Democracy."
Public Administration 83, no. 3: 573–96. https://doi.org/10.1111/j.0033
-3298.2005.00463.x

Smith, Alison, and Zachary Spicer. 2017. "The Local Autonomy of Canada's
Largest Cities." *Urban Affairs Review* 54, no. 5: 931–61. https://doi.org
/10.1177%2F1078087416684380

Sorenson, Eva, and Jacob Torfing. 2005. "The Democratic Anchorage of
Governance Networks." *Scandinavian Political Studies* 28, no. 3: 195–218.
https://doi.org/10.1111/j.1467-9477.2005.00129.x

Tausanovitch, Chris, and Christopher Warshaw. 2014. "Representation in
Municipal Government." *American Political Science Review* 108, no. 3: 605–41.
https://doi.org/10.1017/s0003055414000318

Taylor, Zack, and Sandra McEleney. 2017. "Do Institutions and Rules Influence
Electoral Accessibility and Competitiveness? Considering the 2014 Toronto
Ward Elections." *Urban Affairs Review* 33, no. 1: 83–97. https://doi.org
/10.1177/1078087417703753

Tiebout, Charles M. 1956. "A Pure Theory of Local Expenditures." *Journal of
Political Economy* 64, no. 5: 416–24. https://doi.org/10.1086/257839

Tindal, Richard C., and Susan Nobes Tindal. 2004. *Local Government in Canada*,
6th ed. Toronto: Thomson Nelson.

Trounstine, Jessica. 2010. "Representation and Accountability in Cities." *Annual
Review of Political Science* 13: 407–23. https://doi.org/10.1146/annurev
.polisci.032808.150414

van Popering-Verkerk, Jitske, and Arwin van Buuren. 2016. "Decision-Making
Patterns in Multilevel Governance: The Contribution of Informal and
Procedural Interactions to Significant Multilevel Decisions." *Public
Management Review* 18, no. 7: 951–71. https://doi.org/10.1080/14719037
.2015.1028974

Zeemering, Eric. 2012. "The Problem of Democratic Anchorage for Interlocal
Agreements." *American Review of Public Administration* 42, no. 1: 87–103.
https://doi.org/10.1177/0275074010397532

PART THREE

Interpreting Democracy: Critical and Postmodern Approaches

CHAPTER TEN

Hatred of Democracy

Dan Bousfield

INTRODUCTION

This chapter begins by outlining a foundation for a critical approach to evaluating democracy. Unlike democratic theories that define democracy as a form of governance, this chapter will look at democracy as a radical claim of equality *against* governance. This entails an examination of the tensions between rational approaches to the study of democracy and affective or emotional approaches that highlight minority groups' relationships with majoritarian sensibilities. By examining a series of competing claims against governance, this critical approach argues that non-expert and non-authoritative claims made against elites are a series of democratic moments that provide important alternative ways to think about politics. Using the insights of iconoclast Jacques Rancière, this chapter adopts a bricolage methodology – that is, it draws conclusions based upon a diverse range of available examples from the world around us (Kincheloe 2011). It uses a series of "everyday" examples of how democratic claims are made in the "popular" and non-expert realm to show how anyone, anywhere, can make democratic claims. Moreover, each of these cases can help to foreground how race, gender, class, settler colonialism, and capitalism continue to define who can speak and how they can be heard. It uses this method to flatten or democratize examples as equally important for inclusion, without deciding on which ones are most valuable.

This chapter argues that democracy as a principle of equity is betrayed by efforts to govern. In ancient Greece, "democracy" was used pejoratively, expressed as a hatred (*misos*) toward those who rejected the idea that birthright or ability should determine who governs. Hatred was not individual anger, but a separate feeling directed toward a certain type of person whom everyone could agree was incorrigible, such as the thief, the informer, or the democrat (Konstan 2007). This chapter examines the persistence of these feelings in the context of resurgent anti-elite populism and the challenges this poses to the possibility of governance.

WHAT IS A CRITICAL APPROACH TO DEMOCRACY?

Canadian international relations scholar Robert Cox famously lamented that academics create "subdivisions of social knowledge" in order to have domains of expertise over which they preside (1981, 126). He argued that specialization and professionalization have produced competing tracks of inquiry: the approaches that "[take] the world as [they] find it," attempting to solve problems within the world, versus those that question "institutions and social and power relations" in order to embed them within larger critical processes (129). This chapter adopts the latter "critical" approach as a way to understand the persistence of democracy as a pejorative concept, or the ways in which demands for equity are rejected by the status quo. This approach involves critically reassessing democracy as a persistent demand for equity against those who make authoritative claims about what democracy is and how we should think about it. This approach also argues against democracy as a problem-solving process, and instead sees it as a way of challenging the status quo and the established view of politics. As a rejection of the need for elites, democracy continues to evoke emotional responses (hatreds), as it represents a demand that cannot be reasoned with, dominated, or simply wished away (equity). Democracy as a demand for equity produces excessive and emotional responses that result in political attitudes that help explain the proliferation of extreme ideas today. Unlike love (*philia*), which for Aristotle is directed at individuals, hatred is an organizing principle directed at groups that can be made by urban elites against rural commoners, liberal democrats against racist xenophobes, but also by the poor against an elite global liberal order (Konstan 2007, 182).

Critical approaches to democracy are not necessarily declarative claims about the importance of the status quo; instead, they aim to frame issues in terms of injunctive relief. In other words, they can express an emotional demand without having to propose a rational solution. In *How to Do Things with Words*, Austin argued that performative sentences can be either contractual ("I bet") or declaratory ("I declare war"), but both rely on a distinction between what is written or said, and the internal emotional difference between the language used and the intentionality behind it (such as in Hippolytus's famous claim, "my tongue swore to, but my heart did not") (Austin 1962, 9–10). The ability to speak and be heard is an appeal to legibility, to have a voice that is commensurate with the status quo in order to be both heard and understood. This is why Martin Luther King Jr. famously called the riot a "language of the unheard," where frustration with not being heard resulted in an outpouring of violence. Herein lie two reasons for the critical approach proposed here, following the work of Jacques Rancière. First, not all claims can be understood by those representing the status quo. Second, democracy as a demand for equity produces moments in which the injunction against the status quo (such as the chant "Whose streets? Our streets!") presents the possibility of reconfiguring who can speak and how. This critical approach to democracy does not necessarily propose a new way to govern, but, rather, makes a claim about how existing governance is anti-democratic. This is a rejection of Plato's argument that only a small minority can rule well (as discussed in chapter 2 of this volume), and instead proposes that the radical equality of the masses is a refutation of the need for rulers. This is the persistence of the ancient Greek hatred in which elites believe they have the right to rule but the masses believe that governance is anti-democratic.

YouTube is an example of the inherent tension between democracy as a demand for equity and the need for governance. The ethos behind the YouTube platform is a radically democratizing impulse: the ability of anyone, anywhere, to share videos and ideas using the internet. This injunctive ethos allows people to bypass authoritarian governments, censorship, corporate control of media, concentration of ownership, and access to media infrastructure because they can broadcast videos from cell phones. Yet, those same users often want to regulate offensive, anti-social, harassing, racist, and misogynist content that can lead to deadly ideas and claims. They want to protect their own ideas from theft and to adjudicate disputes between users. These impulses stem from the inherent equality that comes from opening up a platform to everyone, but they require a range of attitudes toward governance and regulation. Democracy as a call for equality is in tension with the desire for governance. Moreover, with the advent of technology, equality can increase the possibility for manipulation, subterfuge, and foreign disruption of the social order. In 2013, YouTube worried that the high number of automated bots masquerading as users on their network would cause their bot-detection technology to start misidentifying humans as bots if they became a minority of users (Read 2018). Democracy online foregrounds the problem of identifying who should be able to speak. YouTube's goal as a commercial platform is to promote channels that grab and keep one's attention, even if these channels cause social disruption. In 2017, YouTube was found to have placed ads for major brands such as Verizon, AT&T, and Walmart alongside videos containing "heinous material, including disinformation sites, hate speech, extreme political content, and terrorist, racist and anti-Semitic publications and videos" (Zuboff 2019, 476). When combined with conspiracy theories, anti-vaccination advocacy, racism, and white supremacy, this democratic equality can be corrosive to governance and social order and can magnify and exploit the basest and most repugnant dynamics of its users. YouTube is an example of the tension inherent in the relationship between, on one side, the critical and problem-solving approaches to the equity of democracy and the ethos of equality that allows anyone to participate, and, on the other, users wanting governance over contested and socially corrosive ideas. The critical approach is one that looks for alternatives, while also explaining the persistence of frustration with a governing order. Those who embrace a problem-solving approach would like to develop reasonable and rational responses to and explanations for these events.

HOW CAN STUDYING DEMOCRACY REFLECT EQUALITY?

Developing critical sensibilities about democracy during a period of social upheaval creates a series of challenges. If you are being critical in a period of social change, does that make you conservative? Does political activism produce a new form of regulation that undermines its democratic potential? These are the types of questions that French philosopher Jacques Rancière wrestled with in the wake of the global anti-war and civil rights protests of 1968. As someone dedicated to critical thinking in a period of radical change, Rancière broke with Louis Althusser, his French Marxist teacher, over the importance of class as a foundation of politics. Instead, he chose to study politics without relying on pre-existing frameworks and ideologies (Tanke 2011, 16). He was an iconoclast interested in challenging existing beliefs rather than establishing a new ideology through which to interpret the world. Rancière argued that the capacity for critical politics always exists, and by returning to classic Greek thought he claimed he could expose those voices that have been omitted or excluded by the dominant telling of history, politics, and education. In one of his first books, *The Ignorant Schoolmaster: Five Lessons in Intellectual Emancipation*, Rancière argued that we are often taught about democracy by experts who wish to govern, and thus this teaching perpetuates anti-democratic norms and substitutes democratic moments for truly democratic politics (Rancière 1991). Think of the ways in which political education is so concerned with the proper way to govern, rarely stopping to ask why policies fail before searching for a better solution. So what does a democratic form of education look like? Rancière turns to French Enlightenment philosopher Joseph Jacotot, who believed that true equality stems from a few basic precepts. First, everyone has a similar level of intelligence and we are capable of self-instruction. Second, we are capable of figuring out what we do not know. Finally, there are enough clues in the world for us to figure out how the world works without relying on deities, intermediaries, or experts to tell us (Suoranta 2017, 10). In the Enlightenment tradition, democratic education is a rejection of the idea that only a select few are capable of enlightenment, as well as a rejection of the necessity of the expert to develop sound political decision-making. An example of this is the English-only computer tablets dropped off in an Ethiopian village in 2012; within a few weeks the children figured out how to work the tablets and access the settings, and they subsequently began to learn English with no instruction or guidance (Talbot 2012). This example suggests that learning about democracy in education needs to be reflected in *how* we teach, not just *what* we teach (Brehm and Silova 2010, 30). So, while the Ethiopian children may have missed the opportunities of organized, structured instruction, they also were able to access the values of play, experimentation, and autonomy. Within the idea that we can teach ourselves is a notion of radical equality, an injunction that both Rancière and Jacotot used to challenge the educational hierarchies embedded in institutional thought. Rancière argued that inequality of information is often the basis for domination because it assumes that those who have access to information are better at making decisions for others than those who do not have it. The rise of the #MeToo movement provides a glimpse into how authority, expertise, and power make fundamentally inequitable power relations that have long dominated our perceptions of the world seem normal and sensible. Tacit and explicit hierarchies of gender norms are under scrutiny for facilitating rape culture and the tying of normalcy to gender roles (PettyJohn 2018). One strategy that worked against these institutional structures was the shared, open-source Google spreadsheet that women crowdsourced by anonymously providing information about sexual misconduct, workplace harassment, and rape, using the internet as a strategy of equity. However, a defamation lawsuit was subsequently filed to try to expose anyone who contributed to the list, because mechanisms like an anonymously sourced spreadsheet provide little room to examine the veracity of the claims or to provide redress against false accusations (Kaminsky 2018). The lawsuit is aiming to use institutional power to undermine the anonymity of the internet. As an iconoclast, Rancière's goal is to demonstrate how anti-democratic sensibilities have, since the Greeks, embedded themselves into what we think is politically possible and practical (Rancière 2013). The scandal of Donald Trump's lack of political qualifications exposes the extent to which the equality of democracy confronts the hatred embedded in the need for expertise. Moreover, those who support his presidency are undeterred by experts or by evidence of his inability to govern "properly"; instead, they are emboldened by emotional appeals to inequity and the power of *doxa*, the common beliefs and popular opinion of the masses.

ASKING STUPID QUESTIONS

Exposing the democratic principles embedded in institutional knowledge can be as simple as exploring the supposed precepts upon which democratic thought is based. Rancière's vision of democracy is not based on the proper procedures of voting and eligibility (see chapter 7 in this volume) or shared understandings of deliberation (see the discussion of Rawls in chapter 2), but on the "willingness to treat politics afresh" (Chambers 2012, 304). Within this framework, democracy is seen not as a "form of government, or a set of rules on how to live a moral life," but as the way in which political subjects can act to change what constitutes the status quo and the realm of permissible action (Friedrich et al. 2010, 572). Democracy functions as a demand for equity, and politics is a rare event by which those who have no right to speak make themselves heard (May 2008, 41). As Rancière explains:

> Politics does not exist because men, through the privilege of speech, place their interests in common. Politics exists because those who have no right to be counted as speaking beings make themselves of some account, setting up a community by the fact of placing in common a wrong that is nothing more than this very confrontation. (1999, 27)

Seen in this way, democracy is found in moments when equality is demanded by those who have no right to speak. Democratic *practices* are key to this approach and the critical demand for equality explicitly rejects the notion of a universal theory of what democracy should be or how it should function. It is "critical" because it rejects problem-solving approaches as containing tacit or explicit political violence in the attempt to govern. This governance stems from Aristotle's distinction between speech and voice, according to which animals can use voice to express pain or pleasure, but only people have the capacity of speech to distinguish between useful and harmful, good and evil (Rancière 1999, 1). Recall, for example, that the Northwest Territories in Canada did not provide the vote for women until 1951, and Quebec did not provide the vote for Indigenous people until 1969. Such restrictions on full political participation have long been maintained through the distinction between voice and speech. *Logos*, the capacity for reason, provides the basis for a shared political community, so reasonableness becomes the boundary between one community, political body, or citizenry and another. Aristotle states that citizens are those who have a role in the act of governing and being governed, and that while slaves might understand the language of rulers, they themselves do not possess this language (Rancière 2013, 12). In this way, attempts to determine who comprises the legitimate political community (the *demos*) are always fundamentally inaccurate because they fail to include the broader sensibilities and common sense (the *doxa*) of those who are excluded from political participation. This is what Rancière calls the democratic scandal – the fact that there will never be a single principle of community that does not exclude someone or some group. As outlined in chapter 7, the constituting of a community depends on the practice of delimiting those who can speak for that community, and thus there is a constant tension between the equality of community members and the exclusion of people who fall outside the boundaries. Democracy as a principle of equity is betrayed by the efforts to establish governance.

WHAT DOES CRITICAL RESEARCH LOOK LIKE?

The critical approach introduced here takes the view that democracy, when it gets implemented, always fundamentally miscounts those who can speak. This approach has the following research goals: first, identifying who is excluded; second, explaining why those exclusions continue to exist; and third, explaining these exclusions in terms of their emotional (or non-rational) outcomes. Thus, even though Aristotle's citizens often form the basis for our reflections on democracy, slaves, women, the infirm, foreigners, and non-persons are always missing from speech (Feola 2014, 509). Representative government is inherently undemocratic because it excludes voices in order to justify decisions made in pursuit of governance (such as the distinction between a citizen and a foreigner). The policing structures of governance frame how we think about social majorities and minorities, those who can be converted into willing participants versus those who cannot, the elites versus the unwashed (uneducated and uncultured) masses, the experts versus the ignorant fools (Rancière 1999, 14). The bifurcated approach to democracy provides several ways to investigate these issues, which are addressed below. On the one hand, this oversimplified vision of democracy provides a powerful critique of the efforts to reform or normalize inherently unequal or unjust institutions and ideas. For Rancière, governance is the "given distributions of social positions, hierarchies, functions, visibilities and invisibilities, characteristic of any social order understood as a partition of the perceptible" (Plot 2014, 96). For example, the #BlackLivesMatter movement emerged from the efforts to make visible the structural and institutional problems that result in disproportionate impacts on a minority community. The ensuing debate about appropriate responses to #BlackLivesMatter indicates the extent to which normalcy can be reconfigured in more equitable ways. Advocates on both sides of the issue have been unsatisfied with the shift in what is perceived as normal. Consequently, political representation has an inherently aesthetic element, which is to say that often what seems possible is determined by status quo thinking about the present moment. When traditional kinds of representation fail, voiceless communities look to emotional forms of expression, like art, music, and culture, in order to reach equality through extra-reasonable measures. Introducing the aesthetic element of politics is both liberating (anyone can produce alternative visions of the world through art) and dangerous, as the aesthetic can be used to produce mass conformity (such as the Nazi appropriation of the swastika from Asia). Consequently, the research program supporting a critical approach to democracy is to examine the ways in which the status quo attempts to appropriate popular demands for equity, and the ways in which those demands will inevitably remain unmet. In this way we can see the animating grievances that allow demands for equality to take place, on the one hand, and those who would resist and deny those demands, on the other. Defending ignorance in an era of anti-elite populism produces highly divisive claims, which will also be assessed throughout this chapter.

HOW DO WE POLICE EMOTION?

Given the bifurcation between the rational and emotional, how does one go about studying democracy without reproducing the notion of expertise against which so much of this approach is premised? There are a range of methodological avenues that stem from the equality of *doxa* (the common belief or popular opinion of the masses), and the tensions that emerge from efforts to govern the demand for equity. The first is a rejection of the idea of political expertise, or a rejection of the idea that there is a group of elites who "know better" about equality than those who participate in making claims for equality. Next, the role of affect as a form of political mobilization challenges the dispassionate view of politics as a superior form of politics. Finally, while similar to "everyday life" perspectives, Rancière's view of critical pedagogy rejects the academy as a source of political action. This stems from a deep suspicion that governance and representation seek to turn equity into new hierarchies.

Rancière's experience with French Marxism made him profoundly critical of the notion that elite-led politics was the foundation for emancipation (Suoranta 2017, 3). Consequently, the demand for equity serves as a limit on those would make definitive claims about what democratic governance should look like, assessed in terms of the persistence of exclusions upon which that governance is based. Traditionally, philosophers have been opposed to political intervention, or have seen the role of reflection as distinct from the mechanisms of conventional politics, a kind of Platonic reflection that is distinct from the practical implementation of ideas (Rancière 1999, xii–xiii). Plato's hatred of democracy stemmed from the way that the *doxa* scandalizes the virtues of the *demos*, the way appearances can pleasure the people, who then make decisions based not on logic and reason, but rather on the impulses of the masses (Rancière 1999, 9–10). With the rise of the internet, it has been easier for elites to blame outside interference in the electoral process for the rise of anti-elite populism than to address the common sensibilities that have proliferated in the changing information landscape of social media and the declining role of elite-driven news. A key aspect of the "attention economy," as an advertising-driven model, has been to apply sophisticated engineering and behavioural technologies to drive higher and higher levels of affective responses to online content. The political consequences of this affective computing have been under-examined until recently, but they magnify the importance of non-rational decision-making as techniques to encourage consumerism are applied to political choices (Zuboff 2019, 276).

WHAT IS A RATIONAL APPROACH TO STUDYING EMOTION?

The study of the hatred of democracy follows the rise of an affective literature in political studies. These approaches seek to rebalance the idea that rational and deliberative models of decision-making have largely been built on the unfounded prioritization of cognitive over sensory responses (Marcus 2000, 7–8). Since the late 1800s, research into crowd psychology and group dynamics in political mobilization has argued that we need to understand emotional registers alongside rationalist framings of politics (Le Bon 1897). The role of affect is to highlight the ways in which subjective values, deference to authority, leadership, and nostalgia operate alongside and often in opposition to rationalist and narrative framings of politics (Brennan 2004, 19). The democratic scandal of Trump supporters in the United States is that they reject a reasonable, truth-based politics for a common-sense deference to what they feel is right. As affective systems tend to set the terrain for cognitive choices, emotions tend to inform decision-making, not the other way around (Marcus 2000, 9). Consequently, emotion has a cohering effect on divided communities, solidifying the division between those who are part of the community and those who are not. Hatred has a unique role in naming outsiders as enemies and allowing the community to unite around others. As Ahmed has argued, hatred personalizes politics in a way that prompts members to interpret their own victimization as a reason to act (Ahmed 2001, 346–7). The rise of the internet has created feedback loops of hatred and victimization and has allowed members to reinforce their ideological predispositions in a group by blaming non-members and radicalizing the group against others (Davidson 2019). As hatred is an outward expression of difference, it helps to solidify the boundary between those who should belong, reinforcing identity-based politics in opposition to perceived others (Ahmed 2001 353–4). The democratic paradox presents itself in recognition of the need for the ability to speak, and the communities in which that speech can be heard.

WHAT DOES LOOKING AT EMOTIONS ENTAIL?

The preceding paragraph described the problem of trying to legitimate knowledge through the disciplinary mechanisms of expertise and the academy. Why does a discussion of emotion need to ground itself in rational analysis? Methodologically, the rational model draws its strength from expertise, referencing, and peer review, all of which reinforce the value of elite attitudes about appropriate ways of thinking. This model lacks all affect. Hatred is a common process that functions in real-world scenarios involving everyday people and challenges expertise (as *pathos* undermines *logos*). An appeal to reasonableness in a debate about the meaning of wearing a MAGA (Make America Great Again) hat misses the affective point. The examples in this chapter draw on ideas from critical pedagogy, bricolage, and everyday life to prioritize the non-expert in the interest of having more equality in our understanding of the world. Critical, everyday life perspectives in social history emerged as a method for foregrounding the accounts of people who had traditionally been omitted from elite perspectives (like those in the Greek *demos*). The tension inherent in everyday life perspectives is that they remain filtered through the narratives of academic expertise, and as such often fail to capture the resistance and non-conformity of personal feelings and experience (Highmore 2002, 5). The examples selected in this chapter follow the idea of bricolage, a non-linear, patchwork perspective that allows the meaning of a text to draw upon multiple and conflicting narratives (Markham 2005, 815). Bricolage highlights "research as a power-driven act" and is an effort to "respect the complexity of the lived world" so as to resist "understanding that operates without variation in every context" (Kincheloe 2005, 324). Drawing on the idea of interdisciplinarity, bricolage proposes a kind of equality in the idea of not having a proper starting point or single privileged viewpoint when discussing where democracy can take place (Thumlert 2015, 124). Much of the history of the internet has emerged from the "do-it-yourself" vision of politics in the absence of traditional norms (like the emergence of cryptocurrencies as an internet-based vision of money). The rise of "fake news" and disinformation exposes the tension inherent in the idea that people are learning from non-traditional sources and therefore undermining the social cohesion that results from the existence of norms, even if we recognize the elitism and exclusion inherent in those norms.

Consequently, critical pedagogy follows the democratic demand for equity in trying to render visible the exclusions in everyday life. Critical pedagogy develops critiques of our democratic participation in capitalism, our role in inequality, and the oppressions that persist in an effort to spur action or counter-education (Biesta 1998, 500–1). The weakness of these approaches is that they must either refer to themselves as sources of authority, or they must attempt to demystify the world in a way that presupposes expertise. Rancière's work attempts to move away from the notion of the mastery of ideas, and instead examines how people can make a contribution to the world in a way that allows them to "escape from the minority" (Biesta 2010, 46–7). This approach involves highlighting moments in which those who normally play no part in the production of norms demand to be heard without claiming expertise over those actions.

The idea that everyone has the right to think, challenge, and disrupt the functioning of normalcy does not imply a better political project, just that minority ideas can challenge and disrupt majoritarian ones (Lambert 2012, 215). The benefit of critical approaches over problem-solving ones is that they can highlight demands for equity without having to propose new mechanisms of governance, and that is an integral part of the process of democratic politics. This approach challenges Churchill's dictum that "democracy is the worst form of government except all those other forms that have been tried from time to time" as a problem-solving approach primarily concerned with governance and not the practices of democratic engagement.

WHY ELITES HATE DEMOCRACY

The hatred of democracy stems from the disdain expressed by elites for supposedly ignorant and uninformed opinions counter to what they believe is correct. In brief, the experience of Greece in the lead-up to the 2015 bailout referendum is an excellent example of the way in which rationality was used to trump democratic demands for equity. After the Greek election in early 2015, the country's finance minister, Yanis Varoufakis, met with European officials from the European Commission (EC), the Washington-based International Monetary Fund (IMF), and the European Central Bank (ECB). During this meeting the three institutions opined that they did not believe the election of a new Greek government should significantly impact the terms of the bailout. They were not interested in discussing changes to the debt relief programs, as they argued that these programs had been "accepted by the previous government," adding that "we can't possibly allow an election to change anything" because "we have elections all the time, there are 19 of us, if every time there was an election and something changed, the contracts between us wouldn't mean anything" (Lambert 2015). Reasonableness was framed as an explicit rejection of an equitable and democratic political decision by the Greeks. Given the ongoing turmoil related to the country's debt levels after its entry into the eurozone and the unwillingness of European officials to renegotiate any deals, the Greek prime minister and Parliament proposed a referendum, to be held in June 2015, on the bailout conditions. Elected on a left-leaning platform, the Greek prime minister argued: "We should respond to authoritarianism and harsh austerity with democracy, calmly and decisively ... Greece, the birthplace of democracy, should send a resounding democratic message to the European and global community" (Yardley 2015). Framed explicitly in terms of the people's need to make choices about the country's future, the referendum's result was that 61 per cent rejected the bailout conditions. The response from the Eurogroup was a punishing set of conditions more severe than those that had been rejected by the referendum, with new language that explicitly stated that all further proposals would require consultation with European officials before being submitted to the Greek public and Greek Parliament (Krugman 2015). The final agreement contained larger pension cuts and tax increases than what had been rejected by the referendum, and was criticized by the IMF for not adequately dealing with debt levels (Spiegel 2015). The failure to deal with debt levels stemmed from substantial ownership of the debt by German, French, Italian, and Spanish banks, which is to say that the rationality of the Eurogroup was weighted in the interest of their community, not the Greek populace. The institutions of European integration normalized the poor lending practices of the Eurogroup and made the Greek debt a problem of the Greek populace, a populace that was explicit in wanting different political outcomes. Recalling how the affective informs the rational, the self-interest of the creditors was framed as the rational choice while the democratic will was framed as impossible.

WHAT CAN HATRED TELL US?

A miscounting lies at the heart of governance and the rationale of this miscounting is what generates the emotional response from those who are miscounted. The demand for democratic equity will always appear unreasonable to those who are governing. In the Greek debt situation discussed above, democracy is always subordinate to the nation-state, which means that power is to some extent always placed outside the control of the people, and that "every state is oligarchic" (Rancière 2006b, 71). The idea that democracy is foreign to citizens of other countries is a normalization of inequity and elite rule. Reason is on the side of those who rule, and emotion is relegated to the passions of consumerism and the excesses of anti-elite populism and common sense. Take the example of fandom and the excessive identification with a sports team, an interest, or a collectible, reinforced through consumerism and individualism. These emotional connections are encouraged and facilitated through sport, patriotism, and consumerism in an effort to unite people through a shared experience of an event that produces a form of equality. Yet, at the same time those efforts are carefully managed to minimize political outcomes, as the collective outpouring of support, mobilization, and face-to-face interactions do not produce a recognition of the power of collective action, public spaces, or popular mobilization. After the First World War, there was a concerted effort to develop the so-called Worker Olympics, an alternative to the explicitly bourgeois and exclusive Olympic Games. The principles of these games were to give working people the chance to partake in healthy recreation in a comradely atmosphere, and while the 1932 Olympics had 1,408 athletes in competition, over 100,000 workers participated in the Worker Olympics in Vienna a year earlier (Riordan 2002, 105). Moreover, these games were open to all workers regardless of gender or race in an attempt to provide a co-operative international space based on shared solidarity and participation, a counter to private amateur sporting clubs and competitions (106). However, the rise of the Second World War and the subsequent Cold War made state-based competition the norm, and sport became an effective way to develop patriotism at one another's expense. Workers' sports associations persist in Finland, France, and Austria but are largely ignored by the press as they do little to bolster the consumerist spectacle of the modern Olympic Games. The Olympics typify the way in which the democratic spectacle of sport can draw people together (through the Olympic truce) but also how host nations' publics are expected to financially support the private accumulation of wealth. Though not a primary impetus of the debt crisis, the public debt born by Greece for the 2000 Olympic Games did not result in greater economic prosperity and helped fuel the financial crisis described. The equity of the democratic impulse of sport is in constant tension with the inequity of wealth, which continually regenerates new bases of cynicism and disenchantment with the possibility of public action (Rancière 2006b, 77). Moreover, as the spectacle of fandom invigorates nationalism and patriotism, anti-elite populism as a political strategy contorts the equality of participation into governance.

DEMOCRACY AS CRITIQUE

Rancière's approach is designed explicitly to avoid a new political foundation for governing democracy. His project is to examine moments of political claims, rather than to establish a new foundation for governing (Chambers 2012, 304). This approach is useful to examine specific interruptions and political backlash, not to help configure more effective forms of governance (Chambers 2012, 320). Immigration policy and advocacy have been one of the key sites for examining claims about equity. The "No One Is Illegal" global network of refugee advocates has long argued that immigration status should not impact the political or human rights of individuals. This injunction that everyone deserves equality regardless of their citizenship is a claim that says little about the specifics of what needs to be done. Moreover, the audience for the claims being made by the advocates is unclear. Is it the country of origin? The country of current status? Here the distinction between speech and voice is central, as most communities do not like the idea that non-community members should have equal political status. When activists are arrested for leaving supplies along the routes used by undocumented migrants, should the prohibition of those acts trump the migrants' right to life? Questions such as these help make visible the democratic claims inherent in everyday practices, even if they fail to develop into traditional policy-making outcomes. The tension between the normalcy of settler-colonial states choosing to restrict access to immigration exemplifies the tension inherent in democratic claims. Thus, when a critical approach exposes the fundamental unevenness between the two sides, it helps foreground the limits of normalcy and the failure of political alternatives.

HATRED AS MOBILIZING FORCE

Rancière encourages us to think about democracy beyond the liberal democratic state. Rancière's radical democratic project is an effort to move beyond the state and capitalism as mobilizing horizons for action. Democracy is a way to interrupt and perhaps modify the existing ruling order without seeking a new form of order (Purcell 2014, 171). The demand for equity has strong affinities with populist movements but omits the desire to establish a new foundation for policing or governance.

So, while we could detect demands for equality in the populist backlash and rise of far-right leaders around the world, their efforts to utilize power, hierarchy, race, and class to establish their political agendas are a betrayal of equity. Additionally, the more liberal and cosmopolitan elites blame the masses for populist movements, the more they reinforce this divide. As Rancière has argued recently, politicians and the popular press redouble their elitism by denouncing populism and disdain for popular mobilization and anti-elite politics (Rancière et al. 2016, 102). He claims that populism is more like "a certain attitude of rejection in relationship to prevailing governmental practices" (101) than a type of partisan movement. Indeed, as Dean has argued, this approach is not "pragmatic" enough and is chastised, condescendingly, as "childishly petulant" (2009, 23). Thus, while anti-elite populism often adopts patriotic rhetoric and rejects foreigners, this does not necessarily have to be the case. Moreover, to the extent that a political claim is being made for those who have no part in the political system, this claim often results in a convergence of the extreme Right and the radical Left. The proliferation of conspiracy theories about global elites is a common foundation for the populist rejection of issues of global consensus, whether it be global warming or global military interventions.

HATRED AND GLOBAL ELITES

The role of elites in establishing rule is not synonymous with democracy but remains a point of contention for populist movements and anti-state activism today. There is an extensive academic literature beyond strictly Marxist analyses that identifies the relationship between global elites and the contemporary hegemonic world order. This literature points to the idea that the virulent populist agitation against the global hegemonic order is not without foundation. If a critical reading of the liberal world order is possible, it aligns with the idea that hierarchy opposes equity. From Robert Cox's analysis of the role of American ideology in shaping the postwar order, to Gill's analysis of the Trilateral Commission's activities in setting elite leadership agendas, to Sklair's exploration of an emerging transnational capitalist class, the idea of ruling global elites managing global liberal democracy poses a constant legitimacy problem for supposed democratic institutions (Cox 1987; Gill 1991; Sklair 2001).

The postwar bloc of liberal institutions, ideas, and elites that established a consensus about the value of "embedded liberalism" produced the idea that having a global consensus on key issues in free trade, international institutions, and intervention is the norm (Ruggie 1982). More recent examinations have given further credence to the idea that "epistemic communities" can create private hubs of policy-making, coordination, and regimes (Hass 1992). When combined with historical examinations of groups such as the Mont Pèlerin Society (Mirowski and Plehwe 2015) and policy coordination through mechanisms such as the IMF, the World Bank (Woods 2006), and the European troika (IMF, EC, ECB), the idea of a "democratic deficit" is easily popularized (Follesdal and Hix 2006). In the wake of the 2008 financial crisis, the politics of global austerity, combined with the continued growth of income inequality, has reinforced the ease with which the Occupy movements, Donald Trump, or climate change deniers can feel hatred of global elites. As policy efforts attempted to address the global crisis, the perception of a "one size fits all" global economic order reinforces "dissensus" tendencies among the masses. As May argues, "In a world dominated by neoliberalism, those who are not conversant with the workings of the market need to yield their political involvement to those who are. Where politics is a matter of proper economic administration, only those with economic expertise are qualified to participate fully in the political realm" (2008, 159). As economic elites popularized austerity policies as the only viable economic strategy in the wake of the 2008 crisis, this norm reinforces the privatization of public policy. This norm of austerity politics has promoted the idea that "a pure market economy is structurally stable and that only inappropriate public interventions trigger public finance crises" (Boyer 2012, 310). As faith in government intervention is attacked by neo-liberal policy-makers and elites, the democratic impulse of dissensus and anti-elite populism returns, and often in a more polarized form. These broad anti-elite attitudes are an important way in which democracy continues to be valuable, even as it faces challenges from illiberal forces. Rancière's argument is that elites, both those in global positions of power and those who tap into hatred, are in direct opposition to the idea of democracy and democratic rule. He argues that "societies, today as yesterday, are organized by the play of oligarchies. And, properly speaking, there is no democratic government. Government is always practiced by the minority on the majority" (Rancière 2006a, 297). Populist groups in France, Germany, Hungary, Italy, and the

United Kingdom have all campaigned against the idea of a global economic consensus to boost their support and to propagate the idea that the global liberal regime is the cause of economic problems. For example, in June 2018 Hungary passed a "Stop Soros" law aimed at making it illegal to help migrants, naming the law after the billionaire philanthropist George Soros, and basing it on the idea that his Open Democracy organization was contributing to the country's problems (Kingsley 2018). Combining global elitism, liberalism, and crisis is a powerful tool that can be used by leaders willing to tap into the affective power of hatred.

CONCLUSION

This chapter has argued that by viewing democracy as a series of injunctive claims against governance, we can see the importance of affective and emotional responses to the democratic scandal. This scandal is the way in which problem-solving approaches to democracy reinforce the rule of elite governance and delegitimize democratic moments in which claims for equity are made. As a critical approach, Rancière's insights allow us to explain the tensions of anti-elite populism and non–expertise-based authority that is emerging in opposition to a global elite that is seeking to stabilize the status quo. This critical approach uses a methodology highlighting a diverse set of popular issues and events (bricolage) to demonstrate how non-expert claims clash with those who seek to stabilize normalcy and order. Examples from everyday life can demonstrate how this approach can help us identify current populist trends and the persistence of elite sentiments that will continue to define global democratic debates.

REFERENCES

Ahmed, S. 2001. "The Organisation of Hate." *Law and Critique* 12, no. 3: 345–65.
Austin, J.L. 1962. *How to Do Things with Words.* Toronto: Oxford University Press.
Biesta, G.J. 1998. "Say You Want a Revolution … Suggestions for the Impossible Future of Critical Pedagogy." *Educational Theory* 48, no. 4: 499–510. https://doi.org/10.1111/j.1741-5446.1998.00499.x

Boyer, R. 2012. "The Four Fallacies of Contemporary Austerity Policies: The Lost Keynesian Legacy." *Cambridge Journal of Economics* 36, no. 1: 283–312. https://doi.org/10.1093/cje/ber037

Brehm, W.C., and Silova, I. 2010. "The Ignorant Donor: A Radical Reimagination of International Aid, Development, and Education." *Current Issues in Comparative Education* 13, no. 1: 29–36. https://www.tc.columbia .edu/cice/pdf/25597_13_01_Brehm_Silova.pdf

Brennan, T. 2004. *The Transmission of Affect.* Ithaca, NY: Cornell University Press.

Chambers, S.A. 2012. *The Lessons of Rancière.* New York: Oxford University Press.

Cox, R.W. 1981. "Social Forces, States and World Orders: Beyond International Relations Theory." *Millennium* 10, no. 2: 126–55. https://doi.org/10.1177 /03058298810100020501

– 1987. *Production, Power, and World Order: Social Forces in the Making of History,* vol. 1. New York: Columbia University Press.

Davidson, B.I., Jones, S.L., Joinson, A.N., and Hinds, J. 2019. "The Evolution of Online Ideological Communities." *PloS One* 14, no. 5. https://doi.org /10.1371/journal.pone.0216932

Dean, J. 2009. "Politics without Politics." *Parallax* 15, no. 3: 20–36. https://doi .org/10.1080/13534640902982579

Feola, M. 2014. "Speaking Subjects and Democratic Space: Rancière and the Politics of Speech." *Polity* 46, no. 4: 498–519. https://doi.org/10.1057 /pol.2014.24

Follesdal, A., and S. Hix. 2006. "Why There Is a Democratic Deficit in the EU: A Response to Majone and Moravcsik." *Journal of Common Market Studies* 44, no. 3: 533–62. https://doi.org/10.1111/j.1468-5965.2006.00650.x

Friedrich, D., B. Jaastad, and T.S. Popkewitz. 2010. "Democratic Education: An (Im)possibility That Yet Remains to Come." *Educational Philosophy and Theory* 42, nos. 5–6: 571–87. https://doi.org/10.1111/j.1469 -5812.2010.00686.x

Gill, S. 1991. *American Hegemony and the Trilateral Commission,* vol. 5. Cambridge: Cambridge University Press.

Haas, P.M. 1992. "Introduction: Epistemic Communities and International Policy Coordination." *International Organization* 46, no. 1: 1–35. https:// doi.org/10.1017/s0020818300001442

Highmore, B., ed. 2002. *The Everyday Life Reader.* New York: Routledge.

Kaminsky, M. 2018. "The 'Shitty Media Men' Defamation Lawsuit Is a Danger to Both Free Speech and the #MeToo Movement." *Forbes,* October 22.

Kincheloe, J.L. 2005. "On to the Next Level: Continuing the Conceptualization of the Bricolage." *Qualitative Inquiry* 11, no. 3: 323–50. https://doi.org/10.1177/1077800405275056

– 2011. "Describing the Bricolage: Conceptualizing a New Rigor in Qualitative Research." In *Key Works in Critical Pedagogy,* edited by K. Hayes, S. Steinberg, and K. Tobin, 177–89. Rotterdam: Brill Sense.

Kingsley, P. 2018. "Hungary Criminalizes Aiding Illegal Immigrants." *New York Times*, June 20. https://www.nytimes.com/2018/06/20/world/europe/hungary-stop-soros-law.html

Konstan, D. 2007. "Anger, Hatred, and Genocide in Ancient Greece." *Common Knowledge* 13, no. 1: 170–87. https://doi.org/10.1215/0961754x-2006-045

Krugman, P. 2015. "Killing the European Project." *New York Times*, July 12. https://krugman.blogs.nytimes.com/2015/07/12/killing-the-european-project/?_r=0

Lambert, C. 2012. "Redistributing the Sensory: The Critical Pedagogy of Jacques Rancière." *Critical Studies in Education* 53, no. 2: 211–27. https://doi.org/10.1080/17508487.2012.672328

Lambert, H. 2015. "Yanis Varoufakis Full Transcript: Our Battle to Save Greece." *New Statesman*, July 13. https://www.newstatesman.com/world-affairs/2015/07/yanis-varoufakis-full-transcript-our-battle-save-greece

Le Bon, G. 1897. *The Crowd: A Study of the Popular Mind.* New York: Macmillan.

Marcus, G.E., W.R. Neuman, and M. MacKuen. 2000. *Affective Intelligence and Political Judgment.* Chicago: University of Chicago Press.

Markham, A.N. 2005. "'Go Ugly Early': Fragmented Narrative and Bricolage as Interpretive Method." *Qualitative Inquiry* 11, no. 6: 813–39. https://doi.org/10.1177/1077800405280662

May, T. 2008. *Political Thought of Jacques Rancière: Creating Equality.* Edinburgh: Edinburgh University Press.

Mirowski, P., and D. Plehwe, eds. 2015. *The Road from Mont Pèlerin: The Making of the Neoliberal Thought Collective, with a New Preface.* Cambridge, MA: Harvard University Press.

PettyJohn, M.E., F.K. Muzzey, M.K. Maas, and H.L. McCauley. 2018. "#HowIWillChange: Engaging Men and Boys in the #MeToo Movement." *Psychology of Men & Masculinity* 20, no. 4: 612–22. https://doi.org/10.1037/men0000186

Plot, M. 2014. *The Aesthetico-Political: The Question of Democracy in Merleau-Ponty, Arendt, and Rancière.* New York: Bloomsbury.

Purcell, M. 2014. "Rancière and Revolution." *Space and Polity* 18, no. 2: 168–81. https://doi.org/10.1080/13562576.2014.911591

Rancière, J. 1991. *The Ignorant Schoolmaster: Five Lessons in Intellectual Emancipation.* Stanford, CA: Stanford University Press.

— 1999. *Disagreement: Politics and Philosophy.* Minneapolis: University of Minnesota Press.

— 2006a. "Democracy, Republic, Representation." *Constellations* 13, no. 3: 297–307. https://doi.org/10.1111/j.1467-8675.2006.00402.x

— 2006b. *Hatred of Democracy.* New York: Verso.

— 2013. *The Politics of Aesthetics.* New York: Bloomsbury.

— 2015. *Dissensus: On Politics and Aesthetics.* New York: Bloomsbury.

— 2016. "The Populism That Is Not to Be Found." In *What Is a People?*, edited by A. Badiou, J. Butler, G. Didi-Huberman, S. Khiari, J. Rancière, and P. Bourdieu, 101–5. New York: Columbia University Press.

Read, M. 2018. "How Much of the Internet Is Fake? Turns Out, a Lot of It, Actually." *New York Magazine*, December 26. http://nymag.com/intelligencer /2018/12/how-much-of-the-internet-is-fake.html

Riordan, J. 2002. *The International Politics of Sport in the Twentieth Century*. New York: Taylor & Francis.

Ruggie, J.G. 1982. "International Regimes, Transactions, and Change: Embedded Liberalism in the Postwar Economic Order." *International Organization* 36, no. 2: 379–415. https://doi.org/10.1017/s0020818300018993

Sklair, L. 2001. *The Transnational Capitalist Class*, vol. 306. Oxford: Blackwell.

Spiegel, P. 2015. "IMF Criticises Greece Bailout Deal with EU." *Financial Times*, July 15. https://www.ft.com/content/444a0bc8-2a46-11e5-8613 -e7aedbb7bdb7

Suoranta, J. 2017. "Jacques Ranciere on Radical Equality and Adult Education." *Encyclopedia of Educational Philosophy and Theory*, 1–12.

Talbot, D. 2012. "Given Tablets but No Teachers, Ethiopian Children Teach Themselves." *MIT Technology Review*, October 29. https://www .technologyreview.com/s/506466/given-tablets-but-no-teachers-ethiopian -children-teach-themselves/

Tanke, J.J. 2011. *Jacques Rancière: An Introduction*. New York: A&C Black.

Thumlert, K. 2015. "Affordances of Equality: Rancière, Emerging Media, and the New Amateur." *Studies in Art Education* 56, no. 2: 114–26. https://doi .org/10.1080/00393541.2015.11518955

Woods, N. 2006. *The Globalizers: The IMF, the World Bank, and Their Borrowers*. Ithaca, NY: Cornell University Press.

Yardley, J. "Greek Referendum Plan by Alexis Tsipras Tests His Power and Conviction." *New York Times*, June 29. https://www.nytimes.com/2015 /06/30/world/europe/greek-premiers-referendum-call-tests-his-power-and -conviction.html

Zuboff, S. 2019. *The Age of Surveillance Capitalism: The Fight for a Human Future at the New Frontier of Power*. New York: PublicAffairs.

CHAPTER ELEVEN

Rethinking Democracy

Nandita Biswas Mellamphy

INTRODUCTION: A CRITICAL APPROACH TO DEMOCRACY

What is democracy? and *How do we study it?* These two questions form the epicentre of this book, but they are by no means the only ones we must confront. In attempting to answer these questions, a whole series of other, more specific and subtle interrogations may arise depending on who is asking, as well as when, where, how, and why the questions are being posed. "Different people mean different things by *democracy*. They may all want to achieve or promote democracy, but they disagree about how to do this because they disagree about what democracy truly is" (Ball et al. 2013, 16). Not only do semantic questions about meaning complicate efforts to define the term, but normative questions about the value of democracy often clash with more descriptive questions concerning the way democracies actually function (Cunningham 2002, 11). In approaching the study of democracy, it matters which orientation is taken: whereas scientific theories are *empirical* (meaning they describe and explain aspects of the world), political ideologies are *normative* (meaning they *prescribe* what people ought to do). Different orientations have resulted in different approaches to conceptualizing the term; abstract characterizations of democracy might tend toward the drawing of dichotomies (such that anything matching the characterization is democratic and anything else is not democratic), while others might want to think of democracy as a matter of degree (Cunningham 2002, 4). According to the philosopher W.B. Gallie, democracy is an *essentially contested concept* that cannot be reduced to one point of view and for which there is no consensus definition. Concepts such as democracy, freedom, and justice, for instance, cannot be defined without dispute, and these debates cannot be settled by appeal to empirical evidence, linguistic usage, or the canons of logic alone (Gallie 1956). Essentially contested concepts are internally complex and include a variety of possible components or features; they can be described and defined in many ways and the existence of multiple alternative meanings are not absurd or contradictory (Gallie 1956, 171–2). Although the term originally comes from the ancient Greek *demos*, meaning "people" or "common people," and the verb *kratein*, "to rule," the divergence of meanings suggests that democracy is fundamentally an open-ended concept, and that it requires study from various points of view as well as across different historical and ideological contexts. The concept of democracy has been understood variously, for instance, as a type of constitution and/or government, as the spirit of popular sovereignty, as a system of free elections, and as a political attitude or orientation, etc. For the ancient political thinker Aristotle, democracy was a flawed form of government associated with the rule of the many poor, while for the nineteenth-century diplomat Alexis de Tocqueville, democracy (exemplified by America) was understood as popular sovereignty and the will of "the people"; in the twentieth century, by contrast, economist Joseph Schumpeter argued that democracy was not an ideal but a method for selecting public officials that depends on giving individuals power to decide by means of a competition for votes (Cunningham 2002, 7–10). As these historical examples are meant to suggest, democracy is not a single thing and has no singular meaning; as such, the concept remains contestable.

When exploring the concept of democracy, the researcher should be open to the ambiguity of empirical material and the complexity of interpretations. Given the contestability of the concept of democracy, no *one* perspective can claim to be wholly neutral or impartial. "There is no such thing as unmediated data or facts; these are always the results of interpretation. Yet the interpretation does not take place in a neutral, apolitical, ideology-free space. Nor is an autonomous, value-free researcher responsible for it" (Alvesson and Sköldberg 2009, 12). A broadly accepted thesis in historical research is that knowledge begins with the knower, that is, data (i.e., "facts") are constructions or the result of interpretations, and culture, language, perception, ideology, and power leave their mark on empirical reality. Thus, knowledge is *perspectival*: "facts" are constructed and contextually framed by ontological and epistemological assumptions, which give these facts meaning.[1] A main task of the researcher is to try to stimulate critical reflection by considering the ontological and epistemological assumptions (e.g., theoretical, linguistic, textual, political, and cultural circumstances) underlying conceptualizations of democracy. This involves paying attention to the way empirical material is constructed, interpreted, and recorded, as well as the way in which different kinds of linguistic, social, political, and theoretical elements combine and inform the research process. Critical approaches would dispute – and even reject – the assumption that empirical "facts" can reflect an objective reality, maintaining instead that societal conditions are neither natural nor inevitable but instead always shaped by the asymmetries of power. Thus, their legitimacy can always be contested. While they can be understood generally as "interpretivist," critical approaches are best understood as the strategic deployment of criticism/critique for the purposes of challenging and/or overturning existing and established interpretations, often with the goal of offering novel and alternative meanings.

More specifically, the critical approach underlying this chapter rejects reliance on dogmatic methods, interpretations, and practices in the research process, and draws instead on post-structuralist, feminist, and decolonial theories that emphasize (to varying extents) the interpretive, perspectival, and ideologically embedded features of knowledge (see e.g., Lyotard 1984; Foucault 1989, 1998; Butler 1990; Haraway 1991; Tuhiwai Smith 1999). The aim of such criticism is to challenge conventional sources and interpretations, and may even involve developing counter-interpretations, counter-histories, and counter-practices of research that disrupt or reject pre-existing normative frameworks. "The idea is to strive for multiplicity, variation, the demonstration of inconsistencies and fragmentations, and the possibility of multiple interpretations" (Alvesson and Sköldberg 2009, 183). Rather than identifying problems and proposing solutions (as in other kinds of approaches), critical perspectives tend to challenge the norms and tools of scientific reasoning that define the academic study of politics (which is why they are often labelled as theoretical "trouble-makers" in social science research – see

Alvesson and Sköldberg 2009, 3). Critically oriented research confronts (rather than ignores) the divergence of conceptualizations; conceptual variations, even if they are conflicting, are instructive because they point to the important role of *context* in research. Critical approaches force the researcher to contest and rethink: that is, to build upon prior conceptions while simultaneously challenging them, thus permitting more complex and nuanced investigations of democracy from various vantage points.

CONTEXTUALIZING DEMOCRACY

The term "democracy" has been used broadly across historical and ideological spectrums, but scholars, especially scientists, often fail to account for how ideologies influence their theories. Ideologies are systems of ideas that shape people's thinking and actions with respect to significant and controversial issues; they help to explain social, political, and economic conditions (particularly in times of crisis), provide cues that influence judgments and decisions, and supply formulas for social and political action that orient identities (Ball et al. 2013, 1, 5, 6). Ideology teaches us what and how to desire, which structures people's judgments and decisions about how best to live and pursue life goals. Ideologies *frame* thinking (Lakoff 2004) – just as contemporary brands and logos influence consumer behaviour by directing the consumer's desires, ideologies are cognitive and linguistic mechanisms that create ideological landscapes that constrain, filter, and focus sensory data so that any information that we receive is already structured by data that are unconsciously processed (Kapoor 2013, 2). Political ideologies organize reality into a coherent story about what to believe in and why. Ideologies not only function at a conscious level through a fairly coherent and comprehensive set of ideas and texts that justify social fictions (e.g., ideologies are meant to help people understand their actual or potential place in society, and provide a program for social and political action), ideologies also function at an unconscious level, filtering our perceptions and shaping judgments, making them very hard to pinpoint and thus difficult to resist.

For the ancient Greeks, *demokratia* signified something very particular: government by the *demos* or common people – that is, rule by the many who were poor and uneducated but who made up the majority of the citizenry. Many understood democracy to be a form of government by and for the working ranks and instead favoured aristocracy, the rule of *aristoi*, those "best" and most suited (that is, wealthy enough) to rule. The *polis* or city-state was the epicentre of political activity in ancient Greece; there was no single country, or government, but a series of self-governing *poleis*. Athens, the largest *polis* in ancient Greece, was best known as a place governed by a democratic constitution that only lasted 186 years (from 508 to 322 BCE) before it was conquered in war by a rival wealthy military society from the city-state of Sparta. In the fifth century, known as the golden age of democracy (Thucydides's masterpiece, *The History of the Peloponnesian War*, is perhaps the best account of this period), citizens – mostly farmers – were paid an average day's wages so that the poor as well as rich could participate in deciding the public affairs of the city-state. Moreover, the filling of political offices was determined not by election (which was a means used by the aristocracy) but by lottery to ensure that any citizen could run for office without barrier and regardless of familial or other ties. However, political participation was exclusive: only free, adult, male Athenian citizens had the right to participate actively in political life; women, resident foreigners, children, and slaves were all excluded from the rights of political citizenship. In fact, only about one in ten inhabitants of Athens was considered a citizen at all (Ball et al. 2013, 17).[2]

The Athenian philosopher Plato (427–347 BCE) believed that democracy is dangerous because it puts the important task of governance into the hands of the poor masses, those whose life circumstances make them unsuitable and without the necessary experiences required to rule skilfully. Plato, who favoured aristocracy, cautioned that democracies tend to be unstable because political power is in the hands of people who have regard only for their own class interests rather than for the common good of all citizens. The masses are more easily swayed by demagogues, self-interested leaders who will flatter and appeal to them, and turn citizen against citizen until such time that democracy becomes anarchy. However, demagogues are likely to be tyrants who care nothing about the common good or the people, only power. As Plato warns, democracy is a perilously slippery slope toward tyranny (see Book VIII of *The Republic*).

Plato's student, Aristotle (384–322 BCE), also considered democracy to be a less than desirable form of rule because the people tend to be poor, fickle, and indifferent to the affairs of the city-state as a whole. In Book V of *Politics*, Aristotle analyses the connection between democracy and tyranny by showing how the former can often turn into the latter. Since monarchy is ideal but rare, the form of rule in which most people benefit is democracy, the rule of the many poor; the best practical form of government is what Aristotle called *polity*, a mixed constitution combining the interests of the few wealthy and the many poor in which both take turns ruling over the other so to be more representative of the common interest of the city-state as a whole. Democracy has thus been associated with popular government and the ideal of the rule of the people for the common interest of both rich and poor. Although ancient democracy was short-lived and was eventually replaced by other forms of rule (especially rule by military oligarchs), this democratic ideal survived in the Roman concept of the *republic* or *res publica*, which in Latin means "public things." The Greek historian Polybius argued that the secret to ancient Rome's success was its mixed constitution; rather than giving power to one, few, or many persons, the Roman Republic divided power among all three. In this way, no *one* group was able to pursue its own interests at the expense of the others. Mixed government allows for some degree of self-government and popular participation in government while making it difficult for any one person to acquire enough power to threaten liberty and the common good (Ball et al. 2013, 21).

Modern democratic ideals borrow much from ancient viewpoints on democracy, particularly the emphases on self-government and the common interest of the public exercising self-government (Cunningham 2002, 9). For instance Alexis de Tocqueville, in his masterpiece on American democracy, notes the importance of anti-aristocratic attitudes for developing a strong sense of popular sovereignty, but he also warns (much like his ancient predecessors) of the problems with unchecked majority rule, especially the oppression or tyranny of the majority over minorities (Tocqueville 2000). In nineteenth-century Britain, arguments in favour of democracy tended to centre on two concerns: self-protection and self-development. The theory of utilitarianism suggests that the duty of government is to promote the greatest happiness for the greatest number through representative democracy, which enables every man to vote for representatives who will protect his interests. A champion of utilitarianism, John Stuart Mill (1806–1873), argued that the opportunity for self-protection through voting rights should also extend to women.

Mill maintained that political participation is valuable because it also provides for self-development. Democracy strengthens virtue among the common people, directs participation at local political levels, and improves people through education and literacy (Mill 1951, 196, 7). Such arguments influenced the granting of the right to vote, which was first extended exclusively to all adult males in Canada in the 1870s and to Canadian women only in 1917 (although Quebec women did not get to cast their first ballot until 1944). Often, these changes came only after heated debate, protest, and violence (Ball et al. 2013, 31–2).

Social and political thinkers, both ancient and modern, have identified several problems with the concept of democracy that have been endemic to practices of democracy: the *tyranny of the majority* refers to the potential of the majority to mistreat, neglect, or ignore minority viewpoints; the *massification of culture and morals* refers to the way the dominant ruling class tries to synchronize and standardize cultural practices and moral codes; *ineffective government* refers to the inability of democracies to pursue and implement large-scale and long-term change due to conflicting interests and scarcity of resources; *demagoguery* refers to the way some leaders use populism (the language of "the people") to manipulate public opinion, carry out authoritarian measures, and justify autocratic rule; and *oppressive rule* refers to democracy's association with a number of political exclusions and the subordination of gender, sexual orientation, or race, etc. (Cunningham 2002, 16–21).

The study of democracy, as such, has to involve more than just the questions of what and how, but also *which* – which class, race, ethno-cultural group, gender, sexual orientation, age, etc.? Scholars have suggested that although democratic ideals have theoretically emphasized equality, liberty, and human rights, in practice these have not always been applied equally to everyone. Whereas liberal normative political perspectives have tended to emphasize the role of mind, intellect, rationality, and reasoning in political life, feminist and critical political theorists have argued that this rationalist-individualist approach privileges reason and mind by de-privileging the body, its emotions, and its experiences, thereby creating the political conditions for unequal power relations, subordinations, and exclusions in social relations (Jaggar 1983). This point was made in the late eighteenth century by Mary Wollstonecraft, who argued that the Declaration of the Rights of Man (1789) did not really apply to women who were still considered to be property of males. Carole Pateman (1988) argues in *The Sexual Contract* that the so-called social contract upon which modern liberal democracies are built, and which was described in the theories of Hobbes, Locke, and Rousseau, is really a "sexual contract," that seeks to subordinate women. Virginia Held (1993), in *Feminist Morality*, argues that social contract theory relies on a conception that is best described as *homo economicus*: a predominantly economic and masculinist viewpoint that, contrary to its claim, fails to represent all persons in all times and places. Charles Mills (1997), in *The Racial Contract*, also calls into question the supposed universality of liberal social contract theories and shows that non-whites have a similar relationship to the social contract as do women (in Pateman's reading). His central argument is that there exists a "racial contract" that determines who counts as full moral and political persons, and therefore sets the parameters of who can access the freedom and equality that democracy promises. Ideology frames the democratic idea and deploys it according to its own particular vision; those who promote ideologies often use their vision of democracy to persuade others to adopt their points of view. While democracy has been associated with tendencies toward anarchy and tyranny, as the ancient political thinkers emphasized, it has also been associated with the idea that every citizen is free and equal to the other.

RETHINKING DEMOCRACY AS CONTESTATION

The democratic ideal survives in two principal forms[3] – liberal and social democracy (Ball et al. 2013, 299) – but the so-called universalization of liberal democracy is "far from complete" (Benhabib 1996, 3). Those who favour liberal democracy continue to stress the importance of privacy, including private property, so that individuals may be free to choose how to live. In contrast, the proponents of social democracy continue to stress the importance of social and economic inequality, claiming that people will not be able to rule themselves unless they have an equal voice in the decisions that affect their lives. But there are also oppositions and antagonisms asserting themselves against these trends in the name of various forms of "difference" – ethnic, national, linguistic, religious, and cultural. "The negotiation of identity/difference ... is the political problem facing democracies on a global scale" (4). Whereas liberal democracies focus on the "negotiation, contestation, and the representation of difference within the public sphere," the politics of ethno-nationalism seek to create new politically sovereign bodies (4). Modern democracy, as such, is intimately connected to the politics of identity and difference; while in some cases, democracies have been flexible enough to allow difference to be expressed without fragmenting identities, in other cases it has led to factionalism, fundamentalism, and extremism.

While some scholars wonder about how much difference is compatible with the democratic ideal, this chapter has emphasized that difference is really at the heart of the democratic ideal. Democracy, in other words, is inherently based on contestation and is *agonistic* (based on the ancient Greek *agon*, meaning "contestation"). "To take difference – and not just identity – seriously in democratic theory is to affirm the inescapability of conflict and the ineradicability of resistance to the political and moral projects of ordering subjects, institutions, and values ... It is to give up on the dream of a place called home, a place free of power, conflict, and struggle, a place – an identity, a form of life, a group vision – unmarked or unriven by difference and untouched by the power brought to bear upon it by the identities that strive to ground themselves in its place" (Honig 1996, 258). An agonistic democratic theory maintains a commitment to the radical contestability and pluralism of values/viewpoints that recognizes the impossibility of deciding upon competing visions of the good, of justice, and of the political without the contestation of opposing viewpoints.

Thus, a critical approach to democracy would not prioritize consensus over resistance to consensus. In fact, liberal democracies are born out of and must preserve the dynamic tension between two different traditions: political liberalism (rule of law, separation of powers, and individual rights) and the democratic tradition of popular sovereignty. Democracy, in other words, is the relentless contestation of cultural and ethical perspectives; the circumventing or cancellation of contestation thus renders civic relations *less* rather than *more* democratic. According to proponents of agonism, a major flaw of a consensual politics of the centre (one that affirms consensus over contestation, such as "third way" and "deliberative" theories of democracy) is the mistaken assumption that contestation impedes politics and is a problem that needs to be solved. "Once the very idea of an alternative to the existing configuration of power disappears, what disappears also is the very possibility of a legitimate form of expression for the resistances against the dominant power relations. The status quo has become naturalized and made into the way 'things really are'" (Mouffe 2000, 5). An agonistic conception of democracy preserves rather than resolves the contestability between the claims of liberalism and those of populism. While democracy has the potential to invite the contestation of identities, an agonistic theory of democracy provides "the best political medium through which to incorporate strife into interdependence and care into strife" (Connolly 1991, 193). Agonism does not eliminate strife but instead privileges the production of opposing viewpoints and thus encourages people to engage with, criticize, and change the status quo. Agonistic democracy does not privilege unity and consensus (or agreement) as democratic ideals, but rather plurality and dissensus, which are seen to provide the possibility of perceiving and relating to the world in novel ways. Some argue that unless it is decoupled from consensus, democracy is at risk of becoming a

> "self-refuting ideal" because the very moment of its realization would coincide with its disintegration ... Pluralism implies the permanence of conflict and antagonism. Indeed, it helps us to understand that conflict and division are not to be seen as disturbances that unfortunately cannot be completely eliminated, or as empirical impediments that render impossible the full realization of a good constituted by a harmony that we cannot reach because we will never be completely able to coincide with our rational universal self ... We have therefore to abandon the very idea of a complete reabsorption of alterity into oneness and harmony ... Instead of trying to erase the traces of power and exclusion, democratic politics requires us to bring them to the fore, to make them visible so that they can enter the terrain of contestation. (Mouffe 2000, 32, 33, 34)

Unlike more reformist theories of democracy, a contestation-oriented democracy can challenge the given social order of values because it views identity not as pre-ordained or fixed, but as constructed and performative, as a complex but changing hierarchy of privileged and subordinated people who are intersected by racial, ethnic, class, gender, and other markers of identity.

CONCLUDING REMARKS: CHALLENGES TO DEMOCRACY IN THE DIGITAL ERA

What are some implications and limitations of this approach to rethinking the concept of democracy? In rejecting consensus over resistance, does agonistic democracy always ensure the pursuit and practice of democratic ideals? How can we be so sure that the contest of pluralisms will enhance rather than erode democratic politics? Agonistic politics are subject to the kinds of objections that the ancients voiced clearly: people are not always just, fair-minded, or critically informed, and they can make mistakes that lead to violence and that harm others. The representation of democracy that political theorists have sought to counteract is the spectre of democracy as lawless and prone to fits of violence. These rebellious and revolutionary ideas have nonetheless extended the boundaries of political participation to include the active involvement of those hitherto excluded or marginalized. Nonetheless, some scholars warn that institutionalization ultimately attenuates democracy: leaders begin to appear, hierarchies are created, experts emerge, as do centres of decision-making, administration, and order that displace spontaneity and exclude some populations. Accordingly, there is a "fugitive" character to democracy (Wolin 1996, 41) that undermines or at least subverts the historically dominating role of the state apparatus as guarantor of peace and security and as symbol of justice and authority (41, 42).

Agonism, by contrast, deprioritizes the state's dominion over legitimacy and asserts an unbridgeable gap between power and legitimacy. The resulting contraction of the state's influence and authority, especially in matters of economy and culture, has led to a splintering of the ideological spectrum, "the individualization of politics into commodifiable 'lifestyles' and opinions," which "subsumes politics into consumption" (Dean 2009, 11). But because economics cannot fulfill all the functions of government, "one element of the state rises to the fore – security. Thus, accompanying the diminished political influence on economic and social policy is the intensification and extension of the state as an agency of surveillance and control" (12). Today's digital information and communication technologies give the impression that they enhance democratic pluralism by welcoming the contestation of ideas and positions. But as Dean argues, digital visions of democracy are actually damaging the historical practices of democracy: "the technologies, the concentrations of corporate power, the demands of financial markets, the seductions of the society of the spectacle that rule in and as the name of the public have created conditions anathema to democratic governance" (2003, 104).

The growing use of digitally networked information and communication technologies has made the access and control of information a central object of governmental, financial, scientific, commercial, and popular struggles for power. And yet, these very same technologies are revealing a power to affect and modulate their users, to prime user perceptions, influence user beliefs and behaviours, and make users subject to an emergent regime of info-gluttony and data-mania. While the expansion and adoption of digital information and communication technologies is making it easier for human beings to connect beyond physical boundaries and national borders, it is also actualizing an emergent logic of accumulation in the networked sphere characterized by often opaque mechanisms of information extraction, of commodification, and of control that alienate people from their own bodies and behaviours, all the while generating new markets of prediction and speculation. While internet, mobile devices, and social-networking apps have been used to create popular revolutions against governments perceived as unjust, mobilize huge swathes of the population, and enable large-scale acts of popular protest, these very same technologies are easily hacked and weaponized. They are, as such, not only platforms for empowerment but also vehicles for the spread of virulent narratives and reactionary ideologies that awake and inflame historical hatreds and cultural traumas, creating enormous upsurges of popular sentiment that are difficult to foresee or regulate (never mind legislate). Ironically, while the new media and communication technologies in widespread use give users the feeling that they are not passive consumers but active creators of information, the new information ecosystem is highly predatory and tends to exploit vulnerabilities and reinforce rather than challenge opinions, biases, and beliefs. Messages can be easily and directly circulated, modified, and amplified without the need for any centralized authority or adjudicating body. And for these reasons, digital communication and new media have become key weapons both for extremist, fundamentalist, and revolutionary groups, as well as for governments who argue that the needs of national security trump the demands of individual civil liberty (see e.g., Herman 2011).

While the historical problems associated with democracy are not necessarily solved by the promise of new media and digital communications, agonism, by making contestation central to politics, provides a strong platform from which to question the belief that democratic politics is principally about prioritizing consensus over disagreement. Consensus entails the disappearance of contestation, and thus of politics itself (Rancière 1999, 102). By focusing on improving governance mechanisms that seek to unify publics and do away with public struggles, consensus-driven approaches divert attention away from the democratic potential of politics. The identification of "democracy" with public opinion polls, for instance, reduces the rule of "the people" to statistical standards presenting "total public opinion as identical to the body of the people" – that is, to "a people transformed into an object of knowledge and prediction," as if the summation of opinions is synonymous with the sum of the parts that constitute it (103, 105). Consensus, generally understood in terms of the mechanics of aggregating the opinions of collectivities, is a system of legitimization that promotes rather than deprivileges the policing functions of the state: "The police is thus first an order of bodies that defines the allocation of ways of doing, ways of being, and ways of saying, and sees that those bodies are assigned by name to a particular place and task ... Policing is not so much the 'disciplining' of bodies as a rule governing their appearing, a configuration of occupations and the properties of the spaces where these occupations are distributed" (28, 29). Democracy is not merely or even principally a system of government; it can also be rethought as the transgressive activity by which the *demos* creates and recreates new trajectories for the political through the unending confrontation of positions and power relations. Democracy, as such, is impoverished when conflated with its policing/statistical functions and mechanisms. By contrast, the *demos* is activated by political contestation in which people participate by transforming the class, status, and value systems that define citizenship and that divide, distribute, and exclude citizens. Contestation, not consensus, is the way the "rule of the people" makes itself *political*.

NOTES

1 Ontology has to do with assumptions about what kinds of things exist (i.e.,
   the form and nature of reality and whether this reality exists independently
   of interpretation), while epistemology deals with what we can know and
   how we can know it. Ontology and epistemology are interrelated because

how one comes to know depends on the nature of the objects of knowledge, while ascertaining what exists depends on the means of knowing.

2 While scholars generally agree that women were excluded from participation in the activities of the city-state, there continues to be debate over whether Athenian women were, in fact, citizens at all. For example, Just (1989) and Loraux (1993) argue that Athenian women were excluded from citizenship, while Hansen (1991, 62) calls women "citizens" but also admits that it was political participation that largely determined Athenian citizenship ("the *polis* was a society of *citizens*. It was a male society from which women were excluded"). According to Campa (2019, 257), "in classical Athens female citizenship looked quite different from male citizenship. Enough so, in fact, that some scholars have argued that women were *not* truly citizens, since they could not participate in any aspect of the political and legal sphere in Athens … In defense of female citizenship, other scholars have argued for a broader understanding … Women's key role in producing citizens, participating in cult and legal protections … are evidence of their citizenship."

3 According to scholars, there are *three* main conceptions of democracy in the modern world (Ball et al. 2013, 34, 35). First, liberal democracy, rooted in seventeenth-century liberalism that emphasizes the belief that people should be generally free from governmental authority, is the rule of a majority of citizens provided that the majority does not try to deprive individuals or minorities of their basic rights, which include the rights to speak and worship freely, to run for public office, and the right to own property. This means that majority rule must be limited. Liberal democracy emphasizes equality of opportunity, which is a consequence of the assumption that all individuals possess the same rights, but rejects equality of condition, the assumption that individuals should have equality of property and socio-economic power, which is incompatible with the individual rights to property and freedom of enterprise. Second, social democracy, linked to socialism, in which the key to democracy is equality, especially equality of social and economic power in society and government, argues that liberal democracy puts poor and working-class people at the mercy of the rich. Wealth makes it possible to run for office and influence governmental policies, so the rich enjoy benefits that are denied to the less affluent. Social democracy tends to advocate for the redistribution of wealth to promote equality, public financing of campaigns and elections, and public rather than private control of natural resources and major industries. Like liberal democracy, social democracy affirms civil liberties and encourages fair competition for political office but denies that these can be realized when gaps between poverty and power continue to prevail. Third, popular/people's democracy is the prevailing version in communist countries. The common people are called the "proletariat," or the working class, and democracy cannot be achieved until government rules in their interests. But this does

not mean that the people directly govern; according to Karl Marx's theory of communism, a dictatorship of the proletariat will prepare the way with a communist party, which will rule for the benefit of working people.

REFERENCES

Alvesson, M., and K. Sköldberg. 2009. *Reflexive Methodology: New Vistas for Qualitative Research.* London: Sage.

Aristotle. 1998. *The Politics.* Indianapolis: Hackett.

Ball, T., and Richard Dagger, William Christian, and Colin Campbell. 2013. *Political Ideologies and the Democratic Ideal.* Toronto: Pearson Education.

Benhabib, S. 1996. "Introduction: The Democratic Moment and the Problem of Difference." In *Democracy and Difference: Contesting the Boundaries of the Political,* edited by S. Benhabib, 3–17. Princeton, NJ: Princeton University Press.

Butler, J. 1990. *Gender Trouble.* New York: Routledge.

Campa, N. 2019. "Kurios, Kuria and the Status of Athenian Women." *Classical Journal* 114, no. 3: 257–79. https://doi.org/10.5184/classicalj.114.3.0257

Connolly, W.E. 2002. *Identity, Difference: Democratic Negotiations of Political Paradox.* Minneapolis: University of Minnesota Press.

Cunningham, F. 2002. *Theories of Democracy: A Critical Introduction.* New York: Routledge.

Dean, J. 2003. "Why the Net Is Not a Public Sphere." *Constellations* 10, no. 1: 95–112. https://doi.org/10.1111/1467-8675.00315

– 2009. *Democracy and Other Neoliberal Fantasies.* Durham, NC: Duke University Press.

Foucault, M. 1989. *The Order of Things.* London: Routledge.

– 1998. *Power/Knowledge.* Brighton, UK: Harvester Press.

Gallie, W.B. 1956. "Essentially Contested Concepts." *Proceedings of the Aristotelian Society* 56, no. 1: 167–98. https://doi.org/10.1093/aristotelian/56.1.167

Hansen, M.H. 1991. *The Athenian Democracy in the Age of Demosthenes.* Oxford: Blackwell.

Haraway, D. 1991. *Simians, Cyborgs and Women.* New York: Routledge.

Held, V. 1993. *Feminist Morality: Transforming Culture, Society, and Politics.* Chicago: University of Chicago Press.

Herman, S. 2011. *Taking Liberties: The War on Terror and the Erosion of American Democracy.* Oxford: Oxford University Press.

Honig, B. "Difference, Dilemmas, and the Politics of Home." In *Democracy and Difference: Contesting the Boundaries of the Political,* edited by S. Benhabib, 257–77. Princeton, NJ: Princeton University Press.

Jaggar, A. 1983. *Feminist Politics and Human Nature.* New York: Rowman & Littlefield.

Just, R. 1989. *Women in Athenian Law and Life.* London and New York: Routledge.

Kapoor, I. 2013. *Celebrity Humanitarianism: The Ideology of Global Charity.* New York: Routledge.

Lakoff, G. 2004. *Don't Think of an Elephant: Know Your Values and Frame the Debate.* Chelsea, VT: Chelsea Green Publishing.

Loraux, N. 1993. *The Children of Athena: Athenian Ideas about Citizenship and the Division between the Sexes.* Princeton, NJ: Princeton University Press.

Lyotard, J. 1984. *The Postmodern Condition: A Report on Knowledge.* Manchester: Manchester University Press.

Mill, J.S. 1951. "Considerations on Representative Government." *Utilitarianism, Liberty, and Representative Government.* New York: Dutton.

Mills, C.W. 1997. *The Racial Contract.* Ithaca, NJ: Cornell University Press.

Mouffe, C. 2000. *The Democratic Paradox.* London: Verso.

Pateman, C. 1988. *The Sexual Contract.* Cambridge: Polity Press.

Plato. 2004. *The Republic.* Indianapolis: Hackett.

Rancière, J. 1999. *Disagreement: Politics and Philosophy.* Minneapolis: University of Minnesota Press.

Thucydides. 1998. *History of the Peloponnesian War.* Indianapolis: Hackett.

Tocqueville, A. 2000. *Democracy in America.* Chicago: University of Chicago Press.

Tuhiwai Smith, Linda. 1999. *Decolonizing Methodologies.* London: Zed Books.

Wolin, S. 1996. "Fugitive Democracy." *In Democracy and Difference: Contesting the Boundaries of the Political,* edited by Seyla Benhabib. Princeton, NJ: Princeton University Press.

Wollstonecraft, M. 2004. *A Vindication of the Rights of Woman.* London: Penguin.

Contributors

Christopher Alcantara is a professor of political science at the University of Western Ontario. He uses qualitative and quantitative methods to explore a range of topics relating to Canadian politics, federalism and multi-level governance, political behaviour, public administration, and public policy. His latest book, *Winning and Keeping Power in Canadian Politics*, is co-authored with Jason Roy and published by University of Toronto Press (2020).

Cameron D. Anderson is an associate professor in the Department of Political Science at the University of Western Ontario and is the English-language co-editor of the *Canadian Journal of Political Science*. His research employs quantitative methodologies in the areas of public opinion, voting behaviour, and elections. He has published articles in many scholarly venues, including the *American Journal of Political Science, Electoral Studies, Nations and Nationalism, Political Psychology,* and *Urban Affairs Review.*

David A. Armstrong II is the Canada Research Chair in Political Methodology and associate professor of political science at the University of Western Ontario. His methodological research focuses on the use of non-parametric statistical tools in social science research. He also does large-N comparative work on conflict and contentious politics. His work has been published in top outlets, including the *American*

Political Science Review, the *American Journal of Political Science*, and the *American Sociological Review*. His book *Analyzing Spatial Models of Choice and Judgment with R* (Routledge, 2014) will see its second edition published in 2020.

Nandita Biswas Mellamphy is an associate professor of political science, as well as an affiliate member in the Department of Women's Studies and Feminist Research, core faculty in (and former associate director of) the Centre for the Study of Theory and Criticism, and current director of the Electro-Governance Group, all at the University of Western Ontario. Her research puts critical social and political theories in dialogue with Continental philosophy, science and technology studies, media/information studies, and surveillance studies. She is co-author and co-editor of several works, including *The Three Stigmata of Friedrich Nietzsche* (2011), *The Digital Dionysus: Nietzsche and the Network-Centric Condition* (2016), "Apps and Affect" (2015), "Larval Terror and the Digital Darkside" (2014), "Cosmopolitanisms, Social Inclusion, and Global Futures" (2018), and "Humancentrism and A.I. Ethics" (2020). Currently, she is associate editor for the peer-reviewed international journal *Interconnections: Journal of Posthumanism* and assistant editor of the *Canadian Journal of Political Science*.

Dan Bousfield is an assistant professor at the University of Western Ontario. He researches social movements, protest, and critical political economy, with an emphasis on psychoanalysis, gender, technology, pedagogy, and resistance. He received his PhD from McMaster University in Hamilton, Ontario, in 2009. His methodological frameworks draw on critical pedagogy to examine the everyday exclusions built into technology and politics through race, gender, and settler colonial sensibilities. He has published articles in *Globalizations*, *Global Networks*, the *American Review of Canadian Studies*, *International Studies Perspectives*, and *Sport and Society*.

Charles Jones is an associate professor in the Department of Political Science at the University of Western Ontario. He is the author or editor of four books, including *Global Justice* (Oxford University Press, 1999) and, with Richard Vernon, *Patriotism* (Polity Press, 2018). His teaching and research focus mainly on normative political theory and the history of political thought. He has published scholarly papers on human rights, global justice, cosmopolitanism, multiculturalism, and nationalism.

Rob Leone holds a PhD in comparative public policy from McMaster University. He currently is an associate professor in leadership and public policy at Niagara University and a public affairs consultant with Earnscliffe Strategy Group. His research focuses on policy, public-sector management, and ethics from comparative and qualitative methods perspectives.

Joseph Lyons is an assistant professor and director of the Local Government Program in the Department of Political Science at the University of Western Ontario. He mostly uses qualitative methods to explore topics related to multi-level governance, local government, and public administration and policy. His recent book, *Local Government in Practice: Cases in Governance, Planning, and Policy* (Emond Publishing, 2020), is co-authored with Zachary Spicer and Kate Graham.

Josh Morgan completed an MA in political science at the University of Western Ontario. His academic research interests include Canadian and local government with a focus on the theory and practice of democratic representation and elections. He is an active member of the London, Ontario, community and was first elected to London City Council as councillor for Ward 7 on 27 October 2014. He was re-elected to a second term on 22 October 2018 with support from 75 per cent of voters. Josh is currently the City of London budget chair for the 2020–3 multi-year budget and an elected member of the Board of Directors for the Federation of Canadian Municipalities. Over the past decade, Josh has served in various leadership roles on a number of London-area boards, including the London Public Library, the Western Fair Association, the Raceway Corporation, Museum London, the Public Utilities Commission, and the Hyde Park Business Improvement Area.

Bruce Morrison is an assistant professor at the University of Western Ontario, where he teaches comparative and European politics. His research efforts concentrate on state formation, political corruption, and democratization at the national and transnational levels. In his work, he tends to employ process tracing and comparative analysis to evaluate causal propositions, refine them, and reflect on the extent of their generalizability. His approach to comparative historical research takes cases as complex wholes, in which timing, sequencing, and actor interpretations are critical elements. He is the editor of *Transnational Democracy in Critical and Comparative Perspective: Democracy's Range Reconsidered* (Ashgate, 2003) and has published in *World Politics*.

Andrew Sancton is a professor emeritus of political science at the University of Western Ontario. His latest publication is the third edition of his textbook, *Canadian Local Government: An Urban Perspective*.

Laura B. Stephenson is a professor of political science at the University of Western Ontario and co-director of the Consortium on Electoral Democracy. Her work focuses on political behaviour, elections, and voting, which she analyses with quantitative methods. She is an expert in survey research and has conducted many national and international surveys. She has published numerous studies of voting behaviour during elections at all levels of government. Her most recent book is a study of the 2015 Canadian election through three provincial lenses, *Provincial Battles, National Prize?* (UBC Press, 2019), which she co-authored with Andrea Lawlor, William Cross, André Blais, and Elisabeth Gidengil.

Richard Vernon is a distinguished university professor at the University of Western Ontario, where he teaches in the Departments of Political Science and Philosophy. He has won the university's awards for both research and teaching. His interests include the history of political thought (especially in France and Britain) and contemporary political philosophy in the analytical style. Major publications include studies of toleration, citizenship, democratic theory, historical redress, global justice, patriotism, and (most recently) intergenerational justice, the topic of his *Justice Back and Forth: Duties to the Past and Future* (University of Toronto Press, 2016).

Index